THE
LANGUAGE
OF
LIBERTY

A Citizen's Vocabulary

THE
LANGUAGE
OF
LIBERTY

A Citizen's Vocabulary

Edwin C. Hagenstein

First Printing: October 6, 2020

The Language of Liberty: A Citizen's Vocabulary
Copyright © 2020 by Edwin C. Hagenstein
All Rights Reserved.

Release Date: October 6, 2020
Softcover ISBN: 978-1-57869-035-0
Hardcover ISBN: 978-1-57869-037-4
eBook: 978-1-57869-036-7
LCCN: 2020903183

Published by Rootstock Publishing
an imprint of Multicultural Media, Inc.
27 Main Street, Suite 6
Montpelier, VT 05602 USA
www.rootstockpublishing.com
info@rootstockpublishing.com

Email the author at languageofliberty1@gmail.com

Interior design by Eddie Vincent (ed.vincent@encirclepub.com)
Cover design by Deirdre Wait/Enc Graphic Services
Printed in the USA

To the memory of my parents,
good Democrats but splendid republicans—

Ann Hill Hagenstein
Perry Reginald Hagenstein

TABLE OF CONTENTS

PREFACE

There was a grand political moment in the United States, for those of us old enough to remember, somewhere around 1965: good economy, expanding opportunities, civil rights gains, and more. It was a time of extraordinary confidence in American government. Not only was our democracy good and free, it simply seemed right, perhaps even natural and inevitable, at least in the United States.

To the degree Americans held this attitude, we took far too much for granted. Democracy is not, in fact, natural; certainly no more so than, say, monarchy, a form of government far more common in human history. For democracy to thrive, it requires cultivated effort, including continuous attention to the health of political institutions. Even more important than institutional health is the capacity of the people for self-government. No society drifts unthinkingly into democracy, nor remains there for long without effort. Self-government must be cultivated and sustained across generations.

Even in good times, this takes real effort. But hardly anyone thinks these are especially good political times or that our civic health is sound. Basic civic virtues, especially respect for others, appear increasingly fragile. Our political discourse is symptomatic, rife as it is with anger and bitterness.

It is not only bipartisan hatred that mars our discourse, but also a lack of comprehension of the fundamentals of our political system. After all, if we want to speak about politics, we should understand its vocabulary, its basic terms. We should have some feel for the differences between the House of Representatives and the Senate, for example, or what a statute is and how it differs from a regulation or an executive order. Likewise with the great ideals we profess. As we throw around terms such as *justice, democracy,* and *rights,* it would help to know better what they mean not only in the abstract, but also in relation to our actual political institutions. Without such understanding, our discourse remains sterile.

This book aims to rebuild this understanding by focusing on the building blocks of our political system: the words and terms we use when we talk politics. It defines and explores a hundred and one of these terms in the belief that a better grasp of our political vocabulary will lead to better understanding of the system as a whole.

My hope is that the book will act, in effect, as a user's guide to the American political system, written for anyone who wants to think more clearly and act more responsibly as a citizen.

ADMINISTRATIVE STATE

> [W]e have a system of government in which our laws are
> made by the folks that we elect, and these laws are enforced
> by judges and juries in the courts. But we have within
> that an administrative state, a state that acts really by mere
> command and not through law.
>
> —Philip Hamburger

To understand the term *administrative state*, start with *administration* or *administer*. According to the dictionaries, administration is the act of carrying out a program or a plan, one created elsewhere. In medicine, for example, a nurse might administer treatments to a patient under the direction of a doctor. Similarly, administration in government is the carrying out of programs, but not the creation of them. Just as nurses carry out the doctor's orders, so administrators administer programs voted into existence by legislatures. In theory, at least, administration is neutral and value-free, a simple execution of the will of the legislature, and thus of the will of the people.

In terms of the national government, the executive branch administers the nation's laws. It does so through its various departments, agencies, and bureaus. The laws they implement cover immense ground: public health, national defense, low-income housing, Social Security, transportation projects, the environment, and much, much more. Through the administration of the nation's laws in all these areas, the government touches every life in the land. As Woodrow Wilson put it, "Administration is the most obvious part of government; it is government in action."

*   *   *

Our national government has had to administer laws since its beginning, but no one would have spoken of an administrative state in the country's first decades.[1] What we call the administrative state really got its start in the late 19th century, reaching maturity later, especially with the New Deal. It came, naturally enough, with expansive new government programs, all of which need administering.

This governmental growth came in reaction to developments that were dramatically reshaping American society by the beginning of the 20th century, and that created enormous social pressures within the nation. These changes included industrialization, urbanization, and mass immigration. Speaking of their combined effects, Supreme Court Justice Louis Brandeis wrote in 1916 that Americans were passing through "an economic and social revolution which affected the life of the people more fundamentally than any political revolution known to history."

In response, government implemented economic and social regulation on a scale never before seen in the United States. The regulations came through freshly minted agencies, such as the Interstate Commerce Commission (ICC), whose mission included regulating the nation's railroads.

The ICC, established in 1887, was the first major national regulatory agency, but it was far from the last. Before long others were added, including the Securities and Exchange Commission (SEC), founded to regulate the stock markets and related matters; the Food and Drug Administration (FDA), which regulates commercially produced food and drugs; and the Federal Communications Commission (FCC), which regulates radio, television, satellite, cable, and other forms of communications. More recently, the Environmental Protection Agency (EPA), the Occupational Safety and Health Administration (OSHA), the Equal Employment Opportunity Commission (EEOC), and others have joined earlier federal regulatory agencies.

These regulatory agencies, the divisions of the administrative state, exist mostly within the executive branch, but they were created by acts of the legislature.[2] In a technical sense, at least, the regulators exist to do Congress's will. However, the relationship between legislative and executive powers in the administrative state is complicated. Congress was not designed to write the kinds of detailed laws that could effectively regulate technical aspects of the vast, modern American economy. For this reason, Congress leaves much of the detail work to those regulatory agencies.

Consider the ICC. The original legislation that gave it life called for the agency to insure "reasonable and just" railroad prices. But Congress was in no position to determine what those prices would be, nor even when the "reasonable and just" criteria were being violated on a case-by-case basis. They left the ICC to make those judgments itself.

In this case and others, Congress delegates a great deal of rule-making power to the administrative agencies. Congress might set goals for what it wants to achieve through regulation, but it allows the agencies to write the actual rules that touch on the actions of people and businesses.

As the administrative state has evolved, the agencies have gained power on another front as well. They now have the responsibility to judge most of the disputes that grow out of the rules they write. For example, if OSHA finds that a private company is violating a workplace safety regulation, it will cite the company and impose a penalty. Having been cited, the company can appeal the citation, but the appeal will be judged by OSHA itself, not by independent courts. And OSHA's ruling will be the last word, except in very unusual cases.

*   *   *

Sharp eyes will notice a serious constitutional danger in these developments. The administrative agencies have evolved in such a way that they hold not only executive power, but also legislative and judicial powers. The agencies write regulations, administer them, and stand as judges when conflicts arise from them. This concentration of powers within government was one of James Madison's greatest constitutional fears. "The accumulation of all powers legislative, executive and judiciary in the same hands . . . may justly be pronounced the very definition of tyranny," he wrote in *Federalist* 47.

This concentration of power is the root of current concern with the administrative state. The vast scope of the regulatory agencies, combined with their concentrated powers, makes them seem like a shadow government unto itself, one divorced from control by the people.

Yet if the power of the agencies borders on the unconstitutional, the administrative state has not grown in a lawless fashion. It has developed through constitutional channels.[3] The legislature and judiciary have ceded powers to the executive branch willingly, under the increasing pressure of trying to govern a tremendously complex society.

It's also worth asking a further question about the administrative state and its powers. If government is to meet the challenge of protecting the common good in today's highly complicated economic and technological society, what are its options apart from the current administrative state? The Constitution is purposely cumbersome. Yet people feel the need for protection of the sort provided through government regulations, and at least we keep electing people who support them. We are caught in a bind in which we, the people, demand more government than our 18th-century Constitution can readily provide. If the Constitution has been stretched to make the administrative state possible, it's unclear where any better constitutional alternative lies.

AMENDMENT

A government, which, in its own organization, provides no
means of change, but assumes to be fixed and unalterable,
must, after a while, become wholly unsuited to the circumstances of the nation.

—Joseph Story, Supreme Court Justice (1812–1845)

Joseph Story, one of the Supreme Court's greatest justices, lived a half-gen-
eration after the Founding of the Republic, close enough to have a strong
sense of the Founders' ideals. A central ideal was this: the people deserve a
constitution that fits their values and aspirations.

But drawing up a national constitution with the proper fit between the
people and their laws was no easy task, especially for a young nation. There was a
natural danger that the Constitution would remain fixed as society evolved, and
thus lose that necessary fit between citizens and government.

For this reason, the Founders wanted an adaptable constitution. However,
the need for adaptability is only half of a difficult dilemma, and Joseph
Story understood the other half as well: "A government, forever changing
and changeable," he wrote, "is indeed in a state bordering upon anarchy and
confusion." To serve its basic purpose, a constitution can never be too fluid.
Governments and their laws must provide stability and command respect if they
are to secure the people against disorder. A society forever disputing its basic laws
is headed for political disaster.

To address these competing needs, the Founders included within the
Constitution terms for its amendment, or changing. According to the terms of
Article V, the Constitution can be amended when (a) two-thirds of both houses
of Congress propose amendments, *or* (b) when two-thirds of the states call

conventions for that purpose; *and* (c) three-quarters of state legislatures or state-wide conventions ratify the proposed amendments. With these as the only options, any path to amendment will be difficult.

Striking a balance between the ease and the difficulty of passing amendments touches on the deepest concerns of government because amendments change the Constitution itself. They add to (or take away from) the Constitution's very language. Whatever the change may be, an amendment becomes as much a part of the Constitution as any other part.

Just as constitution-making marks a new political beginning for any state, so amending a constitution shares in that momentous, creative act. Amendments allow the people to periodically renew their claim to a government that reflects their will. Constitutional scholar Walter Dellinger put it this way: "The amendment process represents a domestication of the right to revolution...."

*   *   *

Practical politics will often defy theory, and the practice of constitutional change has not always matched the expectations of the Founders. For example, some constitutional amendments have brought little in the way of real change to our constitutional order. Consider the 26th Amendment, which ensured that men and women between the ages of 18 and 21 would have the right to vote. This was a milestone in its way, and a clear change in the Constitution. But it hardly changed our political order in any significant way. For example, it didn't give one branch of the government greater powers, nor did it alter the amount of overall power granted to the government.

On the other hand, great constitutional changes have been brought about without amendments. This happens when constitutional language is not rewritten, but is reinterpreted. A critical example concerns the "commerce clause" of the United States Constitution. The clause itself, from Article 1, Section 8, gives Congress the "power to regulate commerce...*among the several states*..." [emphasis added]. Historically, this power was understood to mean that Congress could legislate in ways that made interstate commerce more regular, smoothing the way for increased interstate trade.

In the late 1930s, however, the commerce clause began to be interpreted in a new light. Under it, Congress began to claim the power to regulate economic activity if that activity had virtually any effect on interstate commerce. This new interpretation of the commerce clause was accepted by the Supreme Court, which opened the door to an unprecedented extension of the federal government's regulatory powers. Consequently, through a new interpretation of unchanged constitutional language, Congress's power over the economy grew dramatically.

Without passing through the formal amendment process, our constitutional order was changed in profound ways.

But constitutional change of this sort presents a danger. Dependent on Supreme Court decisions unread by most citizens, they are made under the public's radar, as it were. By contrast, the standard amendment process places constitutional change at the center of a focused debate, in legislatures or state conventions, for example.

Without that level of public scrutiny, constitutional changes such as the reinterpretation of the commerce clause come without building the sort of national consensus that the full amendment process requires. This stealthier change carries a risk that turns a traditional concern on its head. Rather than society changing as the Constitution remains fixed, here constitutional change outpaces the understanding and support of the people. And when the two are out of sync, our political order loses a degree of its coherence.

Amicus Curiae

We are living in the age of the Supreme Court amicus.

—Allison Orr

The term is Latin and means, literally, "friend of the court." The friend in this case is a party that submits a brief, or a statement, to the Supreme Court or other courts of appeal. These briefs are written to clarify difficult legal issues in a given case. The parties that submit amicus briefs are not *directly* involved in the case being decided; they are not litigants themselves. Rather, they are indirectly interested and have some expertise that makes their opinion useful to the justices as they weigh the merits of the case.

If, for example, the Court is trying a difficult case concerning one company's responsibilities under the Clean Water Act, an independent environmental group might submit an amicus curiae brief presenting their views on the law and its effects.

It's not just private parties that file amicus briefs. Governments—local, state, or federal—can as well. For example, the United States Justice Department filed two separate amicus briefs in one of the most consequential Supreme Court cases in American history, *Brown* v. *Board of Education,* which decided the fate of segregation in public schools. The federal government was not a party to the lawsuit, but leaders in the Justice Department understood the importance of the case to the country's future. So they submitted their amicus briefs to the Supreme Court, spelling out the Justice Department's legal understanding of the matter.

The *Brown* decision presented the Court with difficult challenges, involving a complex weighing of the rights of cities and states to set their own education policies against evolving standards of racial fairness. When the Justice Department filed its amicus briefs, it provided legal clarification to the Court. In this sense, the Justice Department's amicus filings lived up to the Latin meaning of their name, with the briefs serving the interests of the Court. At their best, amicus briefs present useful information, much needed by a Supreme Court that faces complex, often controversial, legal choices.

But in the *Brown* case the Justice Department did something else as well: it put its thumb on the scale. Through its amicus curiae briefs, the Justice Department made clear its opposition to school segregation. This highlights a critical aspect of amicus statements. Despite the name, they are not submitted solely out of friendly feeling for the Court. Parties file amicus briefs in order to shape the outcome of the Court's rulings and to advance their own policy preferences. So, for example, the environmental group that files a brief in a Clean Water Act case will likely use its amicus argument to further the goal of a cleaner environment. Its position might well be met and countered by an amicus statement that takes a different view, perhaps submitted by an industry trade association.[4]

These days, in fact, that will almost certainly happen. Though once rare—there were a scant handful filed during the whole of the 19th century—amicus curiae briefs have become a staple of Supreme Court trials. In the ten years between 1946 and 1955, 531 amicus briefs were filed with the Court. In a similar span between 1986 and 1995, close to 5,000 were filed, roughly nine times as many. And the growth has continued since then. As of 2016, there were roughly 800 amicus filings per year, and 95 percent of Supreme Court cases had at least one amicus submission. One case in 2015, which concerned same-sex marriage, set an amicus record, with 148 briefs filed.

So profuse are the "friends of the court" now that a small industry has grown up, dedicated to providing the Supreme Court with the most effective possible briefs for given cases. This industry comes with so-called "amicus wranglers" who review potential briefs, select the most appropriate, and bundle them together for presentation to the Court. When they see fit, wranglers will even recruit amicus statements if interested parties are slow to produce them.

The amicus environment suggests something important about law and policy making in the United States. For starters, the stakes are high enough in Supreme Court decisions that concerned parties will go to great lengths to influence the outcome through their amicus curiae arguments. The Court is seen as more than a disinterested interpreter of the law: it is a key player in policy making.

Also, the huge number and range of "friends" who seek to shape Court decisions suggests that the government and its laws, rules, regulations, and such affect peoples' lives a great deal. The Court would not have so many friends—nor so many enemies—if government were not in such constant contact with us.

APPROPRIATION

This power over the purse may, in fact, be regarded as the most complete and effectual weapon with which any constitution can arm the immediate representatives of the people, for obtaining a redress of every grievance and for carrying into effect every just and salutary measure.

—James Madison, President (1809–1817)

There is no power in government to match that of money. No program will function, no law will be enforced, no army can fight without spending. And before money can be spent, it must be appropriated. That is to say, the lawful go-ahead must be given to move money from the general treasury to the agencies that will use it.

In the American national government, a critical part of this process is carried out through the appropriations committees of the House of Representatives and the Senate. Of all Congress's many committees, these two are among the most powerful, and positions on them are highly sought after.

Both appropriations committees, House and Senate, include twelve subcommittees, each of which handles a different area of the federal government's activities: Defense; Interior, Environment, and Related Agencies; Transportation and Housing and Urban Development, to cite three examples. Together, the twelve subcommittees are responsible for all discretionary spending by the federal government.[5] They review all the agencies and all the projects that fall under their areas of responsibility, account for the spending therein, and allocate funding for them as they see fit. Without the fiscal blessing of the appropriations committees, the federal government's many agencies and projects would have no money to spend and would be dead in the water.

Among the checks and balances of our national government, the power of the purse, held by Congress, is a lynchpin in the whole system. The executive branch, for example, is dependent on the appropriations process. It is one of the federal government's rites to have representatives from the executive branch agencies go hat-in-hand to Congress to justify their favored projects: a new missile for Defense, a new bridge for Transportation, a bigger budget for the National Parks, and so on, down a very long line.

Nor is the blessing from appropriations a one-time deal. Much spending is granted for one- or two-year periods, the better for Congress to keep tabs on how effectively all that money is being spent. If programs are not living up to their original promise, the appropriations process gives Congress a chance to prune the funding, or at least threaten to do so.

As noted above, the appropriations process covers discretionary spending, which is spending that depends on Congressional decisions. It does not cover mandatory spending, which includes the funding of entitlement programs or paying interest on the government's massive loans. Non-discretionary spending now eats up around 70 percent of the federal budget. However, the sky-high demand for relatively scarce remaining discretionary funds allows the House and Senate appropriations committees to maintain their strong influence.

*   *   *

The power of appropriation is great, but it is distinct from the power of writing basic legislation. This distinction is reflected in the lawmaking process in Congress, which has two separate stages. Before money is appropriated, programs must be authorized. Authorization is the fruit of the work done by Congressional committees other than Appropriations. In those committees, members hash out their preferred policies, producing bills that will be voted on by the full House or Senate. So, for example, the House Energy and Commerce Committee might favor a bill that includes a solar energy research project. If the bill passes, the project is said to be authorized: Congress has granted the authority to establish it.

But the project is not yet funded, and thus not yet active. It must go before the appropriations committee (and the fitting subcommittee), to get its funding. Having completed this second stage—but not before—the program can be set in motion, assuming that the president signs the bill when it comes from Congress.

By treating appropriation as a second stage in lawmaking, Congress is better able to see spending as a distinct matter, apart from policy itself. The appropriations committees are responsible for viewing spending in the context of the broader national budget. Without that perspective, spending might be seen only from the narrow perspectives of the other committees, colored by their policy preferences and agendas. To the degree that Congress has a handle on discretionary spending, it is through the appropriations committees that it applies its grip.

ATTORNEY GENERAL

Nothing can more weaken the quality of life or more imperil the realization of the goals we all hold dear than our failure to make clear by words and deeds that our law is not an instrument of partisan purpose.

—Edward Levi, U.S. Attorney General (1975–1977)

Any attorney general who is not an activist is not doing his or her job.

—Eric Holder, U.S. Attorney General (2009–2015)

According to *The Oxford Companion to American Law*, the attorney general is the "chief law enforcement officer of the United States." Some clarity is in order, however. The *United States* Attorney General is at the top of *federal* law enforcement, but there are fifty other attorneys general, each holding a similar position at the state level. Moreover, the title itself is a good deal older than the Constitution, appearing as early as the 15th century in England. As the English crossed the Atlantic and founded colonies in North America, they brought the term with them. Before the Revolution there were attorneys general in several colonies.

Once the Constitution was adopted and the national government formed, the office of national attorney general was created by an act of Congress, the Judiciary Act of 1789, which also established the Supreme Court. Yet the attorney general is not an office of the judicial branch, but is within the executive branch. Presidents nominate their attorneys general, who are then confirmed by the Senate. In the wording of the Judiciary Act, the attorney general should be "a meet person, learned in the law," whose duties include giving "advice and opinion upon questions of law when required by the President of the United States, or when requested by the heads of the departments, touching any matters that may concern their departments."

For decades after the Founding the attorney general worked virtually alone, with no supporting staff. Over the years, however, the legal needs of the federal government increased steadily, placing an ever greater burden on the office. By 1870, the Department of Justice was founded to better meet those demands. That department now has well over 100,000 employees, and overseeing it is one of the attorney general's primary responsibilities.

But the essence of the job is to assist the president in one of his or her key constitutional obligations: to "Take care that the laws be faithfully executed."

*   *   *

To understand better what it means to faithfully execute the laws of the land, consider the different ways in which government actions touch upon the law. For starters, legislatures write laws, which then need enforcement, and making sure the laws are enforced is one of the attorney general's responsibilities. If the Voting Rights Act, for example, is being violated somewhere in the country, it ultimately falls to the attorney general to make sure the problem is investigated and corrected.

The attorney general also has a responsibility to see that in enforcing the law, the government itself acts lawfully. To continue with the Voting Rights Act example, those charged with investigating its transgression must do so without violating constitutional protections against illegal search and seizure.

In addition, the national government can also weigh in on court cases in which it is not directly involved but has a strong interest. One example is the famous civil rights case, *Brown* v. *Board of Education*. In that case, the Supreme Court was weighing the constitutionality of local—not federal—laws, so the U.S. attorney general had no direct interest in the case. But the attorney general at the time supported the Brown suit, and this support from the attorney general, representing the judgment of the national government, was one factor in the Court's decision in favor of school desegregation.

One other responsibility of the office deserves mention. The attorney general has long played a role in screening candidates for judgeships in the federal judiciary, including the critical positions on the Supreme Court. Given the potent political storms that brew up with so many judicial nominations, this is one of the attorney general's most sensitive duties.

*   *   *

There is a duality at the heart of the attorney general's job, one that can lead to political tension. He or she must enforce the laws impartially. But attorneys general will also, inevitably, bring their own preferences to the job. Moreover, having been chosen by a given president and serving at their will, the attorney general will naturally reflect the president's political stances.

We can see how attorneys general can become enmeshed in politics by looking at two who held the office in the tumultuous 1960s. The first, Attorney General Ramsey Clark, who held the office starting in 1967, was an aggressive defender of civil rights, and made a priority of enforcing the Civil Rights and Voting Rights acts. For many Americans, this was a period of bright hope for the advance of racial equality, and Clark was in the thick of the fight.

During his time in office, however, Clark failed to adequately address a worrisome increase in street crime, which rattled a large number of citizens. In 1968, presidential candidate Richard Nixon vowed in his campaign to restore "law and order," and amid a rising tide of disorderly protests, riots, and drug-related crime, his candidacy thrived. After winning the election he appointed John Mitchell as attorney general, who was fully aligned with the presidential promise to crack down on criminal lawlessness.

When an attorney general makes his or her priorities clear, whatever they may be, opponents will have a clear argument to pick: the attorney general has a responsibility to enforce all the laws and cannot simply choose which ones will get their attention.

Politicized law is almost a contradiction in terms, and any drift toward overt politicization of the attorney general's role presents a danger. In a nation as diverse as ours, the law binds us together, and it must be seen as serving the interests of the whole society. When people feel that laws are enforced unfairly or with political ends in mind, it degrades the trust between the political leadership and the people themselves. Though an attorney general might feel pulled toward particular priorities, none is higher for the office than protecting this trust and the good name of the law nationwide.

BILL OF RIGHTS

> The very purpose of a Bill of Rights was to withdraw certain subjects from the vicissitudes of political controversy, to place them out of reach of majorities and officials. ... One's right to life, liberty, and property, to free speech, a free press, freedom of worship and assembly, and other fundamental rights may not be submitted to vote; they depend on the outcome of no elections.
>
> —Robert Jackson, Supreme Court Justice (1941–1954)

For millions of Americans, the Bill of Rights is the heart of the Constitution. The protections found in the Bill are the Constitution's most memorable elements and the ones we can apply most directly to our lives. Even if we cannot remember how Congress overrides a presidential veto, we remember that the Constitution protects our freedom of speech.

But before the Bill of Rights became such a force in our system, it was not part of the Constitution at all. The Bill of Rights is made up the first ten amendments to the Constitution, all added in 1791, three years after ratification of the Constitution itself.

When the Constitution was delivered from the Convention of 1787, without any bill of rights, opposition was stronger than we tend to remember. Its critics feared that the Constitution gave the national government too much power, without strong enough protections against the abuse of that power. The best way to protect against such abuse, opponents argued, would be to add a bill of rights that specified the protections people held against any infringement by the national government.

This idea was hardly new. At that time, several state constitutions already included bills of rights. And British history provided other models, including the Bill of Rights of 1689, grandfather of all the later American ones.

Federalists—supporters of the Constitution—disagreed with the critics. There was no need for a bill of rights since, as Alexander Hamilton put it, "the Constitution is itself, in every rational sense, and to every useful purpose, A BILL OF RIGHTS." While the Constitution did not list specific rights as a bill would do[6], it did, by its nature, limit the reach of government.[7] Moreover, Congress's powers, limited already, came directly from the people. Thus the legislative power of the national government could not be an alien force, threatening the liberties of the people. At least the federalists argued as much.

But those arguments failed to satisfy the anti-federalists, who pounded away during the battle over ratification.[8] The absence of a bill of rights was one of their favored points.

With the two sides at loggerheads, Massachusetts came up with a compromise. At its state convention, where ratification was being debated, delegates decided they would vote for the Constitution as it was, but included a strong recommendation that the new government adopt a bill of rights as soon as possible.

As events unfolded, this compromise won the day. Other states followed suit, and enough support swung toward the Constitution to see it adopted. Once a new government formed, Congress initiated the amendment process to formally add a bill of rights to the nation's fundamental law. From dozens of suggested protections, James Madison and other leaders boiled the proposals down to a much-condensed set of twelve, which passed both houses of Congress. These twelve were sent to the states for their votes, and the states in turn ratified ten. These officially became part of the Constitution on December 15, 1791, and thus the Bill of Rights became federal law.

                              *   *   *

Despite the early furor over the Bill of Rights, the rights themselves raised little controversy in the decades that followed their ratification. The Supreme Court, for example, did not try a single important free speech case until the First World War.

As the 20th century progressed, however, legal fireworks over the Bill of Rights began to erupt. Through the middle and later decades of the century, the courts decided any number of cases that concerned specific rights from the Bill, and in deciding those cases often extended our notions of what individual rights entail.

Consider, for example, the Fourth Amendment. Among its provisions, it establishes the right of a person accused of a crime to have "the Assistance of Counsel for his defense." In a series of Supreme Court decisions, this right was interpreted to mean that legal counsel must be *provided* to defendants who could not otherwise afford it; moreover, that counsel would be provided whether the defendant requested it or not; and, in addition, defendants had the right to counsel not only during trial, but also whenever interrogated by any government agent. So, as the Supreme Court considered the implications of the basic right to counsel, it enlarged upon it in all those ways. Moreover, similar extensions were applied to other provisions of the Bill of Rights, including those associated with free speech, freedom of religion, and so forth.

*   *   *

In sum, the Bill of Rights grew increasingly prominent in American law during the 20th century, and Supreme Court decisions concerning it have led to a dramatic expansion of individual rights.

However, the logic of rights carries with it a corollary: obligations. If American citizens have a First Amendment right to burn flags as a form of protected political speech, for example, offended citizens are obliged to bear that insult, at least as a matter of law. (Those offended can respond with other, non-legislative remedies: grinding one's teeth, shaking one's fists, flipping one's bird, etc.)

Thus, in protecting the individual, the Bill of Rights constrains the community in terms of the legislation that protects majority-supported standards. As constitutional law scholar Akhil Reed Amar states (or perhaps overstates), "the Bill has become a bulwark of rights against all government conduct."

Yet we do govern, and while "rights talk" tends naturally toward absolute claims, society in fact limits even basic rights and always has. We embrace free speech, but its protection does not extend so far as libel; we embrace the right to bear arms, but no citizen is allowed to operate military-grade artillery at home. We test the limits of our rights, with an understanding that no rights are truly absolute. Even the Bill of Rights was born through the give and take of politics.

BUREAUCRACY

> In a modern state, real rule, which becomes effective in
> everyday life neither through parliamentary speeches nor
> through the pronouncements of monarchs but through the
> day-to-day management of the administration necessarily
> lies in the hands of officialdom . . . .
>
> —Max Weber

Bureaucracy is one of the grim, unavoidable realities of modern life. Just as democracy is "rule by the *demos*," or the people, so bureaucracy is "rule by bureau." *Bureau* in this case means "government agency," as in the Bureau of Indian Affairs (BIA), or any of the other agencies that administer government at the federal, state or local level. *Bureau* comes from the French word for desk, and *bureaucracy* as a term is French in origin.

Such agencies as the BIA are a primary place where citizen and government meet face to face. Imagine (if you can bear it) facing a Department of Motor Vehicles agent across an imposing desk or counter seeking help to resolve some snag in your license renewal.

Government bureaucracies swelled in size during the 19th and 20th centuries, as they did with all large-scale enterprises—very big businesses, for example. Growth presents immense organizational challenges. To function, big organizations need an infrastructure of rules, procedures, and well-defined hierarchies of responsibility. In other words, they require bureaucracy.

Nobody much likes bureaucracy, especially in government. It's easy to forget the times it works smoothly—delivering Social Security checks, for example. More memorable is the time wasted in line at the DMV, or the baffling rules we navigate in sorting out Medicare benefits. We wish bureaucracies were easier to deal with, that they were more responsive to our needs. But some of the problems we face with them are built in. Bureaucracies are designed to handle transactions in bulk, and are not by nature well-tuned to meet individual needs.

*   *   *

The unpopularity of bureaucracy in the United States is ironic, because in a very real way we demand it. American citizens demand, through their representatives, a bewildering array of services from their national, state, and local governments. These services stretch from food safety to assistance with affordable housing, environmental regulation, and a thousand others. None of these come without bureaucracy.

When we demand such services, we think little about the difficulties government faces in providing them. We assume that bureaucracies should and will simply do what citizens want. That is how private businesses work: They have customers, and it is their business to serve them as effectively as possible. If they don't meet the customers' needs, they don't survive.

Life is more complicated for government bureaucracies. Ordinary citizens are not, in a sense, their real client. We don't pay them for performing their work—at least not directly—and they are not directly accountable to us.

In the case of the federal bureaucracy, it is Congress who pays the bills, and Congress is the customer who must be satisfied. This makes Congress the backseat driver, and the bureaucratic agencies cannot afford to ignore its demands.

In overseeing the federal bureaucracy, Congress sets all sorts of conditions on how those agencies do their work. For example, Congress imposes tight regulations on the hiring and firing of federal employees, which tie the hands of supervisors in the bureaucracy. In 2010, the federal government fired only 0.55 percent of its employees, as opposed to the roughly 6 percent who were fired in the private sector.

What's more, if a federal agency contracts with an outside firm to provide some product or service, that firm must generally abide by similar restrictions. Imagine private companies bidding to supply the Army with a new weapon. Under current rules, the winner must employ a certain mix of minority and female workers; provide opportunities for the handicapped; meet all relevant EPA and OSHA standards; not be embroiled in substantial legal troubles; and offer to do the work at the lowest cost. Meeting these requirements *and documenting* the process is difficult and significantly complicates the job of supplying the weapon.

*   *   *

The inefficiencies of bureaucracy are maddening. But there is another, rather darker aspect of bureaucratic growth. As bureaucracy grows, citizens are inevitably affected, even changed, by our constant dealings with it.

Consider this. To function well, bureaucracies must carefully order and rationalize their internal functions. But to complete their mission, the agencies also need to project this ethic of organization out into the public, in effect requiring the people to become more ordered themselves, on terms set by the bureaus. If American citizens and businesses want to avoid painful penalties, for example, they will accommodate the demands of the Internal Revenue Service. They must fill out wretchedly complex tax forms and submit them on schedule, at great cost in time, effort, money, and sanity.

And though we grow used to such demands, it is worth noting that it takes training to reach that point, and it doesn't come naturally. To a degree, good citizenship today means being broken to the saddle of bureaucratic government.

CABINET

As an institution, the Cabinet is (to twist Emerson) the lengthened shadow of another institution—the Presidency. The Cabinet is a secondary institution, understandable only in terms of a primary one.

—Richard Fenno

*C*abinet as a political term is a distant relative of the more familiar *cabinet*, of the sort one finds in kitchens. Etymologically, *cabinet* is to *cabin* as *kitchenette* is to *kitchen*. If a cabin is a private, self-contained structure, a cabinet is a similar thing, but diminutive. In an early English usage, a cabinet was a small, secluded room. When the king met with his closest advisors, they often gathered in such a room, or cabinet, where they could speak in strict confidence. For this reason the king's closest advisors were sometimes called the "cabinet council."

Translated into more contemporary and American terms, the president's cabinet is, like the king's cabinet council, a high-level group of advisors and administrators. They include the men and women who lead the fifteen major departments of the executive branch. Cabinet members include the secretaries of the State Department, the Defense Department, the Treasury Department, and other departments, as well as the Attorney General, the head of the Justice Department, and the ambassador to the United Nations. They are all nominated by the president and are chosen to help achieve the president's political goals. Once nominated, potential cabinet members must be confirmed by a vote in the Senate. Cabinet positions are prestigious, and generally go to people who have proven their abilities over the course of substantial careers.

*   *   *

When cabinet members are nominated and confirmed, people pay attention. Then something odd happens: many seem to disappear. Even news junkies go for months without hearing anything about the Secretary of Labor or Transportation. This leads to a question: once they join the president's administration, what do cabinet members actually do?

The first responsibility of cabinet members is to manage the departments they lead. These are very big, very complex institutions. The Department of Defense, for example, is likely the largest single employer in the world, with over three million employees. It is that department's job to provide the nation's defense: build weapons systems, train soldiers, plan for future defense needs, and fight when and where it is deemed necessary. The Secretary of Defense is responsible for overseeing this vast effort, and making sure the department is prepared to accomplish its tasks. The other cabinet members all have parallel responsibilities in their departments.

In running these departments, cabinet members are like the president's ambassadors to these giant organizations, and part of their job is to carry out the president's wishes there. It is also part of the cabinet's job to report back to the president about matters that they, through their work, know more about than the president possibly could. If a president comes up with a bad idea, the cabinet, acting as a sounding board, can provide needed perspective on the plan.

Yet the cabinet and its members have no legal power to control the president. When Abraham Lincoln was in office, he proposed an idea about which his cabinet was skeptical. After some discussion, a vote was called. Then Lincoln reviewed the result: "Seven noes, one aye," he said: "the ayes have it." While a president might seek advice from the cabinet, there is no constitutional requirement to accept it.

*   *   *

Although the cabinet lacks constitutional powers, they are hardly strangers to brute political force. In fact, cabinet members operate along fault lines where three very powerful institutions collide like shifting tectonic plates. One, of course, is the presidency, and cabinet members understand that they are chosen by, and can be dismissed by, the president. A second institution is the department the cabinet member leads. To run their department effectively, cabinet members necessarily interact with its permanent staff. Each department has its own culture and sense of purpose. As the leader of such a department, a cabinet member must learn its ways, even if he or she aims to reform them.

As they learn, cabinet members often adopt, to one degree or another, their department's views and goals. And as this happens, they may be pulled away from the president's orbit. A high-ranking staffer for Richard Nixon described this as having "gone off and married the natives."

The tendency to go rogue is not just a matter of shifting loyalties. The executive departments are home to some of the national government's most experienced policy makers. Among the thousands of employees in the Department of Interior, for example, are some who have spent decades learning about issues related to Interior's mission. Department specialists are far from perfect, but their expertise is hard for cabinet members to ignore.

The other political fault line that cabinet members confront is between their department and Congress. One key fact shapes this relationship: Congress holds the purse strings. Money is the lifeblood of every department, and Congress appropriates the money that pays for it all. Cabinet members must explain the needs of their department to members of Congress who not only determine where the money goes, but will also have their own ideas about what can or should be paid for. The two sides will debate their priorities and reach their compromises in a confrontation that never really ends.

*   *   *

Thus it is the job of cabinet members to navigate the difficult terrain where major institutions of our national government meet. Without great powers of its own, the cabinet seems to be a weak institution, "one of the few organizations of government for which the whole is less than the sum of the parts," as one observer put it. But perhaps there is more to the cabinet's work than meets the public eye. The cabinet serves a crucial purpose in a constitutional system that divides power among its branches. Cabinet members work where institutions confront each other, and facilitate the compromises necessary to making the system work.

CAUCUS

Do you know how to tell the difference between a cactus
and a caucus?

—Morris Udall, U.S. Representative (1961–1981)

The origins of *caucus* are obscure. Historian Alvin Josephy, Jr., traces it back
to the Powhatan people of Virginia, from whom early English settlers
picked it up. To the Powhatans, Josephy says, *caucus* meant "counselor."

But the term's early history is more strongly linked to colonial Massachusetts,
where its modern meaning took shape. There was a Caucus Club in pre-Revolution
Boston, a group that met for drinking, smoking, and talking, with the talk
inevitably turning to politics. In time, the club grew into a semi-secret society in
which talk turned to activism. Samuel Adams was a Caucus Club regular, and it
was in the milieu of such underground political gatherings that Adams and his
Liberty Boys planned the Boston Tea Party.

The word's essential meaning is found here: A caucus is a meeting of a political
party or faction in which members plan ways to advance their causes. However
provincial its origins, the term *caucus* is now used in countries around the world:
Australia, South Africa, New Zealand, even Nepal.

In today's news, at least in America, the caucuses most often mentioned are
those of the United States Congress, and the origins of the congressional caucuses
shed light on the term's meaning.

In the earliest years of the United States government, Secretary of the Treasury
Alexander Hamilton came up with a highly ambitious plan to solve the nation's
deep financial problems. To translate his plan into action, however, Hamilton
needed Congress to pass the necessary laws. So he met in private with sympathetic

congressmen to plot a strategy for passing his program. Under Hamilton's guidance, they drafted specific legislation, deciding who would introduce it and how supporters would defend the plan in debate. This is typical caucus work.

Hamilton had plenty of opponents, and they included powerful figures: Secretary of State Thomas Jefferson was one, as was James Madison, then the leading figure in the House of Representatives. To counter the Hamiltonian program, these opponents also began to meet privately and plan how to foil it. In the efforts of these two camps, we can see the origins of the caucus in Congress, as well as the origins of our first national political parties.

Caucuses today have much the same function. Both Democrats and Republicans have caucuses in each house of Congress (though the Republicans call theirs "conferences"). These caucuses gather behind closed doors to set legislative goals, discuss how best to defend their policies before the public, vote for party leaders, and, of course, plot ways to thwart their partisan enemies.

Party caucuses in Congress can be convened whenever necessary, but are always held after elections, when new members arrive in Washington. In the House, for example, the majority party—the one with the most representatives—will hold a caucus to elect a majority leader and a majority whip. They'll also elect a caucus chair, who will run the caucus meetings during that session of Congress. The majority party in the House will decide on its choice for Speaker of the House, though he or she will be elected in a vote of the whole House. The party out of power will hold a caucus as well, in which it votes for a minority leader, a minority whip, and a caucus chairperson.

It's worth noting that there are Congressional caucuses that are not party-based. Caucuses can form wherever members of Congress share legislative goals or some sense of solidarity with other members. There is, for example, a Congressional Black Caucus, which seeks to unite and strengthen African-American voices; a Congressional Hispanic Caucus; and a Congressional Caucus for Women's Issues. In addition, there is a long list of caucuses that seek to raise the profile of specific issues within the legislature: the Congressional Caucus on Youth Sports is one example, as are the Congressional Cystic Fibrosis Caucus, the Food Safety Caucus, and the Congressional Rock and Roll Caucus.

*   *   *

While caucuses bring together people who share a point of view, they are also the focal point of hot inter-party infighting and back-stabbing. Representative Morris "Mo" Udall was reminded of this in 1971. Udall, an Arizonan, was much admired. Smart, hard-working, and likable, he rose in prominence among House Demo-crats. After ten years in Congress, he decided to run for majority leader. In preparing for the caucus vote, he made the rounds of his Democratic colleagues asking for support and gathering promises for votes. Going into the caucus, he was upbeat.

Coming out was another matter. To Udall's surprise, promised votes failed to materialize, and he fell well short of winning. Despite losing, however, he retained his sense of humor. In a press conference afterward, Udall asked reporters a rhetorical question: "Do you know the difference between a cactus and a caucus?" Not waiting for their reply, he answered himself. "With a cactus, the pricks are on the outside."

CHIEF OF STAFF

Every president knows when he's picking his chief of staff,
my god, he'd better get the right man in that job or he'll
be ruined.

—Theodore Sorensen

There is a piece of modern folk wisdom about chiefs of staff: Anyone "who
really matters" in Washington has one. That is, anyone who has real
power will have enough of a staff that the staff needs its own chief. This
is surely the case for presidents. So when the term *chief of staff* crops up in the
news, chances are high that it refers to the president's top aide. The chief of staff's
responsibility is to act as an interface between the president and the presidential
staff, making sure that it—the staff—effectively supports its leader.

But this is a daunting mission. The presidential staff has grown enormously
over the decades, becoming an unwieldy bureaucracy unto itself. It now includes
any number of officials, and even whole agencies, that advise the president on
national security, domestic policy, economic affairs, press relations, and more.
The chief of staff is responsible for smooth functioning throughout.

Given the importance of the staff to presidential success, it is hard to imagine
that any president could function without one. Yet presidents up through Harry
Truman managed to do so. Dwight D. Eisenhower was the first to have an
official chief of staff. Eisenhower came to the presidency after a career in the
military, where the office of chief of staff has a long history.[9] As the commander
of all American forces in Europe during World War II, and of the invasion of
Normandy, Eisenhower faced huge organizational challenges in which he was
assisted by his chief of staff.[10] When Eisenhower was elected president in 1952,

he brought the office, though not the officer, with him.

To get a sense of a chief of staff's responsibilities, it helps to consider President Bill Clinton's first year in office. As Leon Panetta, who eventually served as Clinton's chief of staff (though not during that opening period) describes it, the scene was "wild," "undisciplined," and "chaotic." Meetings were called without clear agendas. They ran overtime, but without producing decisions. Staffers had surprisingly free access to the president during the day, which Clinton enjoyed. But these informal intrusions left the president making promises on the fly at times and uncoordinated with key staffers. The interruptions also made Clinton's daily schedule, plotted out in 15-minute segments, unmanageable. Taken together, these miscues led to frustration for all, and, most importantly, a loss of effectiveness for the president.

To remedy the situation, Clinton chose Panetta to take over as chief of staff. Perhaps the key change Panetta made was to clamp down on access to the president, reducing intrusions on his time. In a sense, the chief of staff's basic function is to govern the flow of information to and from the president. Without some filter, the flood of information can be overwhelming. As Bob Haldeman, one-time chief of staff for Richard Nixon, put it, "The president shouldn't have ten piles of irrelevant or unrelated paper that he's got to wade through, sort out, and figure out what to do with. That's the staff's function." Then he added:

> The president's function is to take all that information and make a decision on the basis of that. The whole effort that the White House staff person is making every minute of his working day is to ensure that the president is making the right decision for the right reasons. That means getting the right information to him on all sides of an issue, along with the recommendations of those advisors from whom the president wants recommendations on that particular issue.

*   *   *

In addition to managing incoming information, chiefs of staff also handle its flow from the president outward. If a president needs the staff to follow some new direc-tive, the chief conveys the message. If problems with staff members arise, the chief of staff metes out the discipline. As one-time Chief of Staff Dick Cheney put it, "If there is a dirty deed to be done, it's the Chief of Staff who's got to do it."

Presidents will also inevitably put chiefs of staff in an especially sticky situation. Not every idea from a president will be a wise one. And when a president comes up with a bad one, the chief of staff is the first in line for shooting it down. When there is a healthy relationship between the president and the chief of staff, the chief of staff will feel free to speak his or her mind. Failing that, chiefs of staff have been known to resort to subterfuge. Once Richard Nixon, infuriated by leaks from the State Department, insisted that every employee in that department submit to a lie detector test to prove they were not the leaker. The idea was not only utterly impractical, but politically suicidal. After failing to dissuade the president, Chief of Staff Haldeman managed to delay the plan long enough for Nixon to shake off his anger and see how unworkable it was.

Yet deflection of this sort is dangerous in its way. A president must feel complete trust in the chief of staff, which will surely erode if the chief acts deceptively. Above all, the chief of staff has to remember the distinction between the president's authority and the chief's own. The president is put in power by the will of the people, and an enormous amount of faith is invested in the office. The president answers to a constituency of millions. By contrast, the chief of staff is chosen by the president and has a constituency of only one.

CIVIL DISOBEDIENCE

Must the citizen ever for a moment, or in the least degree, resign his conscience to the legislator? Why has every man a conscience then?

—Henry David Thoreau

The term *civil disobedience* is almost, but not quite, an oxymoron—a term so internally illogical it makes no sense. That which is civil is shared in a spirit of accommodation. Civil life, for example, depends on the acceptance of common laws and mutual respect. Disobedience entails nearly the opposite.

But civil disobedience is not really illogical, and even has a storied place in our history. We can trace its origin to a summer day in 1846, when Henry David Thoreau set out from his home in rural Concord, Massachusetts, to get a shoe mended. On the way, however, he ran into an acquaintance, the town tax collector. The two were friendly and their encounter amiable. But it was not without complications, since Thoreau had not paid certain taxes for six years. When the collector asked Thoreau for the money, he added, "I'll pay your tax, Henry, if you're hard up." When Thoreau declined, the collector warned that he would have to be locked up if he didn't pay soon. "As well now as any time," Thoreau answered, and so went off for his famous night in jail.

Money wasn't the problem behind Thoreau's unpaid taxes. His refusal to pay was a protest. To pay the tax would, in his eyes, lend support to a government whose policies he disdained. Thoreau was outraged by the national government's acceptance of slavery in the South, as well as its recent war with Mexico. Unwilling to support such a government, Thoreau chose the direct way to register his defiance: refusing to pay his taxes, thus breaking the law.

There is no sign that Thoreau meant his act to be publicized at the time. When he was let out of jail the next day, he picked up where he left off, getting his shoe mended. But others were intrigued and asked about his jailing, so Thoreau gave a public lecture on the subject, printed under the title "Resistance to Civil Government." Then, nearly twenty years later, the essay was published again with its better-known title, "Civil Disobedience." In time, this term came to describe all such acts, where a dissident refuses to comply with a law as a way to protest government policy, with the expectation that he or she will suffer the legal consequences.

Through his defiance, Thoreau made clear his insistence on holding government to the high standard of his own conscience. And by accepting the punishment for his refusal, Thoreau demonstrated a personal integrity that lent special force to those opinions.

Thoreau accomplished something else as well. He forced the government to act. Thoreau's opposition could not be ignored because of its illegality. This had the effect of elevating Thoreau's views—his conscience—in the public debate. In effect, he confronted the laws of the state with his own moral code, and the state was obliged to respond.

*   *   *

When it was first published in book form, "Civil Disobedience" found few readers. Eventually, however, the essay made its way into the hands of a broader readership, which included an admiring Leo Tolstoy. Later, Mahatma Gandhi recognized the potential in civil disobedience to be more than a matter of individual protest. Gandhi successfully used mass acts of civil disobedience in his campaigns for civil rights in South Africa and for India's independence from Britain.

Of much greater consequence for this country, Martin Luther King, Jr. drew on the civil disobedience tradition to build the civil rights movement of the 1950s and 1960s. As with Gandhi's efforts, King used civil disobedience as an instrument in his broad civil rights campaign, one that pitted the ugly realities of legal segregation against the higher code of the movement itself.

*   *   *

The potential force of civil disobedience was manifest in the civil rights movement, which shook the foundations of segregation. That civil disobedience can have such effects is a tribute to its power within our political system.

This being the case, however, we should ask by what right the civilly disobedient take on their mantle. There are real risks involved in civil disobedience, after all.

Being unlawful sets dangerous precedents if used too often. Moreover, we have a highly refined political system in place, already responsible for the immensely sensitive task of creating legitimate, constitutional power and harnessing it to widely shared ends. Civil disobedience overrides that process and elevates the will of activists over the outcomes of ordinary legislation. From this perspective, those who engage in civil disobedience display a kind of contempt for the system, and, by extension, for their fellow citizens.

And so it is not only worth asking, but it must be asked: what gives the civilly disobedient their authority to wield political power?

Alas, no set answer is possible, not least because the deepest sources of political authority are mysterious. Yet we know it exists and know too that it does not always rest with government, even when government is legitimately constituted. Martin Luther King, Jr. had that compelling authority and Jim Crow did not, despite the support of dozens of state legislatures and city councils. By 1964, the rightful claims of the civil rights movement could not be dismissed.

Civil disobedience thus serves as a reminder of a central truth of our political tradition. No government deserves absolute allegiance or entire submission. Nor can any government, certainly no broadly representative government, match the moral sensitivity of the individual, at least not the Gandhis, Kings, and Susan B. Anthonys among us. Civil disobedience, though it can be used by charlatans and cranks, can also serve as a final redoubt of skepticism toward government, a step taken when the laws themselves breach the bounds of justice.

CIVIL RIGHTS

The civil rights issue is not some ephemeral, evanescent domestic issue that can be kicked around by reactionary and hypocritical politicians. But it is an eternal moral issue which may well determine the destiny of our nation... .

—Martin Luther King, Jr.

The monumental legacy of Martin Luther King, Jr. can leave us with a skewed notion of what civil rights are. In the popular imagination, they are the rights of African Americans—and other minorities, but especially African Americans—to equality with all other Americans, under the law.

There is, however, a more technical definition of civil rights that is worth learning. Civil rights are all the rights guaranteed by the laws of a given government. So, in the United States, civil rights include the rights to vote, to speak freely, to own and use property, to be free of illegal search and seizure, to own firearms, and so forth. The civil rights movement was aimed at making all such rights apply to African Americans equally with all other Americans.

To better understand what *civil* rights are, compare them to *natural* rights. It is useful here to consider one theory of politics—highly influential at the time of the Founding—that clarifies the difference. According to this theory, all people possess rights according to nature, wholly apart from any government. In a pure state of nature, these rights were extensive. People had, for example, the right to use whatever resources they could find for food, shelter, and clothing. People in this natural state also had the right to protect themselves and their property against all threats, by whatever means necessary. These natural rights, so the theory goes, can never disappear, and they remain as the foundation for all the rights we have when we move from a state of nature to life under government.

We must make that transition to a governed society because in a state of nature all those natural rights, though real, are insecure. They are under constant threat from other people, for example, who will all too often steal, murder, or otherwise deprive us of what is rightfully ours. So we form governments to protect ourselves and our liberties. In doing so, we yield some of our rights to the government. We place them in trust, as it were, with the government, on the understanding that it will protect them for all who come together under government's protection. Here we find the origin of civil rights: they are the rights established by civil government, building on the foundation of natural rights.[11]

*   *   *

According to this theory, civil rights, like natural rights, are shared equally by all. At the heart of the civil rights movement was outrage that the government, in making and enforcing laws, failed to treat all races equally. The goal was to change the laws themselves, which the movement achieved with remarkable success. Among its landmark achievements are the 1964 Civil Rights Act and the 1965 Voter Rights Act, both aimed at disposing of laws that discriminated against African Americans.

Having started with African Americans, the civil rights movement expanded in the years that followed to include women, Hispanic Americans, Native Americans, the disabled, and the LBGT community. All shared a common goal: where discrimination could be proven, civil rights advocates sought to change the laws and draw more Americans under the cover of equal protection.

These movements led to dramatic changes in American life, but those changes fell short of full social and economic equality. Troubling racial disparities, for example, remain in income, employment levels, educational achievement, and rates of incarceration for criminal offenses. Faced with these ongoing problems, civil rights leaders have increasingly looked beyond baseline equality before the law and have called for more positive government action to bring minorities a fuller share of society's benefits. Among the most prominent of these efforts have been affirmative action programs.

This more activist approach to civil rights, however, raises concerns. When a right is claimed, there are implied obligations on the part of others. Under affirmative action, for example, the right being claimed might be for preferential treatment in college admissions; the corresponding obligation is to open space in those institutions for the favored applicants.

But the question of who bears the burden of meeting that obligation is critical. If it is a highly qualified young student applying to a prestigious college, must he or she give up a spot at the school to make affirmative action a reality? If so, the root notion of equal treatment under the law is lost.

Concerns about the direction of the civil rights movement have deepened as some of its advocates have grown more ambitious in their demands. Faced with deeply rooted inequalities, some activists describe discrimination in the United States as "systemic." According to this notion, racism permeates all American institutions. "Rooted in a racist foundation, systemic racism today is composed of intersecting, overlapping, and codependent racist institutions, policies, practices, ideas, and behaviors that give an unjust amount of resources, rights, and power to white people while denying them to people of color," according to one standard source.

If problems are systemic, it follows that the system must be changed in fundamental ways for true equality to emerge. Doing so will require "a program of deliberately reconstructing informal norms and cultural meanings," as the *Stanford Encyclopedia of Philosophy* puts it. In other words, to achieve civil rights for all, the culture must be remade, using all available tools, including, presumably, the laws.

If government power is used for such an ambitious project, we can expect a natural tension to arise. Generally we have understood that our government represents the people and will reflect their culture. And it is odd to think that a democratic government would be in the business of undermining "informal norms" and "cultural meanings." But if America's race problems are deeply rooted in virtually all aspects of our social life, systemic reform points in this direction.

CIVIL SOCIETY

> Despotism, by its very nature suspicious, sees the isolation
> of men as the best guarantee of its own permanence. . . . A
> despot will lightly forgive his subjects for not loving him,
> provided they do not love one another.
>
> —Alexis de Tocqueville

If one can imagine a map of society, one that shows our social landscape in a
politically useful way, at least two big features will stand out: the government
and the individual. Civil society is found in the broad area between them.
Civil society is made up of all the institutions, associations, and groups, formal
and informal, which exist there: churches, book groups, labor unions, softball
teams, symphony orchestras, universities, and so on. A nation with a strong civil
society is one in which people join such groups freely and enthusiastically. A
nation with weak civil society is one in which people do less joining, and where
government—or personal isolation—dominates instead.

The concept of *civil* society hinges on the connotations of the word *civil*.
Its etymological cousins *civility* and *civilization* help in understanding. To live
civilly depends on the capacity of people to interact peacefully with one another
in all kinds of circumstances. That cooperation depends on a measure of trust
and mutual respect, the building blocks of any civilization. Such civility does
not necessarily come naturally, and its opposites are all too familiar: bigotry,
suspicion, selfishness or civility's polar opposite, savagery.

Civil society provides a kind of barometer, measuring a country's social
vitality. It rewards people in ways that individual effort cannot. By acting
through the institutions of civil society, people grow out of isolation and into
fuller lives. As Alexis de Tocqueville put it, "Feelings and ideas are renewed, the

heart enlarged, and the understanding developed only by the reciprocal action of men upon one another." The well-being that civil society provides can be found in no other source.

*   *   *

The relationship between civil society and government is complex and depends partly on the nature of the government in question. A vital civil society can be a great boon to the state, providing material and spiritual satisfactions to its people. If we meet our wants and needs through civil society, we put less of a burden on the political system. Where civil society fails, government will find it impossible to fill the vacuum.

Conversely, where government is out of sync with its people, civil society may be a threat to it. Consider the communist governments imposed by the Soviet Union on the Warsaw Pact countries—Hungary, Poland, the old Czechoslovakia, and others. Like bad grafts, the imposed governments never took, poorly fitting the people and traditions of those countries.

From the governments' point of view, civil society in the Warsaw Pact countries was a threat. When unsupervised Poles, Czechs, and Hungarians gathered in any numbers and for nearly any purpose, simmering resentments could boil over. Suspicious of their own people, these governments went to great lengths to infiltrate and disable any associations that seemed remotely disloyal. For example, the Czech government was so unnerved by the subversive message of a Prague rock band, "Plastic People of the Universe," that it banned their concerts and arrested their members.

In the end, these fears were justified, and civil society played a crucial role in undermining the Warsaw Pact regimes. In Poland the confrontation between civil society and government reached an especially high pitch. The trade union Solidarity, with its charismatic leader Lech Walesa, became a focal point of resistance to Poland's communist government. Just as critical to the anti-communist movement was the role of the Catholic Church, led by a patriotic Pole, Pope John Paul II (Karol Jozef Wojtyla). Like Walesa, John Paul also challenged the legitimacy of the Polish regime. As support for both Solidarity and the Church surged, the morale of the government crumbled.

It was a pattern soon repeated elsewhere. When communist regimes throughout eastern Europe fell in 1989, civil society and its institutions were widely honored for contributing to the revolution.

*   *   *

What the Warsaw Pact governments feared, the American political system protects. Under American law, including the First Amendment's protection of the right to free assembly, the strong constitutional bias in the United States is toward freedom for Americans to join together as they see fit, for whatever purposes they choose.

This holds even if some of the groups in question are more or less antagonistic toward the government or the broader culture.[12] Political parties provide an example. Unlike one-party states, we have had two major parties throughout our history, and dozens of smaller ones as well. Those smaller parties include some with strongly subversive beliefs. Even during the depths of the Red Scare in the 1950s, the Communist Party of the USA maintained its legal existence.

Indeed, in the American view, the notion that civil society must conform to government standards, as in the Warsaw Pact, gets matters almost exactly backwards. We could say that civil society is the alpha and the omega of our government. It existed prior to, and provided the intellectual and spiritual seedbed for, our constitutional government. And government itself exists, not for its own sake, but for the sake of the people and their flourishing. That is, to sustain and protect a people and their civil society.

COLLECTIVE SECURITY

What we are striving for is a new international order based
upon broad and universal principles of right and justice—no
mere peace of shreds and patches. Without that new order
the world will be without peace and human life will lack
tolerable conditions of existence and development.

—Woodrow Wilson, President (1913–1921)

In international relations, collective security is one avenue for approaching the
big issues of war and peace. Under collective security, nations agree to treat
security matters in unison, rather than as lone operators; it assumes that any
attack on one member is an attack on all. So, for example, if some "rogue" nation
invades a neighboring country, the proper response under collective security will
be joint action from other states acting together.

There are other approaches to international relations. Some strategists accept
the notion that each nation has its distinct interests and see the underlying
assumption of collective security—that diverse nations share overriding common
interests—as at best, naive, and at worst, as fantasy.

Collective security can take different forms. In some cases, such as the North
American Treaty Organization (NATO), the group of nations is relatively small
and their shared interests relatively clear. In the wake of World War II, NATO
was formed among nations of western Europe and the United States as a bulwark
against Soviet expansion. If the Soviets attacked one of the member states, all
would be obliged by NATO's terms to respond in kind.

In a more thoroughgoing form of collective security, however, the stress is on
the universal: the interests of *all* nations are served by embracing a set of common
standards to guide them toward peace. The rules are not hard to grasp: nations

have a right to self-determination, nations should not invade or subjugate others; weaker nations should not be at the mercy of the strong. Any violation of these rules tears the fabric that protects all. And while these norms may have been broken throughout history, it is our task today to see that international justice is enforced from this time forward, so that violations become increasingly taboo over time.

*   *   *

For millions of Americans today, the doctrine of collective security seems so much like common sense that it is hard to imagine international relations in its absence. Yet collective security is relatively new. Its doctrine arose from the ashes of World War I, and Woodrow Wilson was its prophet.

To Woodrow Wilson, the Great War was made inevitable by the intense, amoral competition among European nations that long preceded the war's first shots: the scramble for colonies abroad, the competition for resources, the arms buildups to gain leverage over other nations. All of these were symptoms of an unsustainable competition among states.

When the war ended, Wilson led a crusade to establish a new basis for international relations. The keystone would be the League of Nations, a forum where representatives of the world's states could gather to air grievances, and where arbitration could preempt violent confrontations.

The hope was that the League, representing the collective will of diverse countries, would overmatch the selfish interests of individual nations and deter aggression. And Wilson believed deeply in its promise. "God grant that the dawn of that day of frank dealing and of settled peace, concord, and cooperation may be near at hand," he implored.

*   *   *

To translate Wilson's ideals into action, however, has been a daunting task, plagued by at least two serious difficulties. First are the demands that collective security places on member nations. To one degree or another, members must subordinate their particular interests to those of the common good. When it comes to real sacrifices (deaths on battlefields, for example), that willingness tends to falter.

Collective security faces another, perhaps even deeper difficulty: the challenge of applying universal principles to specific conflicts.

Consider one of those principles: the right of all nations to govern themselves, free from subjugation to other countries. This right was a keystone of Wilson's hopes for the post-World War I future. According to the doctrine of collective security, when national self-determination was threatened in any corner of the world, other nations would be bound to come to their aid.

But the principle of self-determination will be understood in different ways by different peoples. The Chinese will embrace self-determination vigorously, if it means that they will be left alone to govern their country as they see fit. But they will not accept so readily the notion that the Uighurs, who live within China's borders, should rule themselves. In fact, since the Uighurs are only one of 56 distinct ethnic groups within that country, the doctrine of self-determination has some distinctly troubling implications for China's rulers.

Or consider what self-determination might mean to contemporary Libya. Unlike China, it is a country with no long history of unified, settled government; its current borders were set in the 20th century by Italian diktat. Since the overthrow of its leader Moammar Gaddafi, Libya has descended into civil strife, with various rivals claiming control of different regions and cities. Loyalties to clan and tribe take precedence, so whatever national self-determination means to ordinary Libyans will differ dramatically from, say, American notions of that principle.

In sizing up such complex dynamics, adherents of collective security will always face difficult quandaries. For example, what stake does the world have, if any, in the self-determination of the Uighurs, or of any of China's other ethnic groups? If one violation of international right anywhere is an attack on all, what do we make of situations such as that in China?

The ideal behind collective security "extols the image of a universal man living by universal maxims," as diplomat Henry Kissinger put it. But that image is difficult to reconcile with the claims of history, geography, and all the other circumstances that make the nations of the world as diverse and complicated as they, in reality, are.

COMMITTEE

Congress in session is Congress on display. Congress in committee is Congress at work.

—Woodrow Wilson, President (1913–1921)

When a word is familiar, as *committee* is, it suggests something important: familiar words are ones we use a lot. And the word *committee* is useful because committees themselves are virtually indispensible. We have committees throughout government, at all levels and in all branches. We also have them in business, academia, and pretty much everywhere else when groups of people organize themselves to get something done.

The Latin roots of *committee* help to pin down the word's meaning. It combines the prefix *com-*, which means "together," with *-mittee*. This word-part is derived from the Latin verb *mittere*, "to send." Think *missile*, which is also derived from the same root word. So a committee is a group that comes together and is launched upon some particular project or task. Your local government, for example, likely has a school committee, which is charged with the task of overseeing the local public school system.

*   *   *

Although committees are found throughout government, the focus here will be on the committees found in Congress, the ones we hear about most often in daily political news. As it happens, the first Congressional committee is very nearly as old as Congress itself. About four months after first convening, the House of Representatives set up a select committee on "Ways and Means."

Select committees are, essentially, temporary. Once finished with their given task, select committees disband. Standing committees, by contrast, are permanent.

This select Committee on Ways and Means had to deal with the intricate problems surrounding the nation's finances: state and national debt, the federal government's national credit, and taxes to fund its expenses. These were difficult, highly technical matters, and for the whole House to grapple with them would have been unmanageable. So a committee was formed, where fewer members working with greater focus could come up with its solution to a given problem and report back to the gathered House with its recommendations.

As the nation grew, the complexity of the issues the national government faced, and the sheer amount of business Congress dealt with, expanded enormously: foreign relations, westward expansion, a rapidly developing economy, Native American issues, and much else. To meet the increasing workload, Congress created a number of standing committees, which quickly came to handle the bulk of Congress's legislative burden. By 1825, almost 90 percent of the bills voted on by the House of Representatives were produced by committees.

Of course, the trends toward greater workloads continued, and both houses of Congress have added committees over time to keep pace. Currently there are 20 standing committees in the House and 20 in the Senate, as well as four joint House/Senate committees. Many, but not all, committees have subcommittees, where the workload can be further broken down into manageable assignments.

At times, both houses of Congress also call into existence select committees, which have been used especially to investigate potential misdeeds within government. The Senate Watergate Committee (officially the Select Committee on Presidential Campaign Activities), for example, played a key role in investigating Richard Nixon's involvement in the Watergate scandal.

*   *   *

Committees are sometimes called the "workshops" of Congress, for it is in committees that legislation gets its most thorough review and reworking. In terms of ordinary business, little or nothing happens in Congress without the groundwork being laid by committees.

Legislation begins with bills, proposed by members of the Senate or the House of Representatives. Once proposed, bills are assigned to an appropriate committee. The committee leadership must then decide what to do with it. If they choose to table it, or set it aside, chances are good that the bill will die a quiet death there, and many do. Roughly 5,000 bills are submitted in the House during each two-year session, and a comparable number are submitted in the Senate. Of those, about 500 make their way to passage as laws.

If a bill survives the first cut, the committee (or subcommittee) then begins to debate its merits. They hold hearings, where experts are invited to offer their assessment of the bill and answer questions from the committee. Committee members also haggle with each other about possible changes to the bill. As debate proceeds, members suggest amendments, with some surviving and others not. This is called the "markup" of the bill.

Debate and markup continue until the committee's chairperson is satisfied. Once done, the committee votes on the final language before "reporting" the bill to the full house, either the Senate or the House of Representatives. A bill reported favorably out of committee stands a good chance of passing the full house vote, since committees are controlled by the party that holds a majority in that house.

Because bills coming out of committees are often supported, and because chairpersons are responsible for the operation of their committees, those men and women have been among the most powerful figures in Washington, D.C. One-time Speaker of the House, John McCormack, himself a powerful figure, offered this advice to freshmen members: "Whenever you pass a committee chairman in the House, you bow down from the waist. I do."

*   *   *

There is another reason why committee reports carry weight in the House or Senate at large. On balance, members of Congress are inclined to acknowledge the authority of committees because members of those committees spend much more time focused on given policy fields than do other members. When someone in Congress is assigned to a committee or subcommittee, that member will often burrow in and stay for a considerable period—decades, in some cases. Over time he or she can develop substantial expertise in that area, and that expertise will be acknowledged by colleagues.

Congress is a forum for politics, not a seminar for policy analysis. However, knowledge of the subjects addressed by legislation is necessary for it to have its intended effects. By providing discreet policy arenas where members of Congress can focus their efforts, the committee system goes some way toward building institutional expertise that would otherwise be impossible.

COMMON LAW

Common law is discovered law, and its principles are not imposed from above but extracted from below, by judges whose aim is to do justice in the individual case, rather than to reform the conduct of mankind.

—Roger Scruton

One might read all the editorials in the leading newspapers for a year, and listen to talk radio every day on top of that, without once encountering the term *common law*. Nonetheless, the common law and its legacy are always present, at least in the background, in any discussion about the rights and duties of American citizens. It is deeply embedded in our system of government, like a critical strand of our political DNA. The common law shaped the Declaration of Independence and the Constitution, and has been present ever since.

The common law is not, however, an American product. Before it was anything else, the common law was the "immemorial customary law of England." Its roots go back to the 1100s when King Henry II established a nation-wide system of English courts, and it was in these royal courts that the common law evolved over the next several centuries.

The common law is sometimes described as "unwritten" or as "judge-made" law. This is true in the sense that it is not found in any single code-book. It is more a body of principles and traditions that took shape over time as judges ruled on cases arising in daily life.

These cases often concerned property and the rights related to it. For example: a cow, owned by one farmer, gets loose and damages another farmer's crops. What right does the second farmer have for repayment of his losses? Suppose the owner of the cow had taken precautions against such damage, putting up fences for example, but the fencing was damaged in a storm. Would he still be liable for damages?

As judges around England hashed out such questions, their most important decisions were eventually recorded in "year books," which served as references for future judges. Over the course of centuries, the principles that guided decisions were sharpened and refined, and became the basic logic of the legal system.

The common law guided judges as they made their decisions, but it did something else as well. It led to standardized court procedures. Rules concerning witnesses, representation by attorneys, the handling of evidence, the role of juries, and more evolved within the common law, and did a good deal to ensure the impartiality of judicial proceedings. The phrase "due process of law," familiar to American ears, captures the essence of these rules.

Finally, the common law both reflected and fostered a certain mindset among the English, for whom it made up a critical feature of their governance. It embodied a practical approach to law. It was not a system suited to the reform of society itself, and indeed the common law reinforced customary values of the English. These included "a protective attitude toward private property, a reluctance to impose affirmative duties on individuals, and a respect for personal autonomy," as historian John V. Orth put it.

*   *   *

The expansion of the British Empire spread the common law to dozens of countries around the world, such as Australia, Canada, Jamaica, New Zealand, and the city of Hong Kong. The American colonies were among the places where the common law took root. When faced with the inevitable conflicts, American colonists depended on the legal customs they knew—the common law— to provide justice.

Somewhat paradoxically, this very English tradition led to the separation of colony from motherland in time. The American independence movement emerged in part because of the colonists' sensitivity to their liberties, a defensiveness that had been nourished by the common law. For example, American patriots were outraged when the British Parliament imposed taxes on the colonies without their consent—without due process, that staple of the common law. Frustration with these impositions led to that uniquely American battle cry, "No taxation without representation!"

Once independence had been won and Americans faced the job of building a nation, the common law again proved vital. Consequently, the Constitution is deeply informed by common law concepts. Not least is the core notion that the people have rights and liberties that are protected by "due process of the law." But more specific common law rights can also be found in the Constitution, including the establishment of habeas corpus, the prohibition against self-incrimination in trials, and the right to trial by jury.

Before independence, several of the colonies passed legislation establishing the common law as the basis of their legal system; and after the Revolution, the new states all declared its continuance. So the common law provided much of the content of our laws from the start, as well as the constitutional matrix out of which future law would grow. It is deeply ingrained in American life.

*   *   *

While the common law has remained a force in American life to the present day, laws generated by other means have grown up around it, overshadowing to a degree the common law legacy. The role of statutory law, for example, has grown dramatically in relation to the common law as time has passed, statutes being laws passed by legislature.

Consider the great wave of statutory law-making during the New Deal era, legislation passed in part to combat the effects of the Great Depression. New Deal legislation penetrated deeply into nearly every corner of our economic life, including matters that had previously been ruled according to common law, such as the setting of wages.[13] Or consider later legislation, some of which marks great strides in our social development, such as the Civil Rights Act of 1964 or the Voting Rights Act of 1965.

With statutory law, government has a tool suited to ambitious goals. Where the common law applies customary rules to solve individual legal disputes, statutes provide a way to reform the customs themselves.

For one scholar of the Constitution, James Stoner, the overshadowing of the common law is a cause for concern. By meting out justice on a retail rather than a wholesale basis, and with its deference to the customary, the common law is inherently moderate. It allows reform, but only through slow evolution. It is not the heavy weapon that statutes can be.

Today, with the influence of the common law having been displaced to a degree and replaced with more ambitious legislative agendas, Stoner wonders if we are suffering from the change. The growth in our expectations of what government can and should do perhaps yields something more than we bargain for. "That our lives are so thoroughly politicized today, and thus our politics so bitter," Stoner writes, "might be testimony to the consequences of dismantling the buffer of common law that stood between the individual and the legislative will." Words worth pondering.

COMMUNISM

Communists disdain to make their views and aims a secret.
They openly explain that their ends can only be attained
through the forcible overthrow of all social order up to now.
Let the ruling classes tremble at a communist revolution.
The proletarians have nothing to lose in it but their chains.
They have the world to win.

—Karl Marx

The term *communism* is much less present in current discourse than it once
was. Seventy years ago, communism loomed large as a political issue, and
what to do about the threat it posed was a staple of American debate.

In this country, the adjective *communist* was almost always a slur. Communism
was the ideology of the old Soviet Union and aligned nations, opponents of western
democracy during the Cold War. That ideology ran directly counter to some of
the deepest American traditions. Communists proclaimed their socialism, their
atheism, and their disinterest in individual rights, in terms sure to raise the hackles
on millions of American necks. To be called a communist in the United States in
1950 was to be ostracized as essentially unAmerican.

The term has its nuances, however, and some history might improve our grasp
of them. *Communism* is very much a modern word, coming into currency around
1830 in France, where it referred to political beliefs in which common ownership
of property was the central feature. As the Polish thinker Leszek Kolakowski
notes, little distinction was made early on between socialism and communism.
By the late 1830s, though, communism came to have distinctive connotations.
Generally, communists were "those radical reformers and utopians who demanded
the abolition of private property (at first chiefly of land, then also factories)

and absolute equality of consumption, and who did not rely on the goodwill of governments or possessors, but on the use of force by the exploited." Communists were socialists with a deep streak of absolutism.

By the mid-19th century, Karl Marx, the great architect of socialist and communist thought, had refined the meaning of communism, and it is from Marx's thought that we get much of our sense of what communism actually is. It is, to Marx, the end stage of human history, our destiny.

He explains that we reach this destiny only after long ages of conflict between working classes and those who have controlled the means of production. This conflict started with the earliest systematic agriculture, when great landlords exploited those who worked the fields. It has continued ever since, through all of history's economic revolutions, culminating in the exploitation of the proletariat by the capitalist owners of modernity's great industries.

This dynamic of exploitation and struggle will continue, according to Marx, until, in overturning the system one final time, the workers will gain power and constitute a system in which the age-old class conflict will be resolved. With that resolution, exploitation would be a thing of the past, social solidarity would reign, and even government—of no use anymore—would wither away.

This end stage of civilization was what Marx meant by communism. It would bring not only the "full superseding of private property," but also the "genuine resolution of the conflict of man with nature and of man with man," he wrote. The communist phase of human history would be a time of perfect community: common ownership of property, a sense of shared purpose in the face of adversity, and unity in aspirations.

The appeal of communism lies here, in its expansive promise of human harmony, the breaking down of barriers that divide us, the end of personal alienation. Contemporary writer Vivian Gornick, who grew up in a household sympathetic to communism, recalls the potent appeal of this vision, which gave "the most ordinary men and women a sense of one's humanity that ran deep" and "made life feel large . . . ." Looking back, Gornick adds, "It was this all-in-allness of world and self" that drew people to the communist message.

*   *   *

Marx's belief in a communist destiny was not, in communist eyes, mere wishful thinking. Natural laws would drive us toward that future, as real as the laws of evolution that drive biological development.

This pretense of scientific inevitability, however, put communists in an awkward position as actual, non-theoretical, history unfolded. The expected workers' revolution never quite materialized. To correct for this failure, communist thinkers accepted the notion that a super-committed vanguard, rather than the workers themselves, would lead the way to the communist future.

Yet when Communist parties fought their way to power, even political victory failed to bring society much closer to the harmony Marx's thought predicted. Rulers in those countries found it necessary to continue the class struggle, in order finish off resistance and build the workers' paradise. They relied, for example, on massive propaganda campaigns to instruct the people and to instill the proper enthusiasm for their government. And when that failed, they used sterner methods to bring their people into line. If nothing else, communism in the 20th century was a massive effort in social control.

Indeed, it amounted to a war of sorts, in which government targeted any seats of authority that could plausibly challenge their own dominance. Since communism was, by its nature, a comprehensive system, those governments saw threats in nearly every field: the law, for example, as well as religion, academia, literature, and elsewhere.

In all these areas, the communist state had to destroy competitors and establish itself as master. Obedience was demanded, and it must be total. Poet Czeslaw Milosz felt this pressure firsthand as a young writer in Poland soon after a Soviet-backed regime captured power there. As he wrote in his memoir, *The Captive Mind*, if a writer accepted "only 99 per cent" of the party line, "he will necessarily be considered a foe, for from that 1 per cent a new church can arise."

For communism, dissent was a mortal danger and diversity of belief was the mother of all problems. This was the sinister side to the "all-in-allness" that Vivian Gornick celebrated.

                         *   *   *

As history has unfolded, the big communist project in Europe collapsed by 1991. Since then, the word *communist* has mostly receded from its old prominence in American political discourse. Yet we might look in coming years for something of a resurgence.

That is because, while few look to Soviet-style communism as a model for governing anymore, something of its spirit lives on. The spectre of communism still haunts us, one might say.[14] At any rate, Ryzard Legutko, a contemporary Polish thinker, sees it that way. Legutko grew up under communist rule in Poland, witnessed its demise there, then served in the democratic government that replaced it. He noticed a phenomenon that would seem, at least on the surface, improbable. Former communist officials, without disowning their past, re-entered government after Poland's anti-communist revolution of 1989, and often thrived there.

Nor had they really changed their stripes, at least not entirely. Working within democratic institutions, they continued the long-term project of overhauling society, especially by attacking independent authorities in various walks of life. As Legutko puts it, "...no traditional hierarchies, no spontaneously developed communities, no historically entrenched institutions" are immune; they are all ripe for attack from a new generation of no-longer-Communist communists.

This phenomenon that Legutko observed in Poland has parallels elsewhere, especially in the more aggressive left-wing movements of our day (among some organized anti-fascist groups, for example, and the self-identified "social justice warriors"). While not necessarily communist in the formal sense, they share some of that movement's old spirit: the tendency toward absolutism, the compulsion to politicize all aspects of life,[15] the unwillingness to accept dissenting beliefs, and the contempt for competing sources of authority. This is the old communist "all-in-allness" in replay.

It is worth noting that Ryzard Legutko himself fell afoul of these tendencies, not in Poland but in Vermont. It happened when a talk he was scheduled to give was shut down under pressure from activists unwilling that his voice be heard. Such efforts to police public debate and to demonize political opponents are troubling symptoms of our distressed political climate. They also open a door for the return of the term *communist* to the public square. Look for it to be applied increasingly to today's most zealous activists, at least if our political discourse continues on its current divisive path.

CONGRESS

If, as Emerson said, Congress is a 'standing insurrection,' it is a standing insurrection against the ancient enemies of mankind: war, poverty, ignorance, injustice, sickness, environmental ugliness, economic and personal insecurity. …What higher calling exists? This is the essence of politics: To translate the concerns and the creative responses of a vast citizenry into effective and humane laws.

—Hubert Humphrey, Vice President (1965–1969)

In 1965, when Hubert Humphrey spoke those words, the United States was enjoying a run of mostly good years. In the decades after winning the Second World War, the economy was booming, civil rights were expanding, and we were sending astronauts into space. Such feats and good fortune seemed to promise only more and better times ahead.

Hubert Humphrey was a fitting embodiment of the country's mood at the time. A long-time senator, then vice president under Lyndon Johnson, Humphrey was nicknamed the Happy Warrior for his expansive optimism. Looking back, one is impressed that he thought Congress should take aim at such "ancient enemies" as poverty, ignorance, injustice, and sickness, as if it were possible to aim everywhere at once.

It's worth considering, though, what the authors of the Constitution would have made of Humphrey's attitude. The era of the Founding was also, in its way, a time of optimism, and like Humphrey, the Founders placed a great deal of faith in the capabilities of Congress. They believed that political power must come from the people, and that their will should naturally be expressed through a representative legislature—Congress, here— that would take the lead in making laws for the country.

And Congress was, literally, the first branch of government in the Founders' eyes. In Article I, just after the Preamble, the Constitution grants Congress the power to write the nation's laws. This power even included the power to call into being the government itself. After the election of the first Congress, we did not yet have a government, in effect. For the government to form, Congress had first to gather, and next to pass the laws that established the Department of Treasury, the Department of War and the Department of State, as well as the Judiciary Act of 1789, which created the Supreme Court and the federal judiciary. Our national government was created by an act of the people's will, enacted through their representatives in Congress.

However, though the founders placed real faith in Congress, that faith was limited. The framers of the Constitution took great pains to prevent the concentration of too much power in the government. For this reason, no sooner does the Constitution grant Congress "all Legislative Powers" of the new nation, than it begins to limit those powers. For instance, Congress's lawmaking powers are checked by the president's power to veto laws that Congress passes. Congress's legislative powers are also limited by the judiciary's powers to review the constitutional legality of those laws.

Moreover, Congress's powers are limited by its own internal structure. The framers made Congress bicameral, with legislative power divided between two separate bodies: the House of Representatives and the Senate. Each has its distinct makeup, and each acts as a check on the other. By requiring that bills move through both houses in order to become law, the Founders assured that each bill would be scrutinized and tested from the differing perspectives of the House of Representatives and the Senate.

Congress's powers are not only divided between the two houses, but are also divided within each house among all its members—and this is, perhaps, the biggest limitation of all. These members represent their home constituencies, which means they carry all sorts of differing interests to Washington, economic and cultural. Once in Congress, they also have a basic equality, so all voices get a chance to be heard and to vote on the country's laws.

In order to pass, every piece of legislation must gain enough approval from these highly varied members to win majorities in both the House of Representatives and the Senate. In each house, members debate the bill, propose changes, debate some more, and hammer out compromises over the course of weeks or months before it is voted on. Bills, having been shaped and reshaped in each house, must then be reconciled between House and Senate versions. For a bill to survive this gauntlet is no mean feat.

All this complexity affects the end product. Congress's complicated approach to legislation has the effect of broadening the base of support for laws and effectively requiring compromises for their passage. This generally undercuts highly ambitious legislation. Laws coming out of Congress tend to be pragmatic rather than strictly ideological, and tend to produce incremental, rather than sweeping change. But the congressional process is designed to yield this effect, too: Whatever legislation does pass will have a broad, sustainable, and bipartisan consensus behind it. Congress builds low, but sturdy.

*   *   *

What happens, though, when the country faces challenges that seem to call for ambitious legislation? This has been the case ever since the late 19th century, as the nation underwent industrialization, urbanization, rising international power, and all the stresses that have come with these and other changes. Lacking efficiency, Congress has had trouble keeping up with the demand for legislation to meet all these challenges.

As a result, it has been bleeding power, with much of that power accruing to the presidency. Thinking back on major governmental initiatives over the last century, we recall the presidents who proposed them, and not the Congresses that supported them: Franklin D. Roosevelt and his New Deal, Lyndon Johnson's "Great Society," Ronald Reagan's "revolution," and George W. Bush's "War on Terror" are all examples. Congress played its part in each, but cannot be credited with the real initiative in forming these programs.

Given Congress's inherent limitations, it is no surprise that sweeping legislation flows more naturally from a president, with Congress playing a supporting role. When Congress is aligned with the president, it can pass far-reaching legislation, but at other times Congress seems almost paralyzed in reacting to national challenges. As Congressman Morris Udall once put it, Congress is at times like a sailing ship with all anchor and no sail. This institutional weakness might account for Congress's low approval rating, which in 2016 dipped as low as 13 percent.

It has also led long-time observers to worry about Congress's health. Norman Ornstein sees it as the "broken branch" of the federal government and calls for increased bipartisanship and pragmatism in Congress to make it more effective. Professors Terry Moe and William Howell make a more dramatic suggestion: changing the Constitution itself. They note that national problems fester while the government seems to dither. They add, "With Congress the prime source of dysfunction, it should be moved to the periphery of the policymaking process where its pathologies can do less damage—and presidents should be moved to the center where they can do the most good." Moe and Howell call for a legislative "fast track" in which the president proposes legislation and the two houses of Congress vote up or down, without delay, amendments, or parliamentary maneuvering of any kind.

This more streamlined legislative process would surely lead to more potent policymaking. It is worth keeping in mind, however, the Founders' fear of concentrated governmental power that led them to make our system as convoluted as it is. Likewise, we should remember that the process by which law is made will have an effect on the character of the law produced. Moe and Howell assume that better law would result from their plan, less muddled by congressional tinkering. But by the same token, "fast-track" legislation will allow more ideologically-driven policy. This can be dangerous in itself: what if those uncompromising laws are bad? Such a process might also degrade the long-term consensus support for the laws, something our system of governance depends on. "Low but sturdy" has its uses in a highly diverse nation.

CONSERVATISM

A Conservative Believes: That we do not know the extent to which various traditional forms of social life—family, rituals, nation, religious communities—are indispensible if life in a society is to be tolerable or even possible. There are no grounds for believing that when we destroy these forms, or brand them as irrational, we increase the chance of happiness, peace, security, or freedom. We have no certain knowledge of what might occur if, for example, the monogamous family was abrogated, or if the time-honored custom of burying the dead were to give way to the rational recycling of corpses for industrial purposes. But we would do well to expect the worst.

—Leszek Kolakowski

In explaining what a conservative believes, Leszek Kolakowski was going boldly where angels fear to tread. The term *conservatism* is notoriously difficult to define, and conservatives of different stripes disagree with each other almost as much as they do with liberals and progressives. Social conservatives clash with fiscal conservatives, Main Street conservatives with Wall Street conservatives, neocons with theocons (and paleocons), and others.

We can see how hard it is to locate conservatism in contemporary American politics by looking at the presidential career of Donald Trump. For many political liberals, Trump became the face of conservatism when he won the 2016 election, and hardly differs from other conservatives except for the extra measure of belligerence in his demeanor.

Yet when Trump ran in the Republican primaries during 2016, many conservatives attacked his campaign, and some remain opposed to his brand of politics. Trump is, to those critics, not remotely conservative, but instead a populist, or perhaps a freelance demagogue, whose views fit no meaningful ideological category.

*   *   *

Which leaves the question, what is conservatism? Going by its name, it must be about conserving something, which raises the further question of what exactly conservatives today actually aim to conserve. Yet, whatever comes of this line of questioning will not quite capture the essence of conservative belief. Conservatism is less about programs and agendas than it is about habits of mind or general sensibilities. Conservative inclinations are mostly articulated only when things worth conserving are clearly threatened.

This explains the relatively late birth of modern conservatism. The conservative mindset has always been present, but the actual articulation of conservative principles came in part as a response to the French Revolution. It was especially the writings of Edmund Burke that provided that starting point. The Revolution itself was a full-spectrum assault on many key French institutions, including the Church and the monarchy, but also all manner of customs, traditions, hierarchies, and privileges.

This generalized attack on so many institutions and customs, and the violence of that attack, provoked Burke and set him on the path to defending traditions in general against the Revolution's aggressions. As he did so, one key thought came to the fore: The French were squandering enormous amounts of cultural capital without fully understanding what was being lost. The revolutionaries could point reasonably to the failures of various institutions, but in their attacks they failed to appreciate what goes into the building of institutions, and all manner of traditions besides.

For Burke, the French Revolution, which justified itself on the need for a rational overhaul of French society, stood in the starkest contrast to Britain's embrace of established customs. "[I]nstead of throwing away our old prejudices, we cherish them," he wrote, meaning the preferences, values, and taboos people inherit as members of an organic society. Citizens shorn of these "prejudices" would be vulnerable to all kinds of misjudgment. "We are afraid to put man to live and trade on his own private stock of reason, because we suspect that this stock of each man is small, and that the individuals do better to avail themselves of the general bank and capital of nations and of ages."

In this, one sees a fundamental tenet of conservatism. It looks to history and experience to guide political life, rather than to abstract logic or mere wishful thinking. We have been learning from the school of experience for centuries, and its lessons have been incorporated into our customs and institutions. This has happened in myriad ways. If we searched those lessons out, we could find them reflected not just in our laws and constitutions, but in our manners, literature, crafts, sciences, and elsewhere.

*   *   *

This belief in the value of tradition colors the way conservatives view the relation between the individual and society. Where liberalism celebrates the free and autonomous individual, conservatism sees the individual as living within social contexts and dependent on them. As English philosopher Roger Scruton put it, "conservatism arises directly from the sense that one belongs to some continuing and pre-existing social order, and that this fact is all-important in determining what to do."

What people do will be shaped by that order, which has evolved to meet needs and to provide the means by which people can live fruitful lives. Bookish men and women might choose careers in academia, for example, others in business, and the athletic in the world of sport. The instinctive conservative will accept this, embracing the idea that living a good life amounts to finding a home within the broader social order and living by its rules. In fact, conservatives will not only accept the social order as a home, but tend to be grateful for what it provides and defensive of it in case of attack either from within or from beyond.

In comparison to this conservative position, the liberal stands somewhat apart from the social order. By its nature, liberalism tends to be skeptical of inherited institutions, questioning their purpose and usefulness. Liberalism depends on objective distance, the better to see customs in a clear light. If conservatives are comfortable with the hominess of the social order, liberals, seeing its defects, might prefer to throw open its doors, or perhaps knock down the occasional wall, in order to improve that home and make it more accommodating.

Still further from the conservative position is one we might call radical: the belief that institutions themselves are the source of much of our trouble. Confronted by human failings—greed, bigotry, criminality—we all grasp for explanations. For those unwilling to accept that our failings come from the individual heart, human iniquity must come from elsewhere, and society is the obvious culprit. Far from providing useful guidance, radicals see social institutions as sources of corruption.

There is a corollary here, that human failings can be cured through deep institutional restructuring. Conservatives won't take kindly to that idea, however. The notion that human corruption can be swept away through social reform is, as Leszek Kolakowski put it, "not only utterly incredible and contrary to all experience, but is highly dangerous. How on earth," he asks, "did all these institutions arise if they are so contrary to the nature of man?"

*   *   *

The conservatism described so far is general, and its spokesmen—Burke, Scruton, Kolakowski[16]—have been British and European. When it comes to American politics, however, conservatism takes on some unpredictable expressions. American conservatives may want to protect our basic institutions, but those institutions, including the Constitution, foster a remarkably dynamic, fluid, open, un-conservative society—a liberal one, in essence.

In fact, the American understanding of conservatism is confused enough that genuinely conservative opinions can appear as dissents from the prevailing ethos. Such was the case with the poet John Crowe Ransom, for example. Writing in the mid-20th century, he took a dim view of the American passion for endless economic expansion. Our society, Ransom argued, was born in pioneering, and like all societies we had to struggle early on to wrest a living from the natural world. But we never really stopped our pioneering, and failed to learn how to "live on terms of mutual respect and amity" with nature. To Ransom, it is only when a society stops pioneering and reaches a point of settlement that "the loving arts, religions, and philosophies come spontaneously into being: these are the blessings of peace. But latter-day societies have been seized—none quite so violently as our American one—with the strange idea that the human destiny is not to secure an honorable peace with nature, but to wage unremitting war on nature."

We fail to settle and continue to pioneer, Ransom believed, to the detriment of our civilization. He saw this at work in our abuse of nature, but we might also see it in other trends: our fascination with technological gadgetry, for example, or the way we celebrate iconoclasm in the arts, or even in our current embrace of gender fluidity. It is all "pioneering," to borrow Ransom's terms, and distraction from the deeper endeavor of cultivating our "loving arts."

*   *   *

In confusing times such as our own, we reach for ideologies to clarify where we are heading and what we should do. We have seen in recent decades a flowering of conservative ideologies. But ideology is, in a sense, nearly the opposite of traditional conservatism. Ideologies provide top-down and abstract answers to political questions, while a conservative order grows out of cultural rootedness, and of the accumulated choices made by ordinary people as much as by "elites."

One question for American politics today concerns the strength of this more traditional, non-ideological conservatism. This is a mostly inarticulate conservatism, embodied in the daily interactions of ordinary people and their attachments to family, work, church, neighbors, and our laws. While the Americans who are most engaged in political life seem to be living in the midst of some cultural cyclone, millions of people go about their business without much obvious concern for the furies apparent elsewhere. By doing so, they provide valuable ballast for society as a whole. Whether that gravity is enough to keep our system steady in coming years is a question worth considering.

CONSTITUTION

A constitution is not the act of a government, but of a people
constituting a government.

—Thomas Paine

We might associate the word *constitution* with dry, complex lessons from school, mostly forgotten. But there is drama in the word, as well. In 1938, C. H. McIlwain, a leading constitutional historian, was aware of this: "The world is trembling in the balance between the orderly procedure of law and the processes of force," he wrote, "for perhaps never in its long history has the principle of constitutionalism been so questioned as it is questioned today."

Those "processes of force" have tempted political leaders since humans learned to distinguish law from raw power. But the mid-20th century was a time of special danger. As he delivered the words above, several of the world's advanced nations, including Germany, were shedding legal traditions and succumbing to a sinister lawlessness.

Germany's lawlessness in 1938 was not anarchic. Indeed, German society was highly ordered, and even lawful in its way. But under Nazi rule, its government was lawless not only in depriving an estimated six million Jewish and minority citizens of their rightful protection by the state, but of subjecting them to genocide. The government was unconstrained by the basic law that ought, by all rights, to have held it in check: its constitution.

Constitutions provide law of a particular kind. They embody the fundamental law of a state or nation—the law that establishes government and guides the making, execution, and judging of laws by which a society rules itself. If it is decently just, a constitution will enshrine an evenhanded respect for the people ruled under it and render invalid laws that violate that spirit. McIlwain put it this way: "Constitutionalism has one essential quality: it is a legal limitation on government, it is the antithesis of arbitrary rule, its opposite is despotic government, the government of will instead of law."

By imposing an authority above the government of the moment, constitutions check the force of popular feeling when the public's temper runs high. With the example of Nazi Germany in mind, McIlwain put it strongly. The existence of constitutions "leave open the possibility of an appeal from the people drunk to the people sober," and constitutions exist as a final barrier "if individual and minority rights are to be protected in the periods of excitement and hysteria from which we are unfortunately not immune."

*   *   *

In the case of the United States, our national Constitution and all our state constitutions are written documents. The people, acting through delegates, constituted their government by voting to adopt those constitutions. Governing thereafter flows from that act. Constitutions are created prior to the governments based on them. Therefore, constitutions are also superior in authority to the laws produced by those governments. If legislatures, state or national, pass laws that violate the constitution, those laws are illegitimate and void.

This only works, however, if a constitution has real, authoritative force—something that cannot be taken for granted. Laws passed by legislatures, after all, channel the will of the people in a fairly direct way. So voiding them depends on deep authority, and it is worth considering where that power comes from.

The source is, in a sense, the same. To trump legislation when it crosses into illegality, constitutions rely on the people's will as well. But they must tap that will at a deeper level than legislation does.

At least this is the thought behind American constitutionalism. At the time of the Founding, for example, people understood widely what was at stake: the possible birth of a new nation. In the Constitutional Convention, highly respected leaders from every state were present to write and agree to the document itself. When done, the Constitution was then sent to the states for ratification, or adoption, which involved widespread debate and voting, state by state, on whether to accept it or not.

Of course, the process could not have yielded an authoritative constitution if the content had failed to compel. On this score, the Framers were able to draw on traditions of great vitality, and they integrated its most valued elements: that government should represent the people, for instance, and that the people hold certain unalienable rights, including the right to due process of the law, which no government could legitimately violate. At the time, these principles were deeply rooted in colonial American society. According to John Adams, they were "intimately known" and "sensibly felt" by ordinary men and women. (He added, "it is scarcely extravagant to say they are drawn in and imbibed with the nurse's milk and first air.")

The end result of all the Founding effort was something new: the creation of a nation, under a written constitution that represented, to the greatest extent possible, the will and traditions of the people. Take away any of the founding elements—the hard thought of the Framers and their prestige, their dependence on tradition, the ratification process—and the Constitution might not have worked. Constitutions often don't. But work it did, and elections were held, laws written, Supreme Court decisions handed down, all with enough authority to make them stick.

*   *   *

Creating a constitution with real authority is a severe challenge, but to maintain a constitution's authority through the ups and downs of history is another matter. There is a necessary tension that runs though the life of any constitution, a Catch-22 of sorts. For their authority, constitutions rely on the will of the people, even as the people evolve. Yet the very purpose of a constitution is to anchor society when popular opinion threatens to throw it off course. Speaking of the national constitution, scholar Walter Berns wrote, it is not so much that the Constitution must keep in tune with the times, but rather "that the times, to the extent possible, must be kept in tune with the Constitution. Why, otherwise, have a constitution?"

The measure of a constitution's usefulness comes when the people are most tempted to violate it. The 1930s and 1940s, for example, provided economic and social crises that pushed nations over the brink of constitutional limits, with fantastically regrettable results in Germany, among others.

The United States, by comparison, came through the storms of the mid-20th century in good constitutional health, despite lapses.[17] Here, to a degree, the times were kept in tune with the Constitution, as it were: Our political institutions did not collapse, nor did society give way entirely to the sort of demons that plagued Germany. We should be grateful for this even today and consider the sources of our constitutional stability.

Partly, success begets success, and the Constitution has performed well for more than two hundred years now. But its force has always depended, at a deeper level, on the faith of the people. The Constitution works because most people believe in it, enough that they abide by the laws and judgments formed under its aegis. This faith may be expressed sentimentally at times. Henry Estabrook, a New York attorney early in the 20th century, paid tribute to the founding document in these terms:

> Our great and sacred Constitution, serene and inviolable, stretches its beneficent powers over our land ... like the out-stretched arm of God himself. ... O Marvellous Constitution! Magic Parchment! ... Maker, Monitor, Guardian of Mankind!

Such expressions may be no less genuine for being sentimental, and the Constitution depends in part on such conviction. But we shouldn't place too much faith in the "magic" properties of any constitution. The liberties we sustained through the crises of the mid-20th century had deeper roots than any document. And those roots must continue to be nourished if they are to remain vital enough to hold fast in whatever storms the future likely holds.

CONTRACT

A contract between two parties, in proper form and for a
legitimate object, constitutes, as it were, a miniature statute.

—Lon Fuller

A contract is a formal agreement, binding under the law. By signing a contract, parties agree to some exchange, which should benefit each side. Contracts spell out the give-and-take agreed upon, and if the obligations incurred are not met, legal penalties may follow.

Lon Fuller makes an important point when he states that a contract is, in his words, "a miniature statute." When people enter into a contract, they are making law. In a sense, contract law provides a highly democratic form of governance, giving people the right to legislate in some critical aspect of their lives. We might sign contracts, for example, when agreeing to do a job for another party, and the contract will spell out what we are expected to do and what we can expect for pay.

*   *   *

Contracts seem so commonplace that it is hard to imagine a time when they were not the regular stuff of economic life. Contracts, however, came into special prominence with the economic changes of the 18th century: the rapid development of trade, new industries, and the expansion of the middle class. This growth presented a wide variety of economic opportunities to the public, but also the challenge of structuring the relationships that came with those opportunities. This is the environment in which contract law flourished. Contracts provided a device by which people in the new business classes could organize deals, for example. Thus, they allowed people freedom to seize opportunities as they arose and to chart their own destinies. "The law of contract," wrote American legal historian Lawrence Friedman, "gave more or less free play to individual choice. What people voluntarily agreed with each other, courts undertook to enforce."

By the 19th century, that "free play" was exceedingly energetic. With the support of the courts, a culture of contracts thrived in the American economy, where vast new industries came into existence and provided myriad openings for work, growth, and investment. American economic expansion was built piece by piece through innumerable business agreements, where contracts brought law and order to the freewheeling market. The law of contracts thrived alongside society's broader celebration of individual initiative and the sanctity of property. The contract was one of the "sovereign notions of the 19th century," as Friedman put it.

*   *   *

That would change as the 20th century got under way. In one sense, liberty of contract contributed to its own decline. By providing the legal scaffolding for the American economy, contracts fostered a period of amazing growth. Out of that dynamism, giant corporations were born, some with unprecedented wealth and power: U.S. Steel, Standard Oil, The Great Northern Railroad, Bell Telephone and many others.

Contract law had assumed that partners to a contract would be acting on a field of equality before the law, and that contracts would suit both sides. But when placed alongside the corporate titans, ordinary men and women were anything but their equals. In effect, enormous corporations sat on one side of the bargaining table, while on the other side were independent workers, desperate to survive in a rapidly evolving economy.

Legal reformers took stock of this situation and many found that the mismatch in power mocked the idea of freedom in contract. "Wealth and poverty, plenty and hunger, nakedness and warm clothing, ignorance and learning, face each other in contract, and find expression in and through contract," wrote one. "Much of the discussion about 'equal rights' is utterly hollow," added another. "All the ado made over the system of contract is surcharged with fallacy."

The reformers believed that the economic inequalities had to be rebalanced through "social legislation"—that is, legislation aimed at correcting the broad social inequalities produced by the unrestrained economy.[18] The era's social legislation included minimum wage and maximum hour laws designed to protect workers' interests.

By setting limits on the conditions under which employees could work, social legislation constrained the "liberty of contract." Under maximum hour laws, for example, employers and workers would simply not have the option of agreeing to work weeks of more than 44 (or 40) hours.

By its nature, social legislation restricts the freedom of individual workers and employers to sign contracts according to their own will. In effect, social legislation "shrank the kingdom of contract," as Professor Friedman wrote. "Every new law on the statute book if it dealt with the economy, was a cup of water withdrawn from the oceanic domain of the law of contract."

What's more, we are still at it when it comes to social legislation. In recent decades, for example, regulations concerning civil rights have entered the realm of the contract and have further limited the traditional liberty of contract. Now, major companies have no right to discriminate against workers on the basis of race, gender, older age, or disability.

*   *   *

From the examples above, one can certainly say that the liberty of contract has, over time, retreated under pressure from social legislation. But has contract law gone into terminal decline as some have claimed?[19]

Not really. The American economy is both huge and enormously complex, and despite the growth of government regulation, still retains a strong measure of contractual freedom. Our economy rests, as Friedman puts it, "on a firm basis of private business, private enterprise, and private consumption. A regime of contract, then, survives and is hearty and hale."

CONVENTION

convention [noun]: An assembly or gathering of persons
for some common object

— The Oxford English Dictionary

In American political discourse, the use of the term *convention* rises and falls
in four-year cycles.[20] When the Republican and Democratic parties hold their
national conventions in presidential election years, talk of conventions is all
but unavoidable. The word itself combines the prefix *con–,* meaning "together,"
with the Latin verb *venire,* "to come." Thus, a convention is a coming-together, or
a gathering.

In politics, however, conventions are not mere get-togethers. The deeper
significance of the term is revealed by the business conducted at those national
party gatherings. The crucial work of each party's national convention is to
nominate its presidential candidate.

At the heart of the nomination process is a roll-call vote, in which each state
reports which candidate it supports. As the roll call proceeds, one hears the leader
of a state delegation saying something along the lines of: "The great state of Kansas,
the Sunflower State and home of the Jayhawks, casts its votes for the next president
of the United States . . . . [etc.]" One by one, the states announce their votes until
a candidate attains a majority of the delegates and secures the nomination. Then a
few minutes of mayhem ensue, with dropping balloons and dancing delegates, as
the party celebrates the event.

These days the roll call is mostly theater: generally everyone knows ahead
of time who the candidate will be. But the voting in the convention makes the
nomination official, and is a necessary step to produce the candidate who will

represent the party in the national election. The convention vote is a formality, but a crucial one.

Going deeper, the words *delegate* and *delegation* point toward the core meaning of *convention*. Delegates to the party conventions are men and women who are selected by fellow party members at the state level. In being chosen, these delegates are given the power to represent the party rank and file. Through this delegation, or endowment, of power, national conventions reflect the will of the party faithful all across the country, and the presidential candidate that the delegates nominate will be the party's consensus choice. The popular will borne by delegates is the making of legitimacy.

*   *   *

It is natural to think first of today's national party gatherings when we hear the term *convention*. But the word should also stir thoughts of another, more import-ant example of the word's use, the Constitutional Convention of 1787. In that gathering, delegates appointed by the different states convened in Philadelphia to discuss the founding of a new national government.

The novelty of this effort should not be overlooked. To effectively create a new nation was unprecedented until that event in Philadelphia. Calling a convention to accomplish this task was likewise new; the constitutional convention was an American innovation.

But the Philadelphia convention also raised a sticky question. By what authority did the drafters of the new constitution claim the right to propose a whole new government? It is not given to groups of private citizens, no matter how well-respected, to take on such a profound responsibility. So who actually called the Constitutional Convention, and what gave it the right to reshape the country's government?

The answer in part lies with that convention itself. When all of the states were invited to send delegates to it, the states did so (with the exception of Rhode Island). That willingness of the states to participate lent legitimacy to the convention and to the constitution that it produced. By sending delegates, the states empowered them to represent the people of each state and their interests in the proceedings.

Even more important for the ultimate legitimacy of the Constitution was the step taken after the convention had done its work: ratification, the process of choosing to adopt it. The new Constitution would have been a dead letter unless it was ratified by the states, which held virtually all political authority at the time. And to decide whether to ratify or not, each state used the tool of the moment: the convention. Delegates from around a given state gathered to discuss the constitution before voting yea or nay. The legitimacy of the Constitution grew out of these conventions, in which a state's political authority could be concentrated and the crucial question of the Constitution's future put to the test.

One can see in these cases the meaning that underlies political conventions and why they are important in a democratic system. Conventions provide a mechanism by which political will is channeled from the grassroots, upwards into substantial, responsible institutions. In the process, that will is transformed from shapeless and evanescent, to coherent and stable. Thus conventions have been a lynchpin in building and maintaining some of the basic political institutions in this country, including the national government itself. They have played a critical, if overlooked, role in making our democratic system possible.

CRIME

To label behavior as criminal means, among other things, that government will punish that behavior at its own initiative and expense. A crime is a wrong whose remedy falls to the cost of the state.

—Lawrence Friedman

The persistence of crime in human affairs is a phenomenon to be reckoned with. Judging by the earliest law codes we know of, crime has always existed, and so far as anyone knows, it always will. Its control is one of the fundamental duties of any government. And since crime is virtually universal, all nations have some apparatus to deal with it: police, courts, jails, and so forth.

Informally, we might describe nearly any wrong done as a crime. *It's a crime what that ref did last Sunday!* But the word has a more technical meaning, one that Lawrence Friedman points out in the quotation above. Crimes are not just any wrongs, but wrongs that the state recognizes as harmful enough to society that they need to be controlled by the government itself. In the case of such offenses, the government will take action against the perpetrator(s).

Not every destructive act is a crime, however. For decades, cigarette makers have sold products that are clearly linked to cancer, and are thus implicated in thousands of deaths. Yet it is no crime to produce cigarettes, and so the government has never charged cigarette makers with any criminal offense. The families of lung cancer victims have sued tobacco companies under civil, rather than criminal, laws to get compensation for the harm done to them. But in such cases, one private party is pitted against another, and the state is not directly involved.[21] This is the difference between civil and criminal law.

* * *

It is crucial that government be clear about which acts are actually criminal. Any haziness as to what constitutes a crime opens the door to the abuse of state power. Crimes must be included in our codes of criminal offenses, but that leaves a question of how they get there.

There are two basic ways. Some acts have been understood as crimes for so long that we perhaps never needed to define them as such, though they appear in official government criminal codes. There is a legal term for such offenses: *mala in se*, or "things wrong in themselves." Murder, of course, falls into this category, as do theft, kidnapping, arson and similarly primal offenses.

Such crimes have been outlawed since time out of mind. American law inherited the bulk of its *mala in se* prohibitions when colonists brought the English common law to these shores. Today they are still embedded deep in our criminal code, and form the basis for hundreds of thousands of prosecutions each year.

There are, in addition, many crimes that are not of this primal stock, and there is another legal term that covers them. That term is *mala prohibita*, or, roughly, "wrongs because they are prohibited." Unlike *mala se,* these are acts that have not always been understood as wrong. Some, in fact, might not have been possible in the past. New technologies, for example, make some crimes possible that were never before known. Speeding while driving on the highway is a crime, but it wasn't in horse and buggy days. Likewise, the Internet has opened up new avenues for bilking and harassing individuals and businesses, and hence we have a number of new crimes related to its abuse.

There is a connection between *mala prohibita* and statutory law. Where the oldest crimes have been embedded in the common law for centuries, *mala prohibita* are added through legislative acts, or statutes. For example, a state legislature might recognize an evolving problem, such as Internet fraud, and pass a law prohibiting it. Thus an act that had not been a crime before enters the criminal code, and it becomes the state's business to prevent it.

* * *

With *mala in se* crimes being inherited with our oldest legal traditions, the real action in the development of criminal law now happens with the *mala prohibita*. That action takes place mostly in legislatures, where representatives of the people fight over what should or should not be legal.

For this reason, developments in criminal law make an interesting social barometer. What we choose to criminalize—or decriminalize—reveals changes in our cultural climate. For example, we have lots of laws on the books today against polluting, which reflect a much greater concern for the environment than we had not too long ago. The dumping of toxins in rivers was once commonplace, but anyone who does so today might find themselves on the receiving end of a criminal prosecution.

Or consider what has happened with laws related to our ongoing "culture wars." We were once concerned enough with marijuana use that it was criminalized across the country. Today, a number of states have moved in the opposite direction, legalizing not only its medical use, but in some cases its recreational use. And where we once had anti-sodomy laws on the books in many states—indeed, they were *mala in se* to previous generations—now such laws are effectively outlawed themselves.

Such changes in our criminal laws suggest a culture that is undergoing rapid change. Look for more in the near future—the barometer suggests the stormy weather will continue—and look for criminal law to be one of the forums where our changing society hashes out some of its most contentious disagreements.

CULTURE

The central conservative truth is that it is culture, not
politics, that determines the success of a society. The central
liberal truth is that politics can change culture and save it
from itself.

—Daniel Patrick Moynihan, Senator (1977–2001)

The term *culture* is notoriously difficult to define. Not because culture
itself is elusive; it is more that culture is virtually everywhere. We are
surrounded by it, as fish are by water. If asked for examples of what
culture is, where would we start? Possibly with jazz concerts and modern poetry,
if our minds are tuned to high culture. But, of course, it also includes so much
more, all of it evolving over time, that, as Mario Vargas Llosa wrote, culture as a
concept is "ungraspable," and a "figurative ghost."

One can, however, find a foundation for the concept by looking to the word's
roots. The Latin verb *colere* provides that starting point: it means "to nourish,"
"to tend," or "to care for." This verb had a religious use for the Romans. It covered
all the acts by which priests did their work, tending sacred fires, for instance, or
preparing altars for sacrifices, or anything else along those lines. All such priestly
actions were covered by that verb *colere,* which took the form *cultus* in certain
uses.

Here we see some of the basic elements of culture, ones that are implied
whenever the term is used. Culture involves, for starters, human action and
effort. Culture is also social, involving matters that are learned, practiced, and
passed on to later generations. Also, culture is linked to things we value most:
one doesn't cultivate what one doesn't care about.

Jumping to modern times, we find the term *culture* used in a much broader way. For anthropologists, culture is an umbrella term that covers all the various aspects of a society's way of life. So, for example, the culture of the Inuit includes traditional practices such as hunting techniques, marriage ceremonies, igloo construction, and storytelling. These elements interact, providing a shared framework—a culture—in which the people of that society live and, hopefully, thrive.

Since culture integrates all of a society's various practices, politics can never be separated from it, and politics will always be marked by a society's distinctive cultural character. As a part of culture, politics will also be imbued, as the Latin root reminds us, with deep values: in politics as in everything else, we cultivate what we care most about.

*   *   *

There is much more to say about the relation of politics and culture. Politics is "downstream of culture," as one saying has it. Our laws and governance will, in the nature of things, reflect the beliefs and values of the people, or our culture.

Consider an example taken from our colonial history. In 1648, the Massachusetts Bay Colony published a code of laws that set out the do's and don'ts for that society. At the top of the list of capital crimes, the code calls for the death penalty for witchcraft; there is a similar entry for blasphemy. Elsewhere the code says that no person should "spend his time idely or unprofitably," under pain of criminal punishment; and the code declared gambling illegal, with betting on a game they called "Shuffle-board" singled out for censure. Taken together, these and the rest of the code's declarations paint a picture of Massachusetts culture, what the colony valued and what it abominated.

American culture has changed a great deal since 1648, so our laws differ from those of Puritan Massachusetts. We no longer hang witches, for instance, nor do we fine the lazy. And far from punishing gambling, even Massachusetts now sponsors a state lottery. Cultures do not stand still, and, downstream from culture, laws and governance change as well.

*   *   *

If culture precedes politics and shapes government, the opposite can also be true at times: politics can shape culture. Where much of culture arises unconsciously among a people, embodied in longstanding customs and social habits, politics offers something different. It provides a forum through which society can, with a measure of self-consciousness, correct or shape the broader culture. The great 20th century example here is the civil rights movement, where the instruments of government were used to counteract the racism that had long marred American culture. *Brown* v. *Board of Education* and The Civil Rights Act of 1964 were landmarks in this crucial campaign.

We can also see government at work shaping culture in another vast endeavor: public education. Its goal is two-fold: to give young people the tools—among them, literacy and numeracy—to make their way in the world. But schools also teach the young how to live under our particular system of government. Through the teaching of history and civics, the schools transmit the knowledge and values, or culture, that will in turn shape the ways we govern ourselves as the young grow older.

This is a difficult challenge at any time, but the fostering of a shared civic culture faced an enormous challenge between 1880 and 1920. During that time, millions of immigrants arrived on our shores, most with little experience under anything like American government. This unprecedented wave of new citizens stimulated a massive effort to assimilate them, and especially their young, into American civic life.

Assimilation had two faces. On the one hand, immigrants were discouraged from holding on to practices from their home country. So, for example, children might be forbidden to use their first language in schools. On the other hand, public schools and other institutions cultivated a specifically American identity among recent immigrants. Students were taught to pledge allegiance to the flag, learned about the heroes of American history, and recited the Gettysburg Address.

This effort to define America's civic culture and to assimilate immigrants into it was remarkably successful. The scale of the success was made clear in the Second World War, when hundreds of thousands of young men and women from immigrant families fought and died in that largest of all wars, in many cases fighting against the nations from which their ancestors had migrated. This feat of assimilation is unmatched—unapproached, really—anywhere in history, and is a remarkable example of government shaping culture in a profound way.

*   *   *

Anything like this effort would be very difficult, perhaps even impossible, today. We are not only exceptionally diverse now, we are more sensitive to our multicultural roots and far less inclined to impose any majority point of view than we once were.

We cannot resist trying to use government to shape the culture, however, and in this we see another way politics and culture intersect: politics is a cultural battleground. We—all of us—want laws that reflect our own views and values. This is, to a large degree, what "government of the people, by the people, and for the people" means. Since American government depends on popular will in its lawmaking, the field is open to pressure from all sides; and since government is so powerful, we find it irresistible to use it for our preferred agendas.

Thus government has been a focal point in our ongoing culture wars, fought over such issues as school prayer, abortion rights, free speech, pornography, and, more recently, same-sex marriage and other rights of sexual minorities.

This politicized culture war cannot come to any easy peace, since the public itself is so divided. Nor, for the same reason, can government enact policies that satisfy all competing cultural concerns. We can, for instance, have laws that defend the rights of women to choose abortion under given circumstances, or we can have laws that prevent that, in accordance with the doctrines of various religious faiths. But no laws can do both at once.

Given this basic fact of political life, there will be losers and winners in the culture wars, and we should ask what happens with the losers. If substantial numbers of Americans feel that their deeper devotions are violated by political outcomes, will these citizens find their primary political affiliations somewhere other than in the nation—that is, in sub-national communities? And if so, what rights will those communities have in relation to the broader culture? Will Catholic-sponsored hospitals have the right to refuse abortion services, for example, or will they be forced to provide those services?

As any national consensus on cultural matters continues to decay, look for smaller cultural groups to assert a degree of independence from the broader society and for the rights of those groups to be a growing political concern.

DEMAGOGUE

The demagogue is one who teaches doctrines he knows to be untrue to men he knows to be idiots.

—H. L. Mencken

As long as political words hold their meanings, *demagogue* will be a slur. When the accusation of demagoguery is made, it is, or ought to be, like a warning flare fired into the sky: There is trouble here and we need to pay attention. Demagogues are leaders who inflame destructive passions in the people, thereby corrupting our politics at its source.

The word did not always have this negative cast. *Demagogue* is one of our oldest political terms, with roots in ancient Greece. Its literal meaning is simply *leader of the demos,* or of the people. Etymologically it is close to that other staple of our political vocabulary, democracy. Though *demagogue* was not necessarily pejorative for the Greeks, their philosophers did view the *demos* with a certain distrust. Ordinary people lacked the cultivation to understand the deeper demands of statecraft. In addition, the people were too self-interested and erratic to be politically dependable. Their leaders, *demagogues,* might share these faults, or worse, purposely play to them in order to amass power.

H. L. Mencken shared the ancient opinion of the common man, and carried it to a modern American extreme. His contempt for demagogues grew naturally from his disdain for democracy, its leaders, and indeed for the *demos* itself. "I confess," he wrote, "I enjoy democracy immensely. It is incomparably idiotic, and hence incomparably amusing. Does it exalt dunderheads, cowards, trimmers, frauds, cads? Then the pain of seeing them go up is balanced and obliterated by seeing them come down."

But if scorn for demagogues came easily to Mencken, it comes harder for those who embrace democracy. In siding with democracy, we take something of a gamble. We place our faith in the capacity of the public to act responsibly enough to secure our political future; to discern, for example, who are the trimmers, frauds, and cads, and to avoid voting for them.

Discerning is easier said than done, however, and demagoguery is, in fact, a natural pitfall in democratic discourse. In a democracy, the health of the state is closely linked to the interests of ordinary people. Any aspiring leader in a democracy will pitch his or her rhetoric to the wants, needs, and hopes of ordinary people. We can hardly expect otherwise. Yet the potential for demagogy is obvious when politicians do so, and the line between fair and foul can be difficult to draw. It is the line between the appeal to voters' legitimate self-interest and the appeal to mere self-indulgence.

To a degree, this difference is in the eyes of the beholder. For conservatives, a good deal of progressive rhetoric is inherently demagogic. Free health care, free college, and the elimination of fossil fuels: these positions strike critics as unsustainable and as political pandering.

To progressives, of course, they sound necessary. And as to demagoguery, the shoe is on the other foot, in their opinion. Donald Trump's 2016 campaign promise to build a wall between the United States and Mexico, they think, plays to the worst aspects of American nationalism. To many progressives the wall itself is pure demagoguery in massive, physical form.

Yet even charges of demagoguery can be demagogic. Standing in judgment over fellow citizens is temptation best not indulged too freely. A healthy politics depends on the character traits that see most people through their personal lives: a degree of self-discipline, respect for others, and a sense of limits as to what we can demand of fellow citizens and from the world itself.

Perhaps we find a clue to the nature of demagoguery exactly here, because the rhetoric of the demagogue undermines all of this. It nurtures grievances, contempt for others, and a sense of entitlement. This—playing to our weaknesses—is the mark of the demagogue and the source of the demagogue's power.

*   *   *

To see demagoguery clearly, it helps to look at it from another viewpoint, that of the working politician. The job is two-fold, at least for those who are elected to their positions. First is the task of winning the office itself, and here the uses of demagoguery will tempt them. Flattering the voters, over-promising, and caricaturing opponents are all winning tactics in political campaigns. And if a candidate is unconvinced of that, pollsters and party strategists will set them straight.

The second aspect of the politician's job takes shape after the election, and is roughly at odds with the first. Once elected, politicians need to legislate and make policy. Given the structures of our political system, this inevitably means working with others to hammer out compromises and build a consensus around practical programs.

The difficulty of this task is made worse by rhetorical claims made on the campaign trail. Writing laws that serve the needs of an exceptionally diverse society is not a process that allows every political promise to be honored. When an intransigent politician lands in a working legislature, it is like the proverbial monkey wrench falling into a machine. No legislator, attempting the ticklish job of building a compromise among fractious colleagues, wants to be harangued with campaign rhetoric from a colleague who cannot shift out of campaign mode. As one 20th century senator put it, "Everybody hates a man who demagogues when the doors are closed."

DEMOCRACY

> As I would not be a slave, so I would not be a master. This
> expresses my idea of democracy. Whatsoever differs from
> this, to the extent of the difference, is no democracy.
>
> —Abraham Lincoln, President (1861–1865)

Among political terms, *democracy* has an exalted place, alongside *liberty,* *justice,* and *freedom.* Americans all love democracy, it being very near the heart of our political creed. And as an ideal to rally around, we could do much worse. But democracy also casts something of a spell over us, so that we love it unthinkingly. We should take more care, since democracy has many facets, and if we are to embrace it, we should do so with clear, rather than spellbound, eyes.

In literal terms, democracy means "rule by the people." The word's roots are ancient Greek, with *demos* meaning "people" and *cracy* meaning "rule" or "power." Democratic states are those in which the will of the people determines the course government takes, rather than, say, the will of a privileged class or a monarch. Democracy is government "of the people, by the people, and for the people," as Abraham Lincoln put it in the Gettysburg Address.

While the word is ancient and familiar to all, actual democracy has been scarce on the ground, historically speaking. Ancient Athens was democratic, but its period of democratic rule was brief, just a few decades. Elsewhere, democracy was rare: the cantons of Switzerland have some democratic history, as did some Italian city-states, and medieval Iceland.

This pattern of overwhelmingly non-democratic rule broke in the late 18th century, when revolutions in America and France opened a new political era. In the wave that followed, political power shifted toward representative, popularly elected legislatures in dozens of countries. Today, we find that it is hard to name countries without such representative bodies at the heart of their government.[22]

This rise of democracy implies two essential beliefs. One is that the people as a whole should be sovereign. Any state or nation, after all, belongs as much to the *demos* as it does to anyone, and the health of the state can only be legitimately understood by taking into account the well-being and interests of all its people, not just of its upper classes.

The other understanding is just as basic. To believe in democracy is to believe that the people will have the necessary capacities—intelligence, judgment, courage, steadfastness—to govern. This confidence in the ordinary people is a staple of the American political tradition. We have sung the virtues of Jefferson's yeoman farmer, Franklin D. Roosevelt's "forgotten man," and even Richard Nixon's "Silent Majority," in their time. When it comes time to campaign for office, American politicians have found a very poor market for flattering the upper classes, but plenty of takers when they celebrate the common folk and their wisdom.

This celebration of democracy has been widespread, but one can find the greatest exceptions where we least expect them: among the Founders of the nation. They were *not* especially fans of democracy, having studied its history and found few examples of successful, durable democratic states. "It has been observed that a pure democracy, if it were practicable, would be the most perfect government," Alexander Hamilton once said. "Experience has proved that no position is more false than this. The ancient democracies, in which the people themselves deliberated, never possessed one feature of good government—Their very character was tyranny; their figure deformity."

In this outburst, Hamilton was speaking of direct democracies, where the people assembled in large groups to voice their opinions. Gathered in this way, he believed, people lacked the power to think clearly and to discuss matters rationally. He feared that democracies of this stamp degenerated too easily into anarchy and mob rule, and especially that the people would be drawn toward demagogues and potential tyrants.

In addition, he and other Founders questioned whether the people, once sharing in political power, could resist the temptation to enrich themselves at the expense of others, and thus throw society into chaos. "Pure democracies have ever been found incompatible with personal security, or the rights of property," wrote James Madison in *Federalist* 10, "and have in general been as short in their lives, as they have been violent in their deaths."

Suspicious of pure democracy, the framers included a variety of measures in the Constitution designed to stem the force of democratic impulses, while maintaining a system that still derived its direction and legitimacy from the will of the people. These mechanisms should be familiar from old civics lessons: a bicameral legislature, a Senate relatively insulated from popular electoral pressure, the presidential veto, and a Supreme Court with the power to judge the constitutionality of legislation.[23]

As a final safeguard against the dangers of government in general, including the danger posed by the majority's will, the Founders added the Bill of Rights to the Constitution, which protects fundamental rights and liberties against government encroachment. In our day we tend to link notions of democracy with various freedoms and liberties, but "rule by the people" is not the same as "good government" or "just government." The people, once in power, are not by any means immune to illiberal actions, and a Bill of Rights offers protection against democratic incursions against personal liberties.

*   *   *

The Bill of Rights, along with other limitations on government power, reinforces a deep streak of individualism in American culture. The emphasis, under constitutionally limited government, is on the rights of people to pursue happiness as they choose, and not on the right of a majority to impose their will on fellow citizens.

Thus, for many Americans democracy starts with the individual, and to be a democrat means embracing the idea that individuals possess a certain dignity by which they have every right to lead their lives as best they can and to live with the consequences. However, if American democracy starts with the individual, it cannot really end there. Our lives are interwoven with those of others to such a degree that we must govern not as isolated individuals, but as a society. To govern means making decisions that affect millions of people at a time, decisions about war and peace, environmental protection, trade policy, welfare, immigration, health care, and so on. Big issues with sweeping effects.

When decisions are made on this scale in a democracy, it is people in bulk who shape policy, and the individual can be lost in the crowd.

There is a tension here, deep in modern democracy's inner workings, where the democratic individual meets the realities of mass governance. It is one that political philosopher Richard Wollheim explored. What happens to the democrat in us when democracy disappoints us, when elections go the other way or democratically elected legislatures produce laws we dislike? After all, the odds that decision making in bulk will reflect our individual preferences are very long indeed, and the odds of it meeting everyone's preferences is nil. No one is served perfectly, and some people will find themselves on the losing end of political battles more often than not.

Thus actual modern democracy leaves democrats in an awkward position. We embrace the democratic process and somehow believe that the result of democratic processes is by definition right. And yet one will inevitably disagree with at least some of the results. One embraces and disdains them at the same time. This bind, Wollheim's Paradox, confronts virtually everyone who thinks of themselves as democratic.

And it leads to a provocative question: does anyone, in their heart of hearts, really believe in democracy?

*   *   *

Wollheim's paradox is especially pressing today. One certainty, given our bitterly divided politics, is that after every major election, tens of millions of democracy-loving Americans will wake up aghast at the results and wondering how they came to share their country with so many lunatics.

Caught in this bind, it helps to look at democracy from a different angle. If we judge democracy simply as a maker of policy and ask whether its results suit us, the answer might often be no. Standing in judgment this way, however, is itself somewhat anti-democratic.[24] We might even say that it amounts to an embrace of monarchy: after all, we measure democratic outcomes against a single, presumably infallible, position—our own.

This might be inevitable, but it is also somewhat unwise. Anyone with a measure of self-awareness knows better than to place absolute faith in his or her opinions, especially when confronted by the immensely complex problems that confront contemporary society.

But democracy is something like crowd-sourcing. It submits decisions to testing from all angles, since the views of all voters count. Democratic decision-making will reflect a broad base of thinking and interests. If the results are imperfect, democrats will learn to live with them. To the degree that we really value democracy, we accept that others will have views that differ from our own, and meet them with a measure of tolerance, if not whole-hearted respect. We accept the worth of fellow citizens and the necessity of taking their views into account as we cultivate a decent political society.

DIPLOMACY

> Diplomacy has always been a secret art; its most inspired
> practitioners have loved the darkness and fled the light.
> Free and open debate is essential for the health of democracy,
> but in matters of foreign policy the most important truths
> are often the ones nobody states.
>
> —Walter Russell Mead

In government, diplomacy is the negotiation between representatives of two or
more sovereign countries. It is the effort to smooth relations between nations,
perhaps defusing dangerous tensions, or preparing some mutually beneficial
agreement, such as a trade pact. Diplomacy is likely as old as organized states themselves. Archaeological records give evidence of such negotiations from the reign of
Akhenaten in Egypt, 4500 years ago.

This is a significant anthropological fact. When nations come into contact, a
degree of friction is inevitable: distinct groups and their interests do not naturally
coincide. Given this, it must have occurred to leaders, even early on, that relations
could go one of two ways. Competing groups could employ diplomacy—that is,
the effort to control events through discussion—or a confrontation could be left
"to take its mindless course," as one professional diplomat, Chas Freeman, Jr., put
it. Placing faith in the former option has been a feature of our political world for
45 centuries.

Of course, another significant anthropological fact should be noted here
as well. If a key goal of diplomacy is to avert war, it has a distinctly checkered
record. The mindless course of things, alas, gathers a great deal of momentum, and
diplomacy is no magic wand. It cannot simply dispel the competing interests that
drive nations toward conflict in the first place. In diplomacy, the security of whole

nations may lie in the balance while the most dangerous aspects of human nature are fully in play. Diplomats cannot afford to assume the best about adversaries and their intentions.

*   *   *

In considering matters of war and peace, it is tempting to treat diplomacy and military force as opposites. There is, of course, an obvious truth to this notion. But at a deeper level diplomacy and military force are more like alter-egos, paired in a common effort. That effort is to serve the nation's interests, to do its will, in the scrum of international relations.

It is crucial in both cases that the essential will come from elsewhere. It is not the diplomat's job to determine foreign policy, but to implement it. A nation's international strategy must reflect the will of its people, and any effort by diplomats to implement policies at odds with the wishes of the nation can only end in disaster.

Diplomats can, however, be a crucial resource in shaping, as well as executing, policy. For example, one of their most important responsibilities has been to provide in-depth information about other nations to their home government, and to make clear how this information might affect policy decisions.

A classic example of how diplomatic input can fruitfully shape policy comes from the mid-20th century. In the wake of the Second World War, the United States found itself rather suddenly at odds with its onetime ally, the Soviet Union. With the defeat of Nazi Germany, the Soviets began aggressively pushing their influence west into the heart of Europe, imposing communist governments on Poland, Czechoslovakia, East Germany, and elsewhere.

Strategists in the United States had to shift gears quickly, away from their wartime partnership with the Soviets and toward something new. But opinions about what course to take ranged widely. Some American leaders assumed that we could still work with our recent ally. For others though, a fear of Soviet expansionism gave rise to a much more oppositional, even aggressive, attitude toward the Russians.

One problem with forming a policy consensus was a lack of informed knowledge of the Soviet Union's strengths, weaknesses, and true goals. Into the breach stepped a diplomat, George Kennan. Kennan was a Russian specialist who spent years in that country. In early 1946, frustrated by Washington's misunderstanding of the Soviet government, Kennan fired off one of the most famous communiqués in American diplomatic history, the "Long Telegram."

In it, Kennan disabused those who believed that close relations between the two countries were still possible. He made clear that the Soviets would oppose our interests at every possible point. But while insisting that the Soviets would be implacable foes, Kennan also denied that they posed a unique, overwhelming threat. Stalin's regime was in fact beset by a variety of internal weaknesses that would limit their power in crucial ways.

Moreover, Kennan had the historical perspective to see that Stalin's Soviet Union was not simply the ideological monster of anti-communist nightmares, but in fact had a good deal in common with pre-communist Russia. "The Soviet regime is a police regime par excellence, reared in the dim half-world of Tsarist police intrigue, accustomed to think primarily in terms of police power," he wrote.

Through his deeply informed assessment of the Soviet Union, Kennan calmed fears that the United States faced an existential danger from that quarter. Further, his information provided the solid ground on which a clear strategy, containment, could take shape. The United States would follow that strategy for the next four decades, through to a successful and nonviolent end to the Cold War.

*   *   *

Kennan was an exemplary diplomat, and not just in his success with the containment policy. The information he gave in the "Long Telegram" exemplified an expertise that seasoned diplomats are uniquely positioned to provide. It came from long experience, close study of a foreign nation, and a capacity for dispassionate analysis.

This combination is nearly the polar opposite of whatever wisdom the mythical "man in the street" holds. Diplomacy is the governmental discipline perhaps least consistent with populism, and has historically been the preserve of an elite, trained corps.[25] British diplomat Harold Nicolson, writing in the 1930s, said: "It will be generally agreed that the most potent source of danger in democratic diplomacy is the irresponsibility of the sovereign people. By this I mean that, although the people are now the sovereign authority which ultimately controls foreign policy, yet they are almost wholly unaware of the responsibilities this entails."

We the people cannot be expected to fully grasp those responsibilities, but that does not mean that a detailed understanding of the world is unnecessary in creating foreign policy. The injection into policymaking of "elite" opinions from seasoned diplomats provides information that cannot come directly from the democratic gut. To reject diplomatic elitism out of hand is to limit the resources we use as we make our way in a challenging, sometimes dangerous international environment.

DUE PROCESS

No person shall be ... deprived of life, liberty, or property, without due process of law.

—Fifth Amendment to the U.S. Constitution

The term *due process* appears in the 5th Amendment to the Constitution, as quoted above, and also in the 14th Amendment with similar wording: "No state shall ... deprive any person of life, liberty, or property without due process of law." The two cases point to the same underlying fact: due process is a critical concept in our constitutional history. In fact, the whole Constitution is something like a blueprint for due process, setting out the procedures by which the government lawfully carries out its duties.

The phrase *due process of law* is at least partly self-explanatory. In essence, due process means that the government must follow fair, lawful processes when it makes and enforces laws.

The right to due process insures that people will be protected from unfair or arbitrary treatment at the hand of government. In the case of criminal proceedings, for example, the government must follow impartial procedures in prosecuting its case against defendants. These procedures include filing proper and public indictments, giving defendants the opportunity to confront accusers, protection against self-incrimination, and more. These are citizens' rights, captured in procedures that the government must follow if the proceedings are to be lawful.

Due process rights come from English law and stretch deep into Great Britain's history. The Magna Carta, written in 1215, includes due process principles, for example: "[N]o free man shall be taken or imprisoned or ... outlawed or exiled, or in any way ruined, ... except by the lawful judgment of his peers or by the law of the land." Over the next several hundred years, due process doctrine was elaborated in English law and practice. It was transported intact to the American colonies in the 17th century. Since taking root here, it has been a central concept in our own law from the start.

Over time, two aspects of due process have come into focus. The first is *procedural* due process, the essence of which is described above. Rules and processes have evolved to protect people from arbitrary government, and must be followed whenever the government deprives anyone of "life, liberty, or property."

*   *   *

The second aspect of due process has less to do with the letter of specific procedural protections and more to do with their spirit. We would not have due process rights in the first place were it not for underlying notions of fairness and individual liberties. Supreme Court Justice Felix Frankfurter put it this way in an opinion from 1950: "[T]he Due Process Clause embodies a system of rights based on moral principles so deeply embedded in the traditions and feelings of our people as to be deemed fundamental to a civilized society as conceived by our whole history. Due process is that which comports with the deepest notions of what is fair and right and just."

The second aspect of due process, called *substantive* due process, relates directly to those deeper principles upon which *procedural* due process rests. It is a relatively new way of thinking about due process, one that goes beyond its traditional meaning. It protects citizens against government actions that violate the principles that procedural due process depends on, not just the specifics of given rules.

This is no gauzy or theoretical matter. The doctrine of substantive due process puts a great deal of power in the hands of the judiciary, which decides what those principles mean in action. As judges do their work, this authority has proved to be elastic. As the *Oxford Companion to American Law* puts it, substantive due process brought with it a new era of "unprecedented judicial creativity."

We can see what this means by looking at a prominent case, *Loving* v. *Virginia*. At issue was the marriage between Mildred and Richard Loving, an interracial couple. Their union violated a Virginia state law, the Racial Integrity Act of 1924, which criminalized interracial marriages. The Lovings were charged under the act and sentenced to prison. They appealed the decision, however, and in time, the Supreme Court found the Virginia law unconstitutional, in part for violating the Lovings' rights to due process. Not procedural due process, since the law was passed and enforced by the books. It violated substantive due process by attempting to deprive a couple of a fundamental right linked to due process, the right to marry the partner of one's choosing.

The *Loving* decision, handed down in 1967, came at a time when the Supreme Court used its power to shape national policy with great confidence, in the *Loving* case and elsewhere. This activism pleased some while angering others. To those who were angered, the expansive reading of substantive due process gave the judiciary far too much say over policy, which they argued was properly the job of legislatures. In effect, the judiciary used the substantive due process doctrine to bypass legislators and to undermine the basic premise of legislation: that laws should be written by representatives of the people.

Justice Frankfurter equated due process with everything "fair and right and just" in our political heritage. Substantive due process gives the judiciary great leeway to judge our legislation by those ideals. But it rests on the authority of unelected judges. Even if we applaud the Court's decision in a case such as *Loving*, it is worth considering the political costs involved in such decisions, and asking: How much power should judges have in using due process principles to overturn legislation?

ELECTION

Elections are the great ritual of democracy, its single most important event.

—Lee Hamilton, U.S. Representative (1965–1999)

If democracy is about ordinary people determining their government, elections are the basic means to that end. The mechanics are familiar. We hold elections to fill official positions in government, including the presidency, governorships, mayoralties, and seats in various legislatures. Well before an election is held, candidates declare their intentions and then run campaigns in a bid for voter support. Come the election, citizens go to the polls and cast their votes. After the authorities count the ballots, the winners go on to fill the offices and, presumably, do the will of the people.

Elections provide a critical way for citizens to maintain a government they can tolerate. When people elect leaders, they grant the government a measure of the authority that otherwise rests with the people themselves.[26] We bind ourselves to the government through elections, as an elected government cannot be seen as an alien thing, imposed upon us by some will other than our own.

However, elections should accomplish more than signal consent for government. They should also send a message about what voters expect from our political leadership. Elections provide the government with information about how citizens feel about their leadership and what directions they want government to move in. During campaigns, candidates speak out on matters of importance and advertise their positions or beliefs. Voters in turn weigh the campaign's message before casting their ballots. In this way, elections send a message: This—the victor's positions on the issues—is what we want.

Of course, the message is never precise. Voters support a candidate for any number of reasons, not just a preference for given policies. But elections do provide crucial feedback from the electorate to the political leadership, pulses of information that help to guide the ship of state.

*   *   *

American elections are often big, public events, and the biggest ones engage the hopes and fears of millions of people. Major campaigns exert a powerful force on citizens, pulling them into distinct camps, like iron filings drawn to the poles of a magnet. For our favored candidate to win feels like an affirmation of our identities, while for that candidate to lose can feel like a rebuke from our fellow citizens.

The potent emotions that come with winning or losing do not necessarily square with the actual effects of elections on governance. After the ups and downs of a big campaign, life generally settles back into its ordinary patterns, and much of our governing goes on as before. Of course, elections always have consequences, and sometimes very big ones, but voters on the winning side can hardly be blamed for wishing that elections had a stronger and more immediate impact.

There are, however, good reasons the elections have a less direct and potent effect on governance. For starters, no election, not even the biggest, stands in isolation. In the United States we have around 500,000 elected officials, from presidents down to local school boards. Every time we the people vote, even for the lowest on the ballot, we grant the winners a degree of power. The mixed signals sent to our governments—local, state, and national— through these half-million elections are epic in their complexity. Seeing elections, even those for the presidency, in the context of the whole electoral system tends to undercut any claim to the sweeping mandates that election winners like to make.

To broaden the context even more, the authority delegated by the people through elections has something of a long shelf life. When voters fifty years ago elected their 500,000 officials, the laws those officials passed had, and have, all the legitimacy of laws passed today. Plenty of our most familiar and valued laws have been around for decades, including the Social Security Act, international treaties, environmental laws, and many more. We do not swap out our whole government and all its laws with each major election.

The rolling, ongoing system of elections in our democracy injects fresh information to our governance on a cumulative basis. But it leans away from definitive judgments on the system itself. The United States does not, and cannot, pivot sharply on the basis of any one election. This might dampen the spirits of citizens impatient for dramatic change. They might prefer an electoral system in which the will of the people is focused on a more concentrated test of public support, one that would pack a more seismic punch. Dictators, for example, sometimes base their claims to legitimacy on unique, up-or-down votes on their rule. But our more diffuse electoral system has its merits, at least if one considers stability and durability to be virtues in a government.

ELECTORAL COLLEGE

The - Electoral College is a political wisdom tooth—
a historical relic that stays largely out of sight yet causes
no small pain when it pops up.

—Matthew Daneman

Few terms in American politics can match *Electoral College* in combining obscurity with importance. Though the fate of the highest office in the land rests with it, the Electoral College is opaque in origin, purpose, and function to most Americans. Even the term itself is strange. What, after all, does an election have to do with college?

Only this. The word *college*, according to its Latin roots, refers to a gathering of people who come together for some purpose, such as scholars who come together for academic work. In the case of the Electoral College, a group of electors "gather" to do the actual electing of presidents.[27]

Nor, strictly speaking, do we hold a national vote to elect our presidents. We hold fifty simultaneous state elections, plus one in the District of Columbia. In those fifty-one elections, what actually happens is that voters determine which candidate will get their state's electoral votes, the votes of its Electoral College members. If Candidate A wins in Michigan on election day, then Michigan's electoral votes go to him or her.

The Electoral College is made up of 538 members. Each state gets a specific number of electoral votes: two, matching the number of its senators, plus the same number each state has of Congressional districts, or seats in the House of Representatives. California, for example, currently has 55 electoral votes, since it has 53 representatives in the House and the standard two for members of the Senate.

When the electoral votes are cast and counted, any presidential candidate who wins a majority wins the presidency. With 538 total electoral votes in the College, the magic number to reach is 270.[28] In terms of process, the Electoral College does not actually vote until several weeks after the people do. This gap would seem to give leeway for members of the college to think twice about whether to obey their home state's voters and cast a vote for some other candidate. Yet only rarely in our history have electors gone "faithless" and voted against their state's expressed wishes. Nor have these very few switches ever had any election-altering effect.

The Electoral College has another feature, one that is critically important for election outcomes. In almost every state, elections are winner-take-all. If a candidate wins just 50.1 percent of the vote in California, he or she still gets all 55 of that state's electoral votes.

When presidential candidates plan their campaigns, they must take the Electoral College into account. The popular vote across the nation is essentially irrelevant. Since candidates need 270 electoral votes to win, they think about plausible paths to reach that number. To start, the candidates look at the polls to see which states they are sure either to win or to lose. Having done so, they can mostly ignore those states. Why waste effort when it won't change the final electoral count?

That leaves all the other states. These are the battlegrounds where candidates focus their efforts, all with the magic number of 270 in mind.

The electoral calculations here lead to some otherwise unlikely campaign decisions. Recently, our biggest states, including New York for example, have received relatively little attention from presidential campaigns since candidates know ahead of time who will get their electoral votes. Meanwhile, voters in Colorado, Wisconsin, North Carolina, and other "swing states" get swamped with visits, speeches, advertising and the like. Candidates must campaign where they can gain electoral votes, not where the greatest number of popular votes are.

*   *   *

It is not uncommon for Americans to pause, look at this system, and wonder why on earth we put ourselves through such an arcane process. The Electoral College system is not only complicated, but in some ways unfair. For example, it certainly appears at first glance to give an electoral advantage to smaller states. South Dakota, with a population of about 865,000, holds three electoral votes, or one for every 288,000 citizens. California, on the other hand, holds 55 electoral votes and has a population of 39 million, or one electoral vote for every 709,000 citizens. By this measure, California's voters wield less than half the electoral power that South Dakota's have.

More importantly, the Electoral College can deliver presidents who are, by the popular vote count, losers. A candidate who wins the right combination of states by close margins can take the presidency despite getting fewer votes overall than an opponent. There is no question about the legality of such a win; the Constitution is clear that the Electoral College as the only measure of victory. But in a democracy where government is founded on the will of the people, it grates to see this happen. Nor is this a merely theoretical problem, having happened five times in the past, including twice in recent years. In 2000, Democrat Al Gore lost the Electoral College vote to Republican George W. Bush while winning more votes nationwide. Then in 2016, Hillary Clinton lost the electoral count to Donald Trump, despite winning 2.8 million more of the total votes cast.

In a closely divided, highly polarized nation, these results are more than galling, they are corrosive. One of the key goals of any election is to deliver a victor who has a clear and legitimate claim to support, which is necessary to do the job one is elected for. In these highly charged political times, the Electoral College may be failing on that critical score, and many Democrats have judged the elections of Presidents Bush and Trump to be virtually illegitimate.[29]

For this reason and others, opposition to the Electoral College rises periodically. In the wake of the 2016 election, an exasperated Senator Barbara Boxer, Democrat of California, spoke for many. "[The presidency] is the only office in the land where you can get more votes and still lose the [election]. The Electoral College is an outdated, undemocratic system that does not reflect our modern society, and it needs to change immediately."

Before reforming the system, however, it is worth considering the purposes the Electoral College actually serves. Supporters of the Electoral College believe, for example, that replacing it with the direct election of presidents would disrupt a delicately balanced constitutional system. With direct elections, the presidency would gain in stature, especially in relation to the other offices of government. After all, presidents would have a strong claim to being the ultimate choice as national leader, as demonstrated in a single, clear vote. The Electoral College breaks the hard edge of this claim through its indirection.[30]

There is another reason its supporters prefer the Electoral College over the direct election of presidents. With the current system, the search for electoral votes pushes candidates out from their strongholds and into battleground states. It forces them to make their pitch to undecided and not necessarily sympathetic voters, and to take the concerns of those voters seriously. Thus the Electoral College favors candidates who can appeal to a broad variety of interests and challenges those who depend on a more concentrated core of support. It tends to elect moderate, consensus candidates.

We see this reflected in the roster of presidents we have elected historically. We have, perhaps, chosen more than our share of mediocrities.[31] But we have also largely avoided electing the worst or most dangerous possible candidates. The Electoral College tends to discourage single-issue zealots, for example, and, until recently, the most mercurial outsiders.[32] When we consider reforming our system, we should consider whether the direct election of presidents would have produced such a record.

EMBASSY

> Even in pre-history there must have come moments when one group of savages wished to negotiate with another group of savages if only for the purpose of indicating that they had had enough of the day's battle and would like a pause in which to collect their wounded and to bury their dead. From the very first, even to our Cromagnon and Neanderthal ancestors, it must have been apparent that such negotiations would be severely hampered if the emissary from one side were killed and eaten by the other side before he had had time to deliver his message.
>
> —Harold Nicolson

If British diplomat Harold Nicolson was right about our Cromagnon and Neanderthal ancestors, the essential notion of the embassy has been with us for a very long time. Embassies are delegations that represent the interests of one group to a foreign people. Modern nations, for example, maintain embassies in the capitals of other nations. There, ambassadors represent their government's views to officials in the host country. The term *embassy* can also refer to specific diplomatic missions. If, for example, some international crisis is brewing, the United States might send an embassy to emergency meetings in order to defuse it.

The system of national embassies is not ancient, but took shape in the late medieval period, and especially among the city-states of Italy. Venice, a giant of medieval commerce, was a focal point for the development of diplomatic and ambassadorial customs. In negotiations with other states, the Venetians sought access to ports, safe passage of goods through other territories, the enforcement of contracts abroad, and other commercial necessities.

As the web of trade relations thickened, diplomatic customs grew more formalized. Among the most important of these customs were the formalities that guaranteed the protection of ambassadors. Embassies, by the nature of things, were often located in hostile lands, so their safety was a pressing concern. With the maturation of diplomatic customs, a tradition of inviolability gathered around embassies. Transgressions were a grave matter, worthy of severe retribution.

Out from Italy, diplomatic institutions spread through Europe, and eventually to the whole world. Now, virtually every nation maintains embassies in foreign lands. 193 nations, for example, send ambassadors to the United Nations. There are also 178 foreign missions in Washington, D.C., one of the world's densest concentrations of diplomatic activity.

The United States itself maintains over 300 diplomatic missions abroad. These include embassies—in the host nation's capital, as a rule—as well as consulates, which are smaller satellites of embassies in a given country.

*   *   *

As outposts in foreign lands, embassies have a charged place in international affairs. They are not just guests of the host countries; embassies are the physical property of the nation they represent. By tradition and law, the host country has no right to enter embassy grounds without permission, even to put out fires. In addition, diplomats assigned to embassies hold certain privileges, including immunity from criminal prosecution in the host country.

A recent example illustrates the ideal of embassies as islands of special rights and privileges. In 2012, Wikileaks founder Julian Assange, an Australian staying in the United Kingdom, came under a particular legal threat. The Swedish government wanted to try him for an alleged crime there, and the British agreed to extradite him to face those charges. Instead of submitting to authorities, however, Assange knocked on the door of the Ecuadorian embassy in London and asked for political asylum. Ecuador's president was sympathetic, so Assange's request was granted and Assange entered the embassy.[33]

The British were furious, and police surrounded the building waiting for a chance to arrest the fugitive, should he venture out to the streets. But Assange remained inside. Fully protected, he lived, in effect, under Ecuadorian law as long as he stayed put, which he did for more than six years.

The British abided by the laws pertaining to embassies. However, foreign embassies have always been tempting targets for espionage or violent attack. At times the urge to puncture the shell of security overwhelms diplomatic tradition. In 1979, after the Islamic revolution in Iran, several hundred members of a radical student group attacked and overwhelmed the American embassy in Tehran. In the attack, they took 52 hostages, who were held captive for well over a year, a fact with potent political repercussions in the United States. (In an interesting footnote, several American diplomats escaped the hostage-taking and found refuge in British and Canadian embassies.)

Memories of the embassy takeover have remained strong, both in Iran and in the United States. To many Americans, the 1979 attack was not just a wound, but an insult. In the forty years since, the United States has not re-established its embassy in Iran, making it one of the very few nations—North Korea and Bhutan are the others—without an official American diplomatic presence.[34]

EMPIRE

Empires have clear sovereignty but unclear borders and they
like it that way.

—Charles Hill

There is no one form of government called *empire*. Over the thousands of years they have existed—since the Akkadians conquered the Sumerians more than 4,000 years ago—empires have taken many different shapes. They are defined more by the elements Charles Hill notes above than by any institutional template. Empires are expansive, pushing out beyond their original borders to swallow other lands. They have the practical power necessary to act on aggressive designs. And, as Charles Hill notes, empires like what they do. Empires are defined by their domination of others, and power over others is a temptation that they find hard to resist.

There have been empires all around the world—China, Mali, Mesoamerica— but the linguistic roots of *empire* go back to ancient Rome and to a particular, momentous turn in its political life. That was the shift from the era of the Republic to the era of the Roman Empire. In its early years, Rome had been a relatively small society, mostly agricultural, with a government limited by a complex system of checks and balances. In time, however, Rome expanded, conquering neighboring states, then much of the Italian peninsula, and eventually large swaths of Europe and the Mediterranean world.

To administer this empire, Rome's government grew more centralized, and the focal point of its power was the emperor. Etymologically, the title derives from the verb *imperare*, "to give orders, or to command." The emperor's power was such that his commands were virtually law. John Adams once wrote that an empire is "a despotism, and an emperor a despot, bound by no law or limitation but his own will."

The two terms, *republic* and *empire*, represent a good deal more than differing institutions. They have been stand-ins for competing social and political ideals. We sometimes speak of the republican virtues—self-discipline, devotion to the public good, and a certain modesty. And we contrast those virtues with the qualities associated with empire: grandeur, might, and vast ambition.

As part of our inheritance from the classical world, we have these two ideals, republican and imperial. We also have the understanding that the two sit uneasily side by side. Like oil and water, republican and imperial spirits can mix but tend toward separation.

*   *   *

Rome's story should sound familiar to Americans. We too have made the transition from rustic and relatively powerless to being the center of enormous wealth, military might, and international influence. But in the stories we tell ourselves, we shy away from glorifying those facts. We hold tightly to the notion that we are a republic still, as when we pledge allegiance to the flag, "and to the republic for which it stands." We still relish the story of our founding, how we declared independence from the British Empire and, later, made it our business to oppose Nazi Germany, the Soviet Union, and other empires.

We are haunted, however, by an awareness that this notion is now out of step with crucial realities. When we take a clear-eyed look around the world and consider our role in it, we know the question is not so much whether we are an empire but rather what kind of empire we are.

A few data points highlight this reality. We have the largest military establishment in the world, and our armed forces are active in 80 countries on six continents; our economic power reaches every corner of the globe; we operate an astonishingly powerful global surveillance network; and even American culture has an imperial edge, planting its flag in nations around the globe, and even on the Moon. Today, the United States exerts an inescapable force around the world.

Matters have been moving in this direction for decades. Only the oldest Americans will recall a time before the United States rose to its role as world leader. The roots of that leadership can be found in the rubble of World War II, and the years immediately after the war marked a turning point for the country. In a world of wrecked governments and ruined economies, the relatively unscathed United States had, as many people believed at the time, a responsibility to take the lead in rebuilding.

So the United States launched into the effort of erecting a new order, a Pax

Americana. Its founders hoped that this order would reflect liberal values, including economic freedom and national self-determination. In constructing it, they used such building blocks as military alliances, including NATO (the first such alliance the U.S. entered into), as well as a network of economic and financial institutions, including the World Bank, the International Monetary Fund, and the World Trade Organization, which knit the world economy together in unprecedented ways.

*   *   *

There is, however, an internal contradiction within the notion of a liberal order. To create a world order means bringing many countries, with diverse histories and interests, into alignment. Nations have to conform to the order if they are to take part. Moreover, some leader will call the crucial shots to impose that order. In practice, to be a part of the American-led system means, to some degree, playing by rules set by the United States.

In taking its international leadership role, the United States has many times now resorted to brute military might or clandestine operations. Most recently we have seen this with the invasion of Iraq, and other Middle East interventions, but there have been other examples in previous decades.

The American-led order, however, is held together by less violent means as well. Many countries, for example, pursue alignment with the United States, acting in their own self-interest. Consider the position of Poland and the Baltic nations. They actively seek security under the umbrella of American protection, fearing a resurgent Russian expansionism.

Or consider another example, economic sanctions, which the United States also uses to impose its will abroad. Nearly every nation in the world understands the value of economic relations with America. If the United States establishes an embargo or deprives an opponent nation of access to international banking, those measures can exact a heavy toll.

And sanctions are a tool that Washington finds increasingly attractive, using them for a wide variety of purposes. The United States employs sanctions to combat human trafficking, terrorist activities, and nuclear proliferation, among other international menaces.

When the United States threatens to impose sanctions, other countries must weigh their options with this in mind: Their decisions will be made in the shadow of a terrific imbalance of power, and often in the teeth of hard American politicking. Failure to submit can lead to heavy consequences.

*   *   *

The power of the United States, which spans economic, military, political, and cultural fields, has made it a *nearly* dominant nation. Yet it is not an empire of the older sort. The United States holds no colonies abroad, as earlier powers did.[35] The United States does not extort tribute from subject states, a practice found among the ancients. Nor do we simply send armies abroad to haul off wheat, oil, slaves, Toyotas, or iPhones for our domestic needs.

What binds other nations to the United States is only partly imposed from the center; it is also driven by a kind of gravity that pulls other nations in: the desire for security backed by American might, the need to trade with the United States economy, the attractions of America's free-for-all culture. What results is hard to name. It is "a new beast," as scholar Martin Walker puts it, "the like of which the world has not seen before." What the United States has formed is, in his words, "a virtual empire."

ENTITLEMENTS

We, the people, still believe that every citizen deserves a basic measure of security and dignity. We must make hard choices to reduce the costs of health care and the size of our deficit. But we reject the belief that America must choose between caring for the generation that built this country and investing in the generation that will build its future.

—Barack Obama, President (2009–2017)

When President Obama spoke of "a basic measure of security and dignity" that every citizen deserves, he was speaking of entitlements. Entitlements are government programs that provide benefits—money especially—to citizens who fit certain categories. They are not payments for services rendered, nor gifts. Entitlements are given on the understanding that citizens have a right to them. Medicaid, for example, is an entitlement program that provides the poor with financial support for their medical needs.

Etymologically, *entitlement* is related to the word *title*. Just as a title to a car confirms one's ownership of it, so entitlements establish, in effect, one's ownership of their benefits. When deprived of expected payments, citizens can and will sue the government for its failure to provide them.

Along with Medicaid (1965), American entitlement programs include Medicare (which is similar but provided to older Americans; 1965), Social Security (1935), and the Supplemental Nutritional Assistance Program (SNAP, the federal food stamp program; 1939, 1964), among others. These programs rank among the biggest financial operations on the planet. Social Security payments in 2018, for example, came to 1 trillion dollars. Net Medicare costs for that year were nearly 600 billion.

Entitlements are no longer new, but they were a radical departure for American government when they were introduced in the 1930s. Since that time, entitlements have grown into a fundamental feature of governance, and a wide majority of Americans benefit from them, if not as individuals at least as families.

Having grown used to promised entitlement benefits, most American citizens are loathe to see them cut. The idea behind entitlements has seeped deeply into the public mind and shaped expectations of what government can and should provide. Though the occasional fearless politician might raise the possibility of trimming entitlements for fiscal reasons, they often find little support for their position.

There was, however, one major exception to the sanctity of entitlement programs. For decades, the one called Aid to Families with Dependent Children (1935) was a staple of federal support for the poor. AFDC dated back to the Great Depression and was designed, as its name suggests, to support families struggling with poverty. Under it, those who met the program's criteria were entitled to financial support, according to the number of dependent children in the family.

By 1996, however, criticism of the program had grown to such a point that a Republican-dominated Congress and a Democratic president agreed to its termination. According to critics, AFDC was working less as a support for families in need than it was drawing people into a life of dependency. So in 1996, the old program was terminated and replaced by a new one, Temporary Assistance for Needy Families. Among other features, TANF requires recipients to find work within two years under threat of losing benefits. The old entitlement reasoning, that poor families had a basic claim to government support, no longer held.

*   *   *

The fate of AFDC highlights a critical aspect of entitlement programs. Whatever promises they include, the right to entitlement benefits is far from absolute and does not have equal status with fundamental Constitutional rights. Created by statutes (that is, by acts of legislation), entitlement programs can be terminated the same way. AFDC was born when Congress passed the 1935 Social Security Act, and it ended when Congress voted it out of existence.

By contrast, consider the rights to "Life, Liberty, and the Pursuit of Happiness." We never needed legislation to confirm these, and the idea that the people's right to them depends on Congress's approval seems ludicrous. The fate of AFDC, on the other hand, shows that entitlements live only as creations of our legislative system. If the current entitlement programs grow unpopular, they too could suffer AFDC's fate.

And the future of entitlements bears watching, as they grow ever more expensive. As of 2020, these programs cost about 70 percent of the federal budget, up from 43 percent twenty years before. Since entitlement benefits are promised in legislation, the costs of entitlement programs are baked into future federal budgets. Their costs can only be contained by further legislation, which will always be difficult to pass, since entitlements are popular with the public.

Yet other government programs are popular too, and are being squeezed by the growth of entitlement spending. And the taxes needed to pay for all government programs are always unpopular, which compounds the funding challenge. These conflicting demands on the public treasury place the country in a tightening vise, with no end in sight. In coming years, look for the word *entitlements* to figure prominently in political discussions, as people wrestle over their place in the country's future.

EQUALITY

We hold these Truths to be self evident, that all Men are
created equal, that they are endowed by their Creator with
certain unalienable rights, that among these are Life, Liberty,
and the Pursuit of Happiness … .

—Declaration of Independence

Is equality natural, resting on observation of the facts? Some
individuals are slyer, cleverer, physically stronger, smarter,
more courageous, more ruthless, more charismatic—often
vastly so. Some are more devoted to family, or more capable
of long-term strategy and waiting. Equality has to push hard
and constantly against the facts.

—Joseph Vining

Equality holds a complicated place in American civic life. It is central to
our political self-understanding. According to the great testament of our
political faith, the Declaration of Independence, we believe in equality as a
basic, even self-evident truth: all people are created equal. Having embraced this
ideal, however, we are profoundly conflicted about how to live up to it.

The essential meaning of equality is clear enough. It actually comes to politics
from that clearest of worlds, mathematics. There, equal means the same, or
equivalent. Two plus two equals—is the same as—four. Likewise in political life,
people are equal in the sense that all are the same in some fundamental way, sharing
equally in their irreducible value as humans.

However, political logic is not mathematical. Politics is thoroughly human, with each individual involved, both the governed and the governors, being a unique mix of willfulness, decency, ambition, intelligence, physical disability, and more. Equality as a perfect ideal can never be fully at home here.

Which is not to say that the principle of equality has no place in politics, as the Founders, of course, insisted. John Adams captured the essence of their view when he wrote that we should have a "government of laws, not of men." We shall be governed, he hoped, as equals. We should be judged impartially under the laws: None should be privileged by rank, and none should be burdened by its lack. If the concept of equality has any meaning in American political life, it can be found here.

A rejection of rank and status, however, is not the same as an embrace of equality as an ideal. In the Founders' vision, liberty was the goal: "the first object of Government," as James Madison wrote. Not equality. The free exercise of one's talents, whatever the result, must be protected by law. In this, the Founders understood that freedom would lead to differing—that is, unequal—outcomes for citizens. James Madison said as much in *Federalist* 10: "From the protection of different and unequal faculties of acquiring property, the possession of different degrees and kinds of property immediately results."

We see here a distinction that remains critical in our politics today. The American Founding embraced what can be called the equality of opportunity. People have equal rights under the law to the "pursuit of happiness." But this equality of opportunity is no guarantee of any equality of outcome. In fact, the first insures the latter's absence. As political scientist Harvey Mansfield wrote, "The hard name for equality of opportunity is inequality … ."

*   *   *

That the Founders were not primarily concerned with the inequality of outcome does not mean we must share their point of view. When the differences between rich and poor are sharp, it rankles. Indeed, inequality, when it is stark and grinding enough, sets the stage for civic strife and can present a danger to society.

Inequality especially rankles in America, where a deep vein of anti-elitism runs through our civic traditions. Even at the time of the Founding, concern about the equality of outcomes was stirring here. This incipient feeling found a voice by the mid-19th century, when an embryonic unionism was taking shape. The self-proclaimed Workingmen's Party, for example, rallied supporters with the slogan "Vote Yourself a Farm!," proposing to get land into the hands of the dispossessed.

The movement to use governmental power to enforce greater equality of outcome gained traction as the 19th century progressed. Its successes came in response to the tremendous social pressures of industrialization, which generated vast private fortunes but also a sharpened consciousness of the hardships faced by the poor. This awareness provoked deep resentment and, in time, political action.

That response unfolded over decades and continues to this day. Government programs to address economic inequality have included minimum wage laws, entitlement programs, including Medicare and Medicaid, and Aid to Families with Dependent Children, as well as the development of public schools. More recently, proposed plans for guaranteed basic income, single-payer health care, and free college for all share similar goals: to extend the promise of equality to all Americans.

These efforts have been extensive in their way, but have always had a patchwork quality, having been cobbled together over decades and with a variety of targets: income, health care, education, and so forth. Such egalitarian efforts have also come in the face of strong countercurrents. Government subsidy programs that favor the poor come at some expense to others, thus violating the Founders' commitment to thorough equality under the laws. In short, we struggle to balance these two equalities: that of exact legal equality with that of equality of outcomes. We want people to be equally free to pursue their destinies, and we applaud success, yet we are disgusted by extreme wealth existing alongside deep poverty.

*   *   *

There is another dimension of equality to consider, one distinct from both equality of opportunity and equality of outcome. It might be called equality of respect, and it concerns the way in which citizens regard each other—whether we see each other as equals or as something else.

Democracy depends on this form of equality. Some degree of mutual respect among citizens is necessary for its well-being, indeed for its survival. Mutual loathing is a poor mortar for building a democratic society.

Of course, it is hardly new for politics to be plagued with hatreds. Governing always reflects some of the darker aspects of our nature. Moreover, as individuals we inevitably invest politics with deep feelings of personal identity and our attachment to some in-group.

While politics has often brought out tribal feeling in societies, the politics of identity has a peculiar grip on our spirits today. More even than religion, many Americans today see politics as the crucible in which we fight it out over good and evil. And it is hard to see the place in such an environment for equality, with its implied respect for others.

At least one observer thinks that we face a deep crisis in this regard. "The American republic's essence had been self-restraint toward fellow citizens deemed equals," wrote political scientist Angelo Codevilla in 2018. "Because a majority of Americans no longer share basic sympathies and trust, because they no longer regard each other as worthy of equal consideration, the public and private practices that once had made our Republic are now beyond reasonable hope of restoration. Strife can only mount until some new equilibrium among us rises."

Whether Codevilla's fears are fully justified or not, we would do well to consider what practices—civic, intellectual, or spiritual—might diminish the animosities that wrack our current political life, and restore a measure of equal respect among fellow Americans.

EXECUTIVE

The legislative power is the heart of the State, [and] the
executive power is its brain, which gives movement to all
the parts.

—Jean-Jacques Rousseau

When Rousseau compares government to a person, with a heart and a
brain, he is nodding toward a central theory of government. To see
the task of governing clearly, it helps to break it down into distinct
functions. Rousseau mentions two, the legislative and the executive.[36] In his metaphor, Rousseau compares the legislature to the heart. It is the organ of government that expresses the will of the country, the one that defines what its people
aim to achieve. The executive in government, on the other hand, is the organ that
"gives movement to all the parts." It takes action to achieve those aims.

The distinctions between government's basic functions are reflected in the
United States Constitution, which separates them and places responsibility for
each in different institutions. Article 1 speaks of legislative powers and grants
them to Congress; Article 2 addresses executive functions and places them
under the President; and Article 3 deals with judicial functions, providing for a
Supreme Court and other courts.

Failure in any of these functions might be fatal to a government, but failure
of the executive was a special concern for the Founders. When the country
was governed under the Articles of Confederation, Congress—though weak in
itself—was the only real national institution of government.[37] The country had
no executive office to carry out whatever laws Congress managed to pass. As a
result, the national government was stunted at a dangerous time, and frustration

with that weakness led to the movement for a new constitution. As historian Forrest McDonald put it, "experience taught Americans that safety and ordered liberty cannot exist without competent government and that government without executive authority was no government at all."

Concern for strength in the executive was reflected in the Constitution, which places the executive power squarely in the hands of the president. By centering that power in one office, rather than divided as the legislative power is in Congress, executive power is focused and, hopefully, effective. In addition, individual presidents will be clearly responsible for failures in the execution of government policy. Executive power and responsibility are married in the office of the president.

*   *   *

The separation of powers—legislative, executive, and judicial—is a cornerstone of American Constitutionalism. And a purist might even say that the executive ought, in theory, to have no real will of its own: it exists to carry out the legislature's commands.

Theory, however, is one thing and practice another. In governing, it is all but impossible to completely separate the willing from the executing when government does its work. In practice, the executive inevitably makes choices that go well beyond a rote carrying out of the legislature's wishes. To apply the law effectively means that the executive must have some discretionary authority to make decisions at ground level. In making choices about how to apply general laws, the executive and the legislative functions are blurred to some degree.

Consider, for example, the challenge of land management. The federal government owns enormous amounts of land across the country, totaling some 635 million acres. That land is fantastically varied, and the uses we make of it vary as well. Some lands are set aside as wilderness, and some are used for mining, grazing, logging, or other purposes.

We need laws to guide the use of national lands, and Congress is ultimately responsible for those laws. However, it would be impossible to write laws that fit all the conditions found on public lands. So, while the legislature might define goals and set broad standards for land use, the executive branch will necessarily use its judgment in applying those goals and standards to conditions on the ground. And in applying its judgment—setting rules and regulations—the executive uses power we can rightly call legislative.

There is another, related, dynamic that affects the balance between the legislative and executive branches. Over time, the executive has gained power not just in deciding how legislation will be applied, but in initiating legislation itself. Many ideas for what the legislature should do will actually come from the executive branch, not from within Congress.

The Defense Department provides a good example here. In thinking through future defense needs, military planners are confronted by all sorts of challenges. For example, planners must take into account which nations may constitute a threat in the near or long term, and thus determine the geography of potential battlegrounds. They must also plan for rapid changes in technology. Computers, satellites, lasers, robotics, and metallurgy all have a role in warfare, and planners must understand their potential military uses.

All this information must be digested in order to handle the daunting job of planning weapons systems. We cannot expect members of Congress to take this on. Planners within the Defense Department are far better prepared to take the lead. They will sift the technical challenges, come up with plans, and present them to the legislature. Congress will have the ultimate say over which systems to buy, but the initiative comes from elsewhere. As President Franklin D. Roosevelt said of the chief executive's role, "It is the duty of the President to propose, and it is the privilege of the Congress to dispose."

*   *   *

If so, we might say that Congress is remarkably privileged today, since we are a much more legislatively ambitious nation than we once were. Yet the effect of growing legislative action has not been an increase in the power of the legislature, at least not in relation to the executive. Power has, instead, migrated toward the executive, in part because of the dynamics described above. This shift of power is reflected in the growth of the executive branch itself. Around 98 percent of the federal workforce is employed in the executive branch, with the remaining 2 percent working in the legislative and the judicial. Executive branch employees include 2 million or so civilian workers, plus another 1.5 million serving in non-civilian roles.

Most of these employees work in the big executive departments of the national government. These include the Departments of State, Treasury, and Defense (or War Department), which date back to the founding of the nation. They also include the departments added since: Justice, Interior, Homeland Security, Housing and Urban Development, and others.

In addition, the Executive Office of the President, established in the 1930s, has grown to include hundreds of employees whose mission is to provide support of all kinds to whichever president is serving in office. Finally, there is a third category of offices that are executive in function, but founded with some degree of independence from the president and the rest of the executive branch. These independent agencies include the Federal Reserve, the United States Postal Service, the Environmental Protection Agency, and others.

The size of the executive branch and the scope of its activities almost overwhelm the imagination. As such, its size and scope reflect, for better or for worse, the enormous amount we expect the government to do.

FAILED STATE

A state or society that descends into civil strife or anarchy is a cancer on the international body politic that endangers neighbors and its region.

—Chas Freeman, Jr.

A failed state—a mostly self-explanatory term—is one in which governance has broken down and the state fails at its fundamental tasks: maintaining order, enforcing laws, defending borders, and creating a stable environment for people to live in. Without some level of governance, nations can degenerate, as Chas Freeman, Jr., says, into civil strife or anarchy, creating a lethal environment within its borders and a danger beyond them.

Unlike most political terms, we can locate exactly the point at which *failed state* entered our political discourse. It occurred when two scholars, Gerald Helman and Steven Ratner, published an article, "Saving Failed States," in the winter of 1992. There they took note of a "disturbing new phenomenon" of states that had devolved to the point that internal government had become virtually impossible.

The timing of their article was significant. In the arc of recent history, the acknowledgment of state failure marked something of a turning point. Previously, a more optimistic trust in the powers of self-government had held sway. That optimism was running at full tide in the years after World War II, when the powers of authoritarianism had been defeated, as the story went, by the forces of democracy.

Even more to the point, the post-war years saw a sharp uptick in decolonization, as many nations in South Asia, Africa, and Indochina gained independence from one or another European power. The number of states in the United Nations grew from 50 in 1945 to more than 150 in the 1990s. By then, virtually the entire population of the world resided in independent countries.

This enormous transformation was greeted with high hopes. The United Nations made national self-determination a primary goal, grounded in the belief that "peoples could best govern themselves when free from the shackles" of foreign domination.

By 1992, however, it was growing clear that self-determination was no magic formula for successful, or even sustainable, government. The challenge of state sustainability grew clearer with the end of the Cold War, as well. During that conflict, both the United States and the old Soviet Union dedicated substantial resources to shoring up client states around the world, the better to promote their own interests in that global competition. As the Cold War ended, the flow of resources into developing countries dropped off, and the challenges of maintaining viable government in those allied nations grew accordingly.

In some cases those challenges proved overwhelming. In the most serious ones, such as Somalia, national government effectively disappeared, displaced by regional factions, feuding warlords, and clan loyalties. It was for such cases that the term *failed state* was invented, and it is a sign of the times that it has been picked up and used so readily since it was introduced.

*   *   *

Failed states are different from incompetent or wicked states. Consider the example of Nazi Germany. However appalling it was, it was no failed state, at least not until its collapse. As a state, it maintained enough institutional capabilities to govern effectively until nearly the end of the Second World War. And when the Nazi regime was brought to an end, it was through violent foreign power, not internal decomposition.

What are the basic functions carried out by a non-failing state? All the sorts of things that make governing possible: a police system to maintain order, transportation and communication systems, tax collection, education, a functional currency. Crucially, states also depend on a strong national consciousness and a degree of loyalty to the government among citizens.

There is one other critical element that makes a state a state, and without which it will fail. That is control of territory within its borders. States cannot allow any competitors in this regard. The ability of armed factions to control land and threaten central government is a hallmark of the failed state.

This loss of control can lead to terrible human suffering. In the long civil war in the Democratic Republic of the Congo, running for the better part of 20 years, over 5 million people died, with millions more displaced and refugees spilling over the border into other countries. Wholly apart from the widespread death and displacement, the civil strife that afflicts failed states makes regular life vastly more difficult to pursue.

Chaos within a state leads to another problem as well, one that came into focus in the years after 2001. Failed states can become incubators of terrorist threats. Nations that cannot provide a stable environment will be home to frustrated people who lash out in violence. And regions beyond the reach of responsible government provide the physical grounds where terrorists can organize and train. Thus, according to the 2002 United States National Security Strategy document, the United States is "threatened less by conquering states than we are by failing ones."

This is not a problem that will go away anytime soon. Modern states are highly evolved, exceedingly complex enterprises, built from the ground up, over time, through deep acculturation on the part of whole societies. The conditions necessary for their existence cannot be assumed for each of the world's 150 nation states. Since the term *failed state* entered our vocabulary, it has thrived because it so aptly fits a crucial feature of the contemporary international scene.

FEDERALISM

> The powers not delegated to the United States by the Constitution, nor prohibited by it to the States, are reserved to the States respectively, or to the people.
>
> —Tenth Amendment to the U.S. Constitution

Discontent with our leadership is something of an American tradition, so criticism of "the government" is more or less constant. Such criticisms are always wrong, however. We have *governments*, plural, to complain about, not just one. This is thanks to federalism.

Federalism is the division of government into different, separate levels, national and state, with local government in the mix as well. Strong federalism means relatively greater powers at the state level than at the national. Less federalism means greater concentration of power at the national level. This might seem backwards, since the terms *national* and *federal* can be and are used interchangeably when we speak of the "federal government." But one must live with the inconsistency.

Federalism has two virtues, one positive and one negative, or perhaps preventative. On the positive side, federalism allows a greater closeness between government and people, and thus a better fit in policymaking. An agriculture policy that suits Iowa, for example, will not suit Rhode Island. The governments of those two very different states can address their agricultural needs with a dexterity that national government cannot match.

As to its negative virtue, federalism acts as a brake on national power by leaving important powers to the states. Dividing powers this way makes it harder for centralized government to grow over-powerful. It splits the power of government power into competing institutions so that none can gather dangerous force.

Federalism deprives the national government of any potential monopoly on power.

Since the Founders were aware of these positive and negative benefits, they made federalism a pillar of the Constitution. This is made explicit in the Tenth Amendment, which emphasizes that powers not specifically granted to the national government shall remain with the states, or with the people.

While the Constitution embraces federalism, it does not spell out any absolute division of labor between the nation and the states. James Madison did propose a starting place, however. "The powers delegated by the Constitution to the Federal Government ... will be exercised principally on external objects, as war, peace, negociation [sic], and foreign commerce ... . The powers reserved to the several States will extend to all objects, which, in the ordinary course of affairs, concern the lives, liberties, and properties of the people; and the internal order, improvement, and prosperity of the State." Though he was a nationalist in comparison to his political opponents in 1787, Madison's vision would satisfy all but the most hard-core federalists today.

*   *   *

If Madison's view provided a starting place, we have moved a very long way from it over the past 230 years. Since the signing of the Constitution, the balance of power has shifted sharply away from federalism and toward nationalized power. The national government now runs vast entitlement programs (Social Security, Medicare, and Medicaid), has a hand in education at all levels, supports transportation projects across the country, runs housing projects, and operates a national police service (the FBI)—all this in addition to the "external objects," or foreign affairs and defense matters, that Madison saw as the special responsibilities of national government.

Another crucial way the federal government dominates the political landscape is through its regulatory power. Washington exerts great pressure on the states to meet national standards on any number of such issues. There is a national minimum wage, for example. States can set their own preferred level, but it cannot be lower than the national standard, only equal to it or higher. Something similar happens on many fronts, including regulations on pollution and worker safety standards. States can exceed national standards, but they cannot go lower.

The drive to nationalize regulations is easy to understand. If one supports a given policy, better to do it on a national scale rather than piecemeal, state by state. If you are concerned about climate change and want laws to control carbon dioxide emissions, you might be happy when one state passes some, but simple math suggests that you will be fifty times happier if the laws are national.

*   *   *

Thus, the nationalization of our politics has strong appeal. But it carries the seeds of real trouble as well. Nationalization, for example, affects the quality of government programs. Legislating at the national level demands compromise, enough to make laws palatable to a wide variety of interests from all across the country. For committed advocates of given policies, the results of the national legislative process almost inevitably seem watered down.

This dynamic has affected health care reform in recent years. Supporters of universal health insurance have wanted a fully public system like that of Canada or the United Kingdom. Such a plan could not pass at the national level, however, and so a complicated, semi-privatized compromise was agreed upon in 2010: the Affordable Care Act (Obamacare). A product of difficult coalition-building in Congress, the ACA never fully satisfied many of its staunchest defenders, and never came close to pleasing its opponents.

Despite the compromises built into it, the fight over the ACA felt like total war, as legislation at the national level often does. Nationalization focuses enormous passion on Washington and its struggles. With so much power concentrated at the national level, who doesn't want their share, and who can afford to lose it?

Thus our highly nationalized politics combines two unfortunate features. On the one hand, it is like mortal combat over every policy decision. At the same time, the resulting compromises are often discouraging even to the victors.

One wonders, as frustration grows with our national politics, whether Americans will look anew at the mostly forgotten virtues of federalism. Early in the 20th century, Justice Louis Brandeis, a pioneer of American progressive thought, wrote approvingly of them. The states, he believed, were natural "laboratories of democracy," where government could experiment creatively to solve difficult problems.

Brandeis also thought there was more at stake than mere efficiency. He yearned for more humane government, for a politics that better suited the fullness of our aspirations. And he believed that federalism could unlock that future. "For a century our growth has come through national expansion and the increase of the functions of the Federal Government," he acknowledged. But, he wrote, "[t]he growth of the future—at least of the immediate future—must be in quality and spiritual values. And that can come only through the concentrated, intensified striving of smaller groups." If what Brandeis said was true in his time, it may be doubly so today, after decades of continued nationalization of both our government and our politics.

FILIBUSTER

> I want to say right now that I would to God I had the power
> to stand here without eating a bite or taking a drink or
> sleeping a wink until twelve o'clock on the 4th day of March
> 1931, if it would keep this iniquitous, infernal machine off
> the people of America. If you call that a filibuster, then I
> am guilty.
>
> —Coleman Blease, Senator (1925–1931)

It cannot be sheer coincidence that the term *filibuster* suggests both busting and bluster. In politics, the filibuster is a maneuver used to stop legislation by talking it to death. In legislative debate, only one speaker can hold the floor at a time, and in a filibuster, that speaker refuses to yield the floor, holding out until he or she exhausts the opposition and causes them to quit.

The right to filibuster is not found in the Constitution, which makes no mention of it, but the Constitution does give the House and Senate the authority to create their own rules. The filibuster is found in the United States Senate and is a product of its rules. The conditions under which senators can filibuster is solely up to the Senate and its Rules Committee.

By their nature, filibusters are frustrating. Despite this, the Senate has been reluctant to curb the practice. Filibustering is deeply rooted in the Senate's sense of purpose. That body prides itself in being "the world's foremost chamber of enlightened debate," as William Safire once put it, and it is where bills, treaties, and presidents' nominations are (or should be) scrutinized with the closest attention. Through extended debate in the Senate, weak bills, for example, should be identified and either strengthened or killed off. As such, the Senate sees itself as the backstop of American lawmaking.

In keeping with the notion that the Senate must thoroughly debate matters before it, its rules allow senators to speak freely, with no effective limits, when they hold the floor. In a filibuster, senators take this allowance and push it to the extreme, ending debate altogether. Thus the filibuster gives individuals (or relatively small groups) the power to derail legislation even when a solid majority supports it. And by stopping business in the Senate, filibusters stop it, period. Bills that do not pass the Senate cannot become law, no matter what happens elsewhere in the government. Thus, the filibuster makes the Senate a choke-point in national government.

The practice of filibustering has led to some remarkable scenes in Senate history. Senators have spoken nonstop through the night, for example, and once Senator Strom Thurmond held the floor for 24 hours straight. Filibusterers have carried on for days on end (with recesses for meals and rest, of course). With all that time to speak, senators have been imaginative in choosing their themes. They have spoken on patriotism, discussed Aztec history, and read Aesop's fables aloud to their colleagues.

Just the threat of a filibuster can make the Senate buckle. In 1903, "Pitchfork Ben" Tillman, of South Carolina, took the floor during debate when he was demanding that the federal government pay his home state money from a long-ago transaction. To prepare, he placed a waist-high stack of books by his desk, sending a clear message about his intentions. Not wanting to test Tillman's endurance, the Senate agreed to the senator's demands. And in fact, filibusters often work this way. Today, when filibusters are threatened, opponents yield without wasting everyone's time on the theatrics.

*   *   *

The filibuster holds a place of honor in Senate lore, but senators have always had a love-hate relationship with the practice. During its first hundred years, the Senate set no real limits to filibustering, but as a practical matter, senators limited themselves out of respect for their colleagues.

By the end of the 19th century, however, that courtesy was wearing off. With the rising legislative stakes of the Progressive Era, filibustering grew more ruthless. In their willingness to defy the will of the majority, practitioners grew "brazen and unblushing," as historian Franklin Burdette put it. And with the filibuster unchecked, the power of the Senate rested "not upon ability and statesmanship, but upon effrontery and audacity."

This mounting audacity naturally provoked angry responses, and the indignation eventually rose to the point where, in 1917, the Senate voted to limit filibustering for the first time. This limit took the form of a rule allowing *cloture,* a formal request to end debate. With a three-fifths supermajority in a Senate-wide vote, opponents could use cloture to end a filibuster and move on.

But that three-fifths is no easy hurdle. For this reason, filibusters have remained a powerful tool in the Senate long after cloture was first introduced.

That remains true today, though less so since 2013. In that year the Democratic majority in the Senate struck a major blow against the filibuster. With a Democratic president, the Senate Democrats grew increasingly frustrated as Republicans used the filibuster to block nominees to federal judgeships. As a result, Majority Leader Harry Reid changed Senate rules so as to disable the filibuster when it is being applied to nominations. The new rule allowed a simple majority to end debate, rather than the previous three-fifths supermajority. It should be noted, however, that the old supermajority vote remains necessary when legislation, rather than nominations, is before the Senate.

What is sauce for the goose is sauce for the gander, however, and Reid's action set a precedent Republicans would use in turn. When Republican Donald Trump was elected and that party held a majority in the Senate, the Senate confirmed a record number of judicial nominees. With no teeth in the old filibuster, the minority (Democratic) senators had no tool with which to stem the flow of Republican nominees to federal judgeships.

This recent history has left the filibuster damaged. Though it is still in place for legislation that comes before the Senate, the filibuster of judicial nominees is all but finished. If, in the future, Senate traditions continue to fray, the practice may completely disappear.

FOREIGN POLICY

> In no field of endeavor is it easier than in the field of foreign
> affairs to be honestly wrong; in no field is it harder for
> contemporaries to be certain they can distinguish wisdom
> from folly.
>
> —George F. Kennan

One primal challenge that confronts every society is how to deal with groups beyond its borders. Foreign policy is the planned, formal effort to accomplish this. It is an exertion of sovereign will—the will of the whole society—and reflects national hopes and fears in relation to other states.

The quandaries presented by international relations are kaleidoscopic in their variety. Other nations might pose military threats, for example. But they also provide opportunities for trade, for partnerships in international policing, for travel and business abroad, and more.

If foreign challenges are kaleidoscopic in their variety, that kaleidoscope is also constantly shifting. Foreign policy must take into account the endlessly evolving circumstances that arise on the international scene. Making sense of these circumstances and plotting the course that will best protect the nation's interest is called strategy.

Grand strategy is the most demanding of political disciplines. To chart a course, the strategist must take into account all the crucial variables in play. For example, how might changes in technology affect foreign relations, including the evolution of military technology? What are the likely economic trends (which nations are growing and which will be struggling)? Demographics, too, are crucial to the prospects of international relations, as is the environment: What should strategists make of global warming, for example, and its potential effects on international agriculture and human migration?

*   *   *

Any mind that could wrestle successfully with such questions would be formidable indeed. Brilliant people disagree on fundamental strategic matters, and even the most dramatic international developments can catch experts by surprise. The fall of the Berlin Wall and the end of the Soviet Union, for example, were effectively unforeseen by the Central Intelligence Agency, despite all its resources and the many sharp analysts there.

If such a thing as a perfect foreign policy strategist existed, it's likely no one would recognize him or her. But if that strategist did exist, and was sent to Washington, it's also likely that he or she would quickly lose their mind. The system we have in place to produce our foreign policy is, emphatically, not suitable for the lone genius to run.

The reasons derive in part from the Constitution, which divides power over foreign policy, as it does power in general. Thus, the president exercises crucial powers over foreign policy as commander-in-chief of the armed forces and as head of the executive branch, which includes the Department of State, center of the American foreign policy apparatus. But the Constitution also checks the president's power. The president's nominee to head the State Department must be confirmed by the Senate, for example, which has the same right over any treaty negotiated with foreign states.

In addition, though the president is head of the executive branch and nominates the Secretary of State, the State Department itself has a strong institutional identity and cannot be steered easily by the president. And even the other big departments have grown to the point where many of them have developed their own foreign policy agendas. The Department of Commerce, for example, has its own distinct interests in foreign trade.

All of which makes the creation of American foreign policy an enormously complex process, one that nearly defies all efforts to impose consistency.

Among the critics of this situation have been foreign policy experts who are frustrated by the system's tendency toward incoherence. One was George Kennan, a seminal policymaker in the mid-20th century. In Kennan's eyes, the power to make necessary decisions had become too fragmented, in a process that favors parochial interests at the expense of the common good. "In this confusion, such a thing as a clear, firm, and prompt decision—and particularly one where all the relevant aspects of national interest are brought together, calmly weighed, and collectively taken into account—is rare indeed," Kennan wrote.

It would be foolish to discount the views of an observer as thoughtful as George

Kennan, but there are other ways of looking at the matter. One starting place is to ask whether the messy process has actually yielded poor results, or whether United States foreign policy has served the nation's interests well, at least in the broadest terms. Here the evidence suggests that, at the very least, the system's faults have not been crippling. The nation survived its fragile infancy and has grown since then to a position of international leadership and unprecedented power. Whatever else this may be, it is no bleak failure. Despite its fragmented structure, the system produced the necessary collective will to survive various threats, including, for example, the challenge of the Cold War.

Noting this record of success, historian Walter Russell Mead speculates that our foreign policy achievements may actually be due, at least in part, to the qualities Kennan decried. Rather than yielding mere incoherence, the complexity of our system works: "[S]omehow a policy—or even a group of sometimes conflicting and sometimes complimentary minipolicies—emerges from the jostling and jumbling of political interests, politicians' egos, economic and ethnic lobbies, regional voting blocs, and random noise that make up the American political process."

The key to success is found in those varied influences, which tend to prevent the domination of any single, and perhaps wrong-headed, approach. Mead continues: "If the results of the process displease a substantial portion of the public, that dissatisfaction will become an increasingly powerful political force that pulls policy back in a direction that reduces dissatisfaction. The system is stable because it is homeostatic."

If Mead is correct, the strengths of American foreign policy are those of our constitutional system as a whole. It is not given to simple, elegant solutions, nor to ideologically satisfying problem-solving. It has, however, shown a capacity for self-correction while pursuing fundamental goals, a combination that has allowed national survival and growth.

GERRYMANDER

See where the hateful serpent of the gerrymander has wound his sinuous course; see where in his glittering folds he has strangled the life out of liberty.

—Henry Johnson, U.S. Representative (1891–1899)

The term *gerrymander,* full of potential political mischief, has become a flashpoint in recent public discourse. It is also, as speechwriter William Safire said, a triumph of American word-smithing. As political lore has it, the term comes from Massachusetts, where in 1811 Governor Elbridge Gerry signed a bill redrawing congressional districts in that state. One new district was made up of a serpentine chain of towns that ran parallel to the rough coastline of northern Massachusetts, but inland. The reason for the unlikely shape was to create a district that favored the Democratic-Republican party over the Federalists, the party that dominated the shoreline harbor towns. The artist Gilbert Stuart sketched an outline of the district for a newspaper editor and compared it to a salamander. "Salamander?" the editor responded. "Call it a Gerrymander!"

Gerrymandering has been with us ever since. To gerrymander is to draw the lines of political districts in ways that serve partisan purposes, rather than those of stricter representation. In the case of congressional districts, states must review the results of every national census and redraw district lines if the data show population growth or decline. Most of our district drawing, outlandish or not, is done by state legislatures. Generally, one political party or another will hold a majority in those legislatures, and thus hold power over redistricting. Whichever party has the upper hand will be sorely tempted to draw lines that favor their own interest.

This favoritism in turn has led to districts with some unlikely shapes. There was the "Monkey-Wrench" district in Iowa, for example, the "Dumb-bell" in Pennsylvania, the "Horseshoe" in New York, and the "Shoestring" in Mississippi. Phil Burton, a powerful Democrat from California, was a force behind that state's redistricting in the 1970s and 1980s. His efforts produced some especially contorted districts, which he called "my contribution to modern art."

While gerrymandering often reflects partisan purposes, it has not always been used to favor one party over another. In the past, some state legislatures drew districts that systematically deprived minorities, especially African Americans, of due representation. In one case from 1957, the city lines in Tuskegee, Alabama went from being a "sensible square on the map" to being a "strangely irregular 28-sided figure," which also managed to exclude from city limits all but four or five of Tuskegee's several hundred African American citizens.

There were plenty of other cases of racial gerrymandering. Eventually they led to lawsuits and, ultimately, to a Supreme Court decision that outlawed the practice. As one justice wrote, the Tuskegee redistricting went beyond the "familiar abuses" found in drawing district lines, and amounted to "fencing Negro citizens out of town" so as to deprive them of preexisting voting rights.

*   *   *

Gerrymandering is, by nature, unfair. It favors some groups of citizens at the expense of others. As seen in the Tuskegee case, the injustice involved can lead to lawsuits, and even to court mandated changes in redistricting. In other cases, however, the federal courts have been reluctant to take on the issue, and with good reason. The Constitution, for a start, is fairly clear about leaving such electoral matters to the states. As Article 1, Section 4 puts it: "The Times, Places and Manner of holding Elections for Senators and Representatives, shall be prescribed in each State by the legislature thereof ... ."[38]

Moreover, the Supreme Court has tended to avoid strictly political cases when possible, leaving such cases to political processes—that is, wrangling by elected legislators—for sorting out. In regard to one case concerning fair representation from the 1940s, Justice Felix Frankfurter put it bluntly. Redistricting has "a peculiarly political nature and is therefore not meet for judicial determination," he wrote, adding: "Courts ought not to enter this political thicket."

So the Court's default position has been to avoid gerrymandering cases. However, as seen in the case of racial gerrymandering, there are limits to what the Court will find legally acceptable. In recent years, gerrymandering has come under increased fire and pressure has risen for the courts to oppose it. Citizen groups in North Carolina, for example, filed a lawsuit to rein in what they saw as unfair redistricting there. In 2018, a panel of three federal judges reviewed their suit, which charged that new district lines systematically deprived Democratic voters of their due representation. The judges agreed, saying: "Partisan gerrymandering runs contrary to numerous fundamental democratic principles and individual rights enshrined in the Constitution," as Judge James A. Wynne wrote for the majority. (It should be noted, however, that the Supreme Court reversed this ruling.)

North Carolina is not alone in facing this issue. Anti-gerrymandering law suits have recently been launched in Wisconsin, Pennsylvania, Maryland, and elsewhere. In June of 2019, the Supreme Court held that partisan gerrymandering cases are generally nonjusticiable, which closed the door on most efforts to fight party-based gerrymandering in the courts. However, a strong animus against the practice remains, and opponents continue to fight against it.

It may yet be that the gerrymander, storied in our political past, will find itself headed for the endangered species list.

HABEAS CORPUS

The writ of habeas corpus ... is the great remedy of the
citizen or subject against arbitrary or illegal imprisonment;
it is the mode by which the judicial power speedily and
effectually protects the personal liberty of every individual,
and repels the injustice of unconstitutional laws or despotic
governors.

—William Rawle

The words *habeas corpus* are Latin and mean "You shall have the body."
The body in question is one's own, which perhaps sounds grim. But
the term refers to a key historical right in the Anglo-American political
tradition. When we speak of habeas corpus, it is shorthand for the "writ of habeas
corpus," also called "the Great Writ." It is a legal device rooted in the notion
that the state cannot arrest and detain people arbitrarily. For example, when an
English king imprisoned a political enemy, lawyers used the writ of habeas corpus
to demand the prisoner's release. If the king could not give good legal reasons for
the arrest, the prisoner had to be be set free. "Habeas corpus"—you shall have
the body—unless the law, and not the king, says otherwise.

Habeas corpus has a long lineage. The term does not appear in Britain's
Magna Carta, but its essential meaning is there: "No Freeman shall be taken or
imprisoned ... but by lawful judgment of his Peers, or by the Law of the Land."
And in 1679, the British Parliament passed the Habeas Corpus Act, which put
the full weight of Parliament behind habeas's core rights.

Along with much other law, habeas corpus was carried across the Atlantic by
the British and transplanted in American soil. It took firm root, so that when the
Framers spelled out the terms of the Constitution, they included a clause that

addressed this essential right: "the privilege of the writ of habeas corpus shall not be suspended, unless when in cases of rebellion or invasion the public safety may require it." Likewise, individual states protect habeas corpus, with all fifty of their constitutions specifically protecting it.

The implications of habeas corpus go far beyond the legal technicalities surrounding imprisonment. As philosopher Adam Smith put it, habeas is "a great security against oppression," and its repeal would "destroy in great measure the liberty" of the people. The power of the state has always been in large measure a matter of controlling people's bodies. To impose its will, the state could imprison, exile, or execute its subjects. To insist on the rights of habeas corpus is to greatly reduce the state's repertoire of techniques for oppression.

Moreover, the logic behind habeas corpus goes to the heart of the relationship between people and their government. If the state has no presumptive claim to control over your body, you are free to act as you choose, short of breaking constitutionally legitimate laws. Where the writ of habeas corpus reigns, there is a presumption of freedom.

*   *   *

As the Constitution says, there are situations where the writ of habeas corpus might need to be suspended in order to preserve the safety of the nation itself. Wartime, for example, challenges the willingness of a government to abide by the limits imposed by habeas corpus. During the Civil War, Abraham Lincoln famously suspended habeas rights, which allowed the government great leeway to detain those it deemed dangerous to the Union cause.

It was likewise during World War II. After the attack on Pearl Harbor, the territorial government of Hawaii (it was not yet a state) imposed martial law and suspended habeas corpus for the duration of the war. And the internment of Japanese Americans in western states surely violated the spirit of habeas corpus on a massive scale.

More recently, the War on Terror raises difficult questions about habeas rights. Unlike more traditional conflicts, the divide between civilian and military is sometimes hard to discern in this war, and so are the cases in which habeas rights apply. For example, we will at times face the question of whether American citizens, captured abroad while fighting against the United States, hold the traditional habeas rights.

Further, we might consider what could happen to habeas corpus if terrorists were to launch a major campaign of violence in this country. If they were to succeed in their goal of terrorizing the nation, the pressure to suspend those rights would mount rapidly. Honoring habeas corpus in good times is far easier than in times of uncertainty and serious danger to the nation.

HOUSE OF REPRESENTATIVES

The House of Representatives is, has been, and if you and
I have our way, will continue to be, the greatest legislative
forum upon the earth.

> —Sam Rayburn, Speaker of the House
> (1940–1947, 1949–1953, 1955–1961)

At the very heart of democracy is the idea that the will of the people must
be the basis of government. By design, it is in the House of Representatives, among all the institutions of the American national government,
where the people's will has the most direct expression. When problems arise in the
country, for example, the House is the place where the people's demand for action
should be most quickly voiced and, perhaps, translated into legislation.

The design in question is, of course, spelled out in the Constitution. Article 1
presents the most basic point: "All legislative Powers herein granted shall be vested
in a Congress . . . which shall consist of a Senate and a House of Representatives."
Thus, all laws must pass both houses of Congress, and no bill becomes law without
being passed by the House.

For a bicameral legislature[39] to work as intended, the two bodies must have
distinct and differing qualities. Each house must debate and test proposed
legislation from different perspectives and with different interests in mind.

The distinctiveness of the House of Representatives is due to the way
members of each body are elected, a process that makes the House more directly
representative of the people than the Senate. For example, each state gets a number
of representatives in the House based on the size its population. States with
large populations hold many seats, and those with small populations get few. So
California holds 53 seats in the House and Texas 36, while, Alaska, Delaware,

Montana, North Dakota, South Dakota, Vermont, and Wyoming each get only one.

The Constitution also mandates that members of the House of Representatives be elected every two years. By doing so, the Constitution makes the House more immediately accountable to voters than either the president (elected every four years) or the Senate (with each member elected every six years). If House members fail to meet their constituents' needs, they might lose their jobs sooner rather than later. This fact encourages a higher level of responsiveness to constituent demands than that of the more insulated Senate.

In addition, and crucially, House members are elected from separate districts across a given state, rather than by statewide elections. This insures that every part of a given state, and every part of the nation as a whole, will get its representation in Congress, from rural upstate New York and downstate Illinois, to big cities such as New York City and Chicago. Moreover, no part of the country gets fewer than one representative. This policy makes for a highly diverse body and an institution in which every district of the country has an equal share in its total power.

*   *   *

When the Constitution was ratified, the nation was made up of thirteen states with a total population of about four million. In the first Congress, the total membership in the House of Representatives came to 65.

The country has grown enormously since then, adding 37 states and reaching a population of around 330 million. The House of Representatives has naturally grown as well, and now includes 435 representatives. The very size of the House determines its character in important ways. For example, such a large body will naturally be busier, more sprawling, and less tidy than the smaller, more personal Senate. In comparing the two bodies, and in an unkind mood, one senator called the House "that glob of humanity" and "that monstrous institution."

To make this "glob" functional, the House needs a tightly structured system of rules to keep it from bogging down. Thus House rules strictly limit the amount of time allowed to debate bills. By contrast, the Senate rules allow much freer and lengthier debate.

The House also has a stiffer hierarchical structure than the Senate, which includes its leader, the Speaker of the House, who has no equivalent in the Senate. In addition, House leaders have a tool to keep the unwieldy body in line. That tool is the majority vote. Business in the institution moves through votes, whether that means electing a Speaker of the House, determining the content of legislation in committee, or ultimately voting by the whole House to decide what bills actually pass.

Through all these votes, whichever party has a majority in the House can, if it holds together, impose its will on the minority. Majority power allows the leadership to push business along, a major achievement given the size of the institution and the sheer amount of business it takes on.

*   *   *

The discipline imposed through House rules keeps a lid on an institution naturally given to fractiousness. The level of conflict in the House of Representatives waxes and wanes, reflecting the intensity of feelings abroad in the country, and the discipline has not always held. Before the Civil War, fights broke out on the floor of the House, and members brought pistols and knives with them for self-protection when they went to work.

Today the American people are living in another divisive period, and it should surprise no one that the House is often in a foul and highly partisan mood. Yet the divisiveness, though rooted in national feeling, is also unpopular, and many people wonder how we can break the spell of partisan anger that afflicts so many national institutions.

Perhaps the House has a special responsibility in this regard. As the most democratic institution of national government, the one where diverging interests come most directly into contact, House members have no choice but to sit alongside colleagues who hold competing, even antagonistic, policy positions. Nor can they simply dismiss the views of those other members, who have equal standing as representatives of the American people. Given their position, House representatives bear a difficult burden, but perhaps also hold an opportunity. The nation needs leadership in finding common ground while honoring the diverse interests found in a nation of 330 million souls. Whether the House is up to this challenge is a critical question, but it is also its unavoidable job to grapple with it.

HUMAN RIGHTS

> We stand today at the threshold of a great event both in the
> life of the United Nations and in the life of mankind. This
> Universal Declaration of Human Rights may well become
> the international Magna Carta of all men everywhere.
>
> —Eleanor Roosevelt

Within the family of rights, human rights would seem to be the primary one—the parent of civil rights, property rights, rights to religious
freedom, free speech, and all the others. Human rights are those rights
that all people can claim simply as humans. They are rights that ordinary people
everywhere are owed by whatever government they live under.

While human rights are in some sense primary, they were not among the first
to be acknowledged. The term only came into common use recently, and under
the pressure of extraordinary circumstances. Those circumstances included the
enormous human *wrongs* of the 20th century: mass civilian deaths in wartime, the
rise of totalitarian regimes, genocide, and ethnic cleansing. More, perhaps, than
any other human catastrophe, the exposure of the Holocaust, with the ghastly
images from the death camps, gave a strong push to the modern human rights
movement.

So in the wake of the Second World War, the effort was made to codify human
rights and to clarify the obligations of governments toward citizens of their own
and all other countries. That movement found a home in the United Nations, and
as one of its first acts, the UN established the United Nations Commission on
Human Rights.

Meeting for the first time in January of 1947, the Commission set out to
draft the document that would eventually be called the Universal Declaration of

Human Rights. Eleanor Roosevelt led this group, whose makeup was thoroughly international.

Theirs was no easy task. "Universal" human rights, the Commission agreed, must apply to all people in all places. They also had to be agreed upon by all commission members, despite their varied historical and cultural backgrounds. As an example of the challenge this presented, the Universal Declaration includes an article that proclaims the equal rights of adults, regardless of race, nationality or religion, to marry and start a family. Yet some Islamic nations found the individualistic language of marriage rights distressing (including Saudi Arabia, which eventually refrained from signing the Declaration).

Eventually, after a great deal of debate, the Commission produced its Universal Declaration of Human Rights, which was approved by the UN General Assembly in December of 1948. The Universal Declaration proclaimed many rights Americans will find familiar, such as the rights to "life, liberty and security of person," the right of all people to equal protection under the law, to freedom of thought and conscience, and to peaceable assembly. In addition, the Universal Declaration lists a number of economic and social rights, such as the right to work, the right to work under just and decent conditions, the right to an adequate standard of living, the rights to leisure and holidays with pay, and the right to security in the event of ill-health, old age, or other circumstances beyond one's control.

*   *   *

As noted, coming up with this list was a challenge, due in part to the sheer diversity of the Commission's members. But the Human Rights Commission faced another problem in reaching its consensus as well. Several larger nations, including the United States and the old Soviet Union, were wary of the potential power of the human rights movement over their own rights to self-government. Acknowledging some higher, international authority implied a willingness to obey it, and not surprisingly, many nations were reluctant to do so.

This is one reason why the United Nations passed a *declaration* of human rights rather than a *treaty* or a *convention* on them. A treaty or convention on human rights would have legally bound signatory nations to meet the obligations defined in the document. Major powers, such as the United States, the United Kingdom, and the Soviet Union used their influence to prevent that outcome,[40] and what we have today reflects their wishes. The Universal Declaration of Human Rights is a symbolic milestone, but it is not legally binding, and the UN makes no provision for punishing violators.

This does not mean that the Universal Declaration has been ineffective. Its terms have informed many national law codes of the post-World War II period, including those of Germany, Japan, and Italy, the Axis nations of the War. The underlying beliefs in human rights have also inspired independence movements among former European colonies, as well as the anti-apartheid movement in South Africa. Also, in a few cases, such as the European Court of Human Rights, international law has gained some traction in bringing charges against at least a few of those who violate the Universal Declaration's norms.

*   *   *

Still, even where there are laws on the books to insure human rights, those laws are of little use if they are not backed up by some government's will and the capacity to enforce them. Take the case of a nation such as Somalia, which has signed a number of international agreements in support of human rights. Whatever commitments it has made, the Somali government itself has been barely functional at times, and its economy is a shambles. Thus the rights of Somali workers to paid holidays, for example, or security in old age, are effectively worthless.

The rights detailed in the Universal Declaration depend on national laws to make them binding. Those laws depend in turn on functioning governments to ensure them. And ultimately, those government and their laws depend on people at all levels to embrace those rights.

As Eleanor Roosevelt understood, the legal side of the human rights movement is only a part, and a secondary part at that, of the advances she hoped for. "Court decisions, and laws and government administration are only the results of the way people progress inwardly," as Mrs. Roosevelt put it. It is through that inward progress that human rights are showing their most important growth.

IDEALISM

'Some men see things as they are and say why? I dream of
things that never were and say, why not?'

—Robert F. Kennedy, Senator (1965–1968)
(quoting George Bernard Shaw)

Words rise and fall in public use, like stocks on the Dow Jones exchange.
Sometimes a word fits the spirit of the day and we use it frequently.
As times change, the word might almost disappear. One doesn't hear
much about idealism these days, for example, but fifty years ago it was otherwise.
In the upheavals of the 1960s and 1970s, when Baby Boomers were reshaping
our political landscape, the word was inescapable. As the nation grappled with
deep problems—racism, war, and poverty—many believed that youth and idealism could usher in a better society if given a chance. Archibald Cox, a Harvard law
professor, expressed this hope when he called the young people of that day "the
best informed, the most intelligent, and the most idealistic generation this country
has ever known."

Idealism is obviously related to the words *ideal* and *idea*. An ideal is a particular
type of idea: a perfect example of something we seek. We hope for the ideal job, for
example, or an ideal marriage.

Ideals hold a special place in political life. They are the qualities we value most
highly for our society. Politicians are keen on ideals, and will wax poetic over them.
They prefer campaigning on the promise of justice or equality, for example, rather
than on grubby self-interest. And voters love them for it, being themselves fully
in favor of justice and equality, as well as decency, charity, martial vigor, and old-
fashioned frugality (without pausing to ask how compatible some of these ideals

might be with one another). Yet despite all the love we lavish on our ideals, we seem never to bring them about in reality, and we might wonder why. Why does the actual existing *is* always fall short of the *ought to be*?

*   *   *

As notions inside our heads, ideas and ideals are obviously distinct from conditions in the world beyond. But we are prone to a certain hubris: we like to think that through our ideas we can control what happens out there, that we can control our present and future through the plans we make. Of course, there is enough truth in this conceit to add to its attraction. We do think about the world and how to make it better. We plan, and execute plans, and by doing so shape our lives.

But social complexities are such that they often challenge our plans, and the more ambitious the plan, the more intractable those complexities. Reality throws up road-blocks, and often ones we never saw coming.

Of all the roadblocks in political life, one of the greatest is also a fundamental reality of life in general: the plans of others. People act in their own interest as they see it, and not necessarily as we imagine they should. Where big, ambitious plans depend on people acting in concord, self-interest may lead them in almost any direction.

One can see the distance between idealism and the opposing force of self-interest in the painful history of school desegregation in Boston during the 1970s. Boston's school districts corresponded to the segregated state of its neighborhoods, and as elsewhere, segregated schools had unequal effects on the quality of schooling provided, with African American students suffering most from the disparities. Motivated by this injustice, the Massachusetts Supreme Judicial Court issued a plan to desegregate the city's public schools by busing students out of their home neighborhoods to schools elsewhere in the city.

But however well-intentioned it was, the plan violated the expectations of many parents in the city. When busing started, it was met with violent protests, and the city quickly saw its social fabric unraveling in the streets. As the Boston Globe put it, "What we prayed wouldn't happen has happened. The city of Boston has gotten out of control."

Massachusetts's idealists were dismayed, but they were unable to prevent the events that followed. Many parents pulled their children out of the public schools and enrolled them in private ones, while others moved out of Boston altogether, beyond the reach of the city's desegregation plan. Far from achieving the lofty goal, Boston's schools settled back into a pattern of sharp segregation, but with much of the white student body having departed.

Whatever the ideals that gave rise to busing in Boston, its supporters had to reckon with its actual outcome. After spending a great deal of money and social capital, the results included a worsening of the city's racial tensions, a loss of trust in city government, and the decline in support for the public schools themselves.

*   *   *

Idealism is especially prone to mistakes of this sort. To the idealist, fixing problems appears straightforward. It means thinking of a solution, then putting that solution into action.

What idealism often fails to see is the complexity of many problems. Those problems are less logical than ecological, to use a metaphor. As in ecosystems, all the elements of societies are interconnected in highly complex patterns, difficult to fully comprehend. Touched in one spot, effects ripple out across the whole, often in unexpected ways.

This lesson can be applied to many political projects. Had we known how difficult nation-building in the Middle East would be, for example, we might have been more circumspect in our efforts in that region after the attacks of 9/11. Making the big *is* out there conform to the *ought to be* in our minds will always be fraught with unexpected dangers.

IDENTITY POLITICS

> The marginalized did not create identity politics: their identities have been forced on them by dominant groups, and politics is the most effective means of revolt.
>
> —Stacey Abrams, Georgia State Legislator (2007–2017)

Politics cannot exist without identity. The United States could hardly have formed if its citizens had not shared a sense of shared identity as Americans, for instance. The same holds for any coherent political state.

Yet while identity and politics have always been entwined, the term *identity politics* itself is relatively new. *Merriam-Webster* puts its first use at 1979, but the core notion was in play for at least a decade before that. Identity politics was the name given to certain political currents born during the upheavals of the 1960s and '70s, specifically among the movements advocating the rights of African Americans, women, gays and lesbians, Native Americans, and other groups.

These movements all shared this feature: In their own eyes, they represented people who had suffered from systematic injustice, not simply as individuals but as groups. According to the *Stanford Encyclopedia of Philosophy*, "Identity politics ... is intimately connected to the idea that some social groups are oppressed; that is, that one's identity as a woman or a Native American, for example, makes one peculiarly vulnerable to cultural imperialism (including stereotyping, erasure, or appropriation of one's group identity), violence, exploitation, marginalization, or powerlessness." For its adherents, identity politics is, as commentator Clifford Humphrey put it, "chemotherapy to eradicate the cancer of various social inequalities."

After the political insurgencies of the 1970s receded, identity politics led a relatively sheltered life. Its central ideas took root in the academy, however, where they were nurtured in campus culture and especially in the various identity studies disciplines: Women's Studies, Black Studies, Chicano Studies, and similar programs.

More recently, identity politics has risen again in the political arena, where it enjoys substantial influence. Everything from Congressional representation to the effects of policies is now scrutinized through a lens of identity politics: How many people of color serve in Congress or in the federal judiciary? How many are women? These and similar questions are rooted in the ideals of identity politics.

Its essential goal is to reduce the oppression of given groups, and to expand their freedoms and protections. Group identity is the key. People are, first and foremost, members of their particular, defining group. An offense against one member is an offense against all. And offenders are not simply individuals acting alone, but are seen as embodiments of deep cultural prejudices against the oppressed group.

*   *   *

Opponents of identity politics find plenty to disagree with in these notions. Not least, they fear the disintegrative implications of identity politics: the emphasis on the solidarity of sub-groups saps the feeling of membership in a broader community.

Whatever the criticisms of identity politics, it is beyond doubt that some groups thrive in our society while others, in comparison, do not, and that the suffering of those who are marginalized is very real. Gays and lesbians have suffered from bitter prejudices; on average African American men do not achieve the same levels of academic success as various other groups; and women still have not found equality with men in all spheres of employment.

Addressing the ills of long-held prejudices presents deep challenges to our political system. One option, which has been followed to some degree, is to pass laws that single out traditionally oppressed groups for preferred treatment in, for example, hiring. Yet by favoring some at the expense of others, such programs turn on its head an essential aspect of the law, its impartiality.

There is another, perhaps even deeper, challenge that comes with identity politics, something that raises the question of whether it is actually a type of politics at all. One primary job of politics is reconciliation. In a country as diverse as the United States, we must find ways for people with very different values, needs and hopes to live in relative harmony. We do so in part through the processes of politics and governing: the making and executing of our laws.

Drilling deeper, we find something more elemental. Politics itself is grounded in a particular action, and that is talk. In Congress, for example, representatives gather, confronting one another with the distinct concerns of their constituents.

Their disagreements are channeled into structured discussions and debate. They might bicker, badger, and threaten each other, swap bluffs and even the occasional lie. But it is all dialogue, and it will, at length, yield some consensus on what our policies will be. Working properly, the deliberation finds common ground and brings people with diverse views together there.

Identity politics fits uneasily in such a system, not least because it views that common ground with suspicion. To its most thoroughgoing adherents, that has been where the marginalized are unwelcome. So working within the political system can seem like a surrender to it.

By its nature, pure identity politics leaves little room for compromise. There is not much to debate when group identity trumps all and the identity in question cannot be shared with others. If, for example, one's identity as a Latina woman sets one apart from all other women, and even more clearly from white men, there is little ground for discussion across those divides. If politics in a diverse society is a sprawling conversation, pure identity politics is a conversation stopper.

IDEOLOGY

Ideology knows the answer before the question is asked.

—George Packer

We ought to be suspicious of ideologies, just as we are of know-it-alls who are sure of answers before questions are even raised. But neither should we underestimate the appeal of ideology. There is something beguiling, after all, about having answers before questions. And if ideologies did not deliver something on that promise, we might not have them in the first place.

An ideology is a belief system, growing out of a core idea that guides a person's views. One applies that core idea to various political issues on the assumption that it will clarify those issues, reducing them to their essences. To some libertarians, for example, many of our social problems can be solved through free markets: health care inflation, energy costs, housing shortages, and so on. For some progressive counterparts, the answer to our problems lies in nearly the opposite direction: rational government controls. At their best, ideologies allow us to formulate coherent responses to political challenges. At their worst, they are rote simplifications we reach for when we are unwilling to do harder thinking.

If ideologies can help individuals get a grip on politics, they are a positive boon to politicians and media commentators. They are tailor-made for mass communication. When candidates are on the campaign trail and need a punchy message, ideology offers a hand. Likewise with talking heads on TV, talk radio, or online editorialists. As with electoral politics, simplicity sells in the news.

So, too, does flattery, and ideology helps here too. Viewers and listeners respond well to hearing that the problems we face have easy solutions. People love to find their own beliefs confirmed by "experts" on TV. Ideology does this in spades, endlessly repeating the same underlying message: Here are the answers, ready for easy consumption.

*   *   *

Not that anyone actually wants to be an *ideologue*. When hurled in public debate, that term is generally an insult, implying rigidity and impracticality. A legislator seen as ideological will be dismissed as too devoted to a pet theory to make common cause with others and actually solve problems.

Yet *ideology* has not always had this unsavory connotation. The term was coined early in the 19th century by a French thinker, Destutt de Tracy, for whom it was anything but negative. De Tracy hoped to find a key, a comprehensive science that would unlock the mysteries of human happiness. Once discovered, this "ideaology"[41] could be put to service in government. Once in place, the solution to political problems would follow with something like mathematical precision.

De Tracy made every effort to construct this philosophy. But the goal proved elusive, and at least one other Frenchman, who faced more than his share of political challenges, grew frustrated with the ideological approach. Napoleon Bonaparte wrote:

> It is to ideology, this cloudy metaphysics which, by subtly searching for first causes, wishes to establish on this basis the legislation of peoples, instead of obtaining its laws from knowledge of the human heart and from the lessons of history, that we must attribute all the misfortunes of our fair France.

Despite Napoleon's early warnings, the hunt for ideological certainties went on. The results included those great political deformities of the 20th Century, communism and Nazism. For all that separated the two systems, each was ideological to the core. Both Communism and Nazism claimed an exclusive understanding of human society. For the Nazis, human relations were driven by national and racial identity. For the communists, they were driven by economics and class conflict. One of the great pathologists of modern politics, Hannah Arendt, observed that "Ideologues pretend to know the mysteries of the whole historical process—the secrets of the past, the intricacies of the present, the uncertainties of the future." The ruthlessness of the 20th century's politics owed a great deal to the "certainties" of its ideologues, as they took control of major nations.

*   *   *

The United States weathered the ideological storms of the 20th century in relatively good health. It's difficult for mass movements to take political control where there are so many ethnic, religious, and cultural differences within the population.

Still, the magnetic pull of ideology is very much at work in our current politics, drawing people into tightly defined camps and amplifying the partisan feelings of our time. Modern media presents a danger here, since ideological messages are so well suited to mass communication. It is worth remembering that both Soviet communists and German Nazis were expert at propagandizing their populations, and could never have reached power without exploiting radio, TV, and newspapers for that purpose.

Today, simplistic political messages flood the Internet and the echo chambers of social media. People gravitate toward media outlets that reward like-mindedness and punish dissent. Ideology thrives in environments where discourse is less a means of open communication and more about enforcing adherence to favored political positions.

Indeed, a useful distinction between ideology and ordinary, principled political views may be found here. For the ideologue, political discourse is not an open dialogue in search of practical policies. It is dictation instead. Presenting a closed circle, ideologies derail further discussion and delegitimize other points of view. And when married to the force of the state, ideologies present an implicit threat to any who stand outside the closed circle.

IMPEACHMENT

> Impeachment is a politically unique device designed
> explicitly to dislodge from public office those who are
> patently unfit for it.
>
> —Gerald Ford, President (1974–1977)

Given our political history in recent decades, *impeachment* ought to be thoroughly understood, but frequent use doesn't mean real knowledge of the word's meaning. Many of us recall, for example, that Richard Nixon was impeached in the 1970s. Except that Nixon was not actually impeached, but resigned from office before the impeachment storm broke on him. And plenty of people assume that Bill Clinton was not impeached, since he never did leave office. But he *was* impeached, though he survived the ordeal and not only stayed in office but thrived there.

Technically, to impeach an official is to formally accuse that person of a serious violation of the public's trust, as part of the process of lawfully removing him or her from office. According to the Constitution, only the House of Representatives has the power to impeach a federal office holder. When a public official is under suspicion of wrongdoing, the House can investigate the matter, calling witnesses and subpoenaing evidence. If the evidence is damning, the House writes up articles of impeachment, which are specific charges against the accused. If a majority in the House votes in support of these charges, the accused official has been impeached.

Then the process moves to the Senate, which convenes as a court that tries the official on all counts set out in the articles of impeachment. Managers from the House of Representatives can present their charges and the House's evidence of impeachable wrongdoing before this court. Meanwhile, the accused official will have an opportunity to rebut the charges. After arguments have concluded, the Senate votes. If two-thirds of the members concur with one or more of the articles of impeachment, the accused stands convicted and must, according to the Constitution, be removed from office. This is the only punishment the Senate can impose in impeachment cases.

Which serves as a reminder: Impeachment is a purely political matter and not a criminal one. It takes place within the political system, carried out by legislators, and not in the legal system. It also serves a political purpose, giving the legislative branch a tool to check the abuse of power in the executive and judicial branches.[42] Above all, impeachment gives the government—and the people—a tool to maintain the integrity of our political institutions and our respect for them. Where there is serious corruption in high public offices, impeachment provides a lawful way to purge the system and secure its well-being.

*   *   *

In our own contentious political era, charges of corruption are far from rare. Faced with these charges, ordinary citizens might be baffled as to which ones justify impeachment and when this political weapon should be triggered.

The Constitution defines impeachable offenses, but it does so in rather uncertain terms. Article 2 cites "Treason, Bribery, or other high Crimes and Misdemeanors" as the basis for impeachment and leaves it at that. While treason and bribery are clear, the other grounds are far from definitive. There is, for example, no clear legal distinction between high and low crimes. And by including misdemeanors, the Constitution suggests that officials can be impeached without having committed any crime at all. By leaving the definition of impeachable offenses partially open-ended, the Constitution grants flexibility to the House of Representatives in deciding when to go forward with the process and when to hold fire.

More specifically, the responsibility for deciding whether to proceed with impeachment generally lies with the majority party in the House of Representatives and its leadership. As for weighing whether given accusations of wrongdoing merit impeachment, those leaders, especially the Speaker of the House, can perhaps best refer to the basic purpose of impeachment: Actions are impeachable when they threaten the integrity of the government in some substantial way.

*   *   *

When making this decision, Congress must keep something else in mind. The impeachment of officials, especially presidents, incurs terrific costs. For starters, the process is a serious drain on government time and energy. The Watergate impeachment drama left government "largely paralyzed for at least a year and a half," wrote historian David Kyvig, and did so without even reaching the point of actually impeaching the president.

The cost goes deeper, however. Impeachment is like a major operation that cuts and destroys even as it works to save the system from corruption. It removes officials who came to their positions through proper channels. When a president is elected, millions of people will have voted for that outcome and have a deep stake in seeing it sustained. Impeachment undoes that result, and when undertaken for merely partisan purposes, reveals contempt for those voters. At its worst, impeachment undermines the unspoken contract that grounds our entire system: We all abide by the results of elections, even when they disappoint us.

Moreover, if impeachment is like surgery, it cannot be a sign of good health that we consider using it as often as we do. Since Richard Nixon's near-impeachment in 1974, several presidents have had close encounters, or worse, with this drastic measure. Ronald Reagan during the Iran-Contra scandal, and George W. Bush after the Iraq invasion, were both subject to serious impeachment threats; Bill Clinton in the '90s, and most recently Donald Trump in 2020, were in fact impeached. Impeachment has become so common in American political life that historian Kyvig calls this "the Impeachment Era." In a pessimistic mood, he wrote:

> I have come to believe that calls for impeachment have been a sort of canary in the mine shaft, an early signal of an increasingly toxic political culture. Both the conduct that has provoked such calls and, more recently, the tendency to think of impeachment as a first response to hints of official missteps have become barometers of the American political climate.

In using impeachment as a purgative, we hope to restore our political health. We need to consider, in each case, whether—or to what degree—such strong medicine is warranted.

INCORPORATION

> I can only say that the words 'No state shall make or enforce any law which shall abridge the privileges or immunities of citizens of the United States' seem to me an eminently reasonable way of expressing the idea that henceforth the Bill of Rights shall apply to the States. What more precious 'privilege' of American citizenship could there be than that privilege to claim the protection of our great Bill of Rights?
>
> —Hugo Black, Supreme Court Justice (1937–1971)

Hugo Black's tribute to the rights of all Americans hardly seems controversial. On the face of it, he is only paying tribute to the Bill of Rights and the liberties they protect. However, his words need unpacking, because enfolded within are the basic terms of incorporation, one of the most consequential doctrines in our constitutional history. Here is the crucial phrase from his statement: "… henceforth the Bill of Rights shall apply to the States." Under incorporation, rights guaranteed by the Bill of Rights become legally binding not just at the national level, but in state law as well.

It was not always so. Before incorporation, the Bill of Rights did not apply to state law. Consider, for example, the concept of religious freedom. The First Amendment says that "Congress shall make no law respecting an establishment of religion." As part of their protection of freedom of conscience, the Founders wanted to prevent the formation of any national church, such as the English had with the Church of England.

Early on, however, this ban on established religion was understood to refer only to the national government and had no bearing on the states. Connecticut, for example, supported the Congregational church with state funds well into the 19ᵗʰ century. At the time, no one doubted the constitutionality of this arrangement, as the Bill of Rights was understood to address national law only.

Matters have changed a great deal since then, and no state could maintain an established church of any sort today. The states no longer have the right to favor particular religious establishment, and are held to the national standard on this matter derived from the Bill of Rights.

A key historical event opened the door to this nationalization: the ratification of the Fourteenth Amendment. It was one of the three great amendments that came out of the Civil War and its aftermath, and it was directly aimed at protecting African Americans from discriminatory *state* laws in the post-war South. The Fourteenth Amendment guaranteed due process and other rights to all citizens of the United States, no matter where in the nation they lived. Compare the language of the Fourteenth Amendment to that of the First. Where the First opens with the words "Congress shall make no law…," the Fourteenth opens with "No state shall make or enforce any law…."

The protections guaranteed by the Fourteenth Amendment were general and open to broad interpretation. It denies states the right to deprive any person of "due process of law," and it assures all Americans of "equal protection under the laws." It protects the "privileges and immunities" of all citizens against infringement by state laws.

After the amendment was passed, a question arose about these general protections. Could the Fourteenth Amendment protections of "due process" and "equal protection" be understood to include, or incorporate, the more specific rights found in the Bill of Rights? Or, to put it another way, could those general rights overrule state laws where those laws violated federal standards on more specific rights?

In a series of Supreme Court trials running through the middle of the 20ᵗʰ century, this question was hashed out, right by right. On balance, the Court ruled that those specific rights from the Bill of Rights were incorporated. Take the famous *Gideon* v. *Wainwright* case of 1963. Clarence Gideon was charged in a Florida court with breaking and entering. Unable to pay for a lawyer, Gideon asked for the court to appoint one. But state law provided such counsel only in cases that might result in the death penalty. After he was found guilty, Gideon appealed the sentence, claiming that Florida law violated his right to counsel, insured by the Sixth Amendment.

Gideon's case went to the Supreme Court, which ruled in his favor. In the summary of its finding, the Court held that a defendant's right to the "assistance of counsel is a fundamental right" and that the prisoner's trial without that assistance "violated the Fourteenth Amendment." The Fourteenth doesn't mention the right to counsel, but the Court held that it incorporated the specifics of the Sixth Amendment under the more general right to due process.

As a result of incorporation, individual rights have gained stronger, nation-wide protection. This is a double-edged sword, however. As Supreme Court Justice John Paul Stevens wrote, incorporation "has transformed the Bill of Rights from a mere constraint on federal power into a source of federal authority to constrain state power." It has played a key role in shifting power away from the states and their legislatures and toward the central government and its courts. By doing so, incorporation strikes a blow against the tradition of federalism in our government, and thus marks an important shift in our basic constitutional order.

ISOLATIONISM

> When others are all over their ears in trouble, who would
> not be isolated in freedom from care? When the others are
> crushed under the burden of militarism, who would not be
> isolated in peace and industry?
>
> —William Graham Sumner

In international relations, isolationism is the practice of avoiding binding alliances with other nations, especially military agreements that obligate the nation to join in wars on behalf of other nations. Isolationism has long had a strong constituency in the United States. Separated by the oceans from much of the world's troubles, Americans have had the option of staying isolated from foreign wars to a degree that other nations might envy. To many Americans, the United States government has not just the option, but a duty, to keep its distance from the world's conflicts.

Isolationism is not an old term, dating only to the early 20th century. It is especially linked with American debates on foreign policy during the 1930s. With Nazi Germany growing more powerful and aggressive, President Franklin Roosevelt nudged the country toward opposition to the German Third Reich and its policies. Recalling the disasters of the First World War, however, isolationists rallied to the cry of "America First!" and pushed back against involvement in Europe's affairs.

The term *isolationist* has been used as something of a slur ever since. Isolationists will, according to critics, ignore international threats in the futile hope that wildfires abroad will never reach the United States. To these critics, isolationism might even contribute to international disasters by preventing early action to head them off.

But many "isolationists" reject the term itself and the historical lesson coded into it. They argue that any implication that the United States was actually isolated between the wars—or at any time in its history—is factually wrong. Wrong too, isolationists believe, is any suggestion that America's policies were responsible for the outbreak of the Second World War. As they see it, the United States cannot control the uncontrollable abroad and should not try. The interests of its citizens should determine America's foreign policy, and those interests generally mean avoiding the horrors of foreign wars.

In any event, to isolationists the mid-20th century was unique, and its lessons should not be our sole guide for foreign policy. They prefer to take a longer view, stretching back to the nation's earliest years.

Their lodestar may be found in George Washington's Farewell Address. As parting wisdom, Washington gave this advice to his fellow citizens: "Observe good faith and justice toward all nations; cultivate peace and harmony with all." Then he elaborated on the theme:

> The great rule of conduct for us in regard to foreign nations is, in extending our commercial relations, to have with them as little political connection as possible. So far as we have already formed engagements, let them be fulfilled with perfect good faith. Here let us stop. ... It is our true policy to steer clear of permanent alliances with any part of the foreign world.

*   *   *

Washington's counsel provided a template for a good deal of our history. We have traded widely all along, but resisted foreign alliances for well over a hundred years after the Founding.[43]

Yet growing American power would make it difficult to remain neutral forever. Having power, one is sorely tempted to use it, and such temptation proved irresistible, especially after the Second World War. With a world desperately in need of physical and political reconstruction and no one else with comparable might, the United States stepped into a leadership role that marked a revolution in the history of its government. That role also set a course that amounted to one long nightmare for American isolationists.

In the wake of the war, for instance, we established a strong military presence in Germany, which remains in place today. And after intervening in the Korean War, the United States likewise left soldiers there as well, with over 23,000 on the Korean peninsula still.

We have extended our commitments in many other areas, too. Worst, from the isolationist perspective, has been the deep American plunge into Middle Eastern affairs, capped by the invasion of Iraq in 2003 and subsequent efforts at nation-building there. One can never know whether matters would have been worse without American intervention in that region, but after deep spending in blood and treasure there, American policymakers must be disheartened: As of 2018, Afghanistan was at war with itself, as was Syria; Libya was a failed state; and Iraq, nearly twenty years after the invasion, was still rife with tensions.

Having invested so much in the Middle East, however, the United States finds it difficult to back away and cut its losses. And therein lies a problem. The role of world leader is impossible to do perfectly and difficult to do decently. Yet it is just as hard to forswear. Nor can it ever be successfully completed: There is no finish line.

The inevitable frustrations that come with international leadership have led to a revival of what has been called "neo-isolationism." This is a fact American strategists should consider as they plan for the country's future foreign policy. The United States has lived in a state of international conflict and crisis almost constantly for more than 70 years. The yearning of many Americans to be free of international burdens and, in the spirit of "America First," to focus on renewal at home rather than commitments abroad, is unlikely to go away as we move through our eighth decade of assumed world leadership.

JOINT CHIEFS OF STAFF

[T]he most powerful person in uniform, actually commands nothing. No tanks, no planes, no ships, no troops. ... He is the chairman of the Joint Chiefs of Staff.

—Robert Burns

If the chairman of the Joint Chiefs of Staff is the most powerful person in the United States military, the rest of the Joint Chiefs are close behind. This council is composed of top leaders from each branch of the armed forces: the Chief of Staff of the Army, the Navy's Chief of Naval Operations, the Commandant of the Marine Corps, the Chief of Staff of the Air Force, and the Chief of the National Guard Bureau. As a group, their primary task is advisory. They are to give the president and other civilian leaders—especially the Secretary of Defense and the Director of the National Security Agency—advice on policy matters that affect national defense.

The Joint Chiefs are led by a chairman chosen by the president from among the group. Once nominated by the president, the candidate for chairman is confirmed by a Senate vote. The chairman is not only the top military advisor to the president, but also the one who sets the agenda for the Joint Chiefs as a group.

*   *   *

The Joint Chiefs of Staff is something of an institutional anomaly. It advises the president but is not part of the presidential staff. The members of the Joint Chiefs are active military, but unlike all other members of the military, stand outside the Defense Department. They retain their rank in their particular service but have no authority to command troops. By design they are independent from immediate military responsibilities and, for that matter, from responsibilities to any other governmental institution. The Joint Chiefs of Staff is free-standing.

It is not an institution grounded in the Constitution, which makes no mention of it. The Joint Chiefs of Staff only came into existence in the mid-20th century during World War II. After the entrance of the United States into that global conflict, it became clear that the American military effort would need coordination among its different branches—Army, Navy, Marines—operating in the different theaters of the war—the Pacific, Europe, and elsewhere. In addition, the Americans needed to coordinate with the British and other allies.

The formation of the Joint Chiefs was driven by this necessity. Faced with the need to coordinate all those moving parts, leaders from the different services, along with civilian leadership, began regular meetings to hammer out wartime strategy. These planners had to assess where to fight, how to allocate scarce resources, enemy strengths and weaknesses, and how to solve all the other military puzzles involved in fighting a global war.

Having taken shape somewhat informally during the war, the Joint Chiefs concept proved useful. When the fighting ended, but with the emerging challenges of post-war leadership in sight, the United States Congress passed legislation to make the Joint Chiefs of Staff permanent. This came with the National Security Act of 1947.

Since then, the Joint Chiefs of Staff has been a fixture in the United States government. With one foot in the active military and one by the president's side, the Joint Chiefs are well-placed to accomplish their top priority: advising the president and other civilian leaders. And in today's world, the flow of advice from the Joint Chiefs of Staff must be almost constant. The United States' role in the world puts it in a state of more or less perpetual low-level military engagement. Beyond current actions, there are always potential threats brewing that might affect the United States, either directly or through its allies. Military and civilian leaders must ask, for example, what the Chinese are planning for the South China Sea, or the Russians for eastern Europe and the Baltic states, and what their plans could mean for the United States and its allies.

So long as the United States plays its current role in global leadership, the president and other civilian leaders will be faced with hard policy choices that involve military options. To make responsible choices, they must have a realistic understanding of what the armed forces can and cannot do in relation to potential conflicts. A minute's thought about the far-flung War on Terror, operating around the world in overt and covert actions, can give a sense of how much ground this understanding covers and how critical the military advice is.

But the role of the Joint Chiefs must be seen in a proper light. Its relation to the president reflects the whole broad relationship between the military and civilian sides of our government. As such, the Joint Chiefs must be strictly subordinate. The military serves the civilian. While the Chiefs represent the armed forces, the president represents the whole country, and it is the will of the people that must drive policy.

JUDICIAL REVIEW

> [J]udicial review, instead of being an American invention,
> is really as old as constitutionalism itself, and without it,
> constitutionalism could never have been maintained.
>
> —C. H. McIlwaine

Judicial review is the power of the judiciary to review laws enacted by the legislative and executive branches and to subject them to this challenge: Are they constitutionally lawful? By demanding this of the laws, judicial review allows government to govern itself, making sure that its laws do not violate constitutional standards, and where the laws fall short of that standard, to invalidate them. In the United States this power is held most prominently by the Supreme Court, but it is also held by lower courts of appeal in the federal system, and by state supreme courts, which hold the power of judicial review over state laws.[44]

However important judicial review is in our system, it is not specifically mentioned in the Constitution itself. What the Constitution does say about the matter appears in Article III, Section 1, which states that "The judicial Power of the United States, shall be vested in one supreme Court, and in such inferior Courts as the Congress may from time to time ordain." The exact meaning of "judicial Power" here can be debated, but it has come to be accepted that it gives the courts the responsibility to interpret the laws and stand in judgment when their constitutionality is in dispute.

In practice, judicial review works in the following way. To start, Congress passes legislation, which is then signed by the president, creating a law. When a law goes into effect, someone, somewhere, will likely be damaged by it. If so, and if that party believes the law is unjust, they can fight back through the courts, by filing a lawsuit, for example.

Once the case hits the courts, judicial review begins. The wounded party makes their case against the law, and lawyers for the government make their case for it. If, after both sides argue their case, a majority of presiding judges finds that the law falls short of constitutional standards, the law becomes invalid and cannot be enforced. This, in short, is judicial review.

*   *   *

An example can put flesh on this bony sketch. In 1989, a protester in Texas who burned an American flag was arrested under state law and charged with vandalizing a respected object. He was tried and convicted, then chose to appeal the conviction, with the appeal eventually reaching the Supreme Court. In trying the case, the Court had to decide whether the Texas state law was valid, or whether the plaintiff's burning of the flag amounted to a form of protected free speech. Weighing the arguments, the Court reached their conclusion: Flag-burning, they decided, was a form of political communication, and the law was not constitutional as applied to the protester's action.

This was not the final word, however. Soon thereafter the United States Congress took issue with the ruling and passed a new, national law, the Flag Protection Act of 1989, designed specifically to outlaw flag-burning as a form of protest. By passing the law, Congress threw down a gauntlet. It confronted the Supreme Court with a law that directly opposed their previous decision and that had the full power of the nation's legislature behind it.

As Congress was debating this law prior to its passage, activists watched intently and anticipated the result. When the law reached the president and was signed into effect, these activists greeted it warmly. That is to say, demonstrators flocked to the streets in cities around the country and promptly set fire to dozens of flags in protest. In Washington D.C., four protesters were arrested and charged with violating the new federal law. They contested the arrests, once again claiming protection under the First Amendment. Now the Supreme Court had to face squarely the issue of whether Congress, representing the will of the people, had the power to enact the anti-flag burning law, or whether that power, great though it might be, should be overruled by the Court's interpretation of First Amendment rights.

In the end, the Supreme Court sided with the protestors again and against the Flag Protection Act. Thus the law was voided, and through the process of judicial review the Supreme Court clarified one stretch of the limits to the government's power over the individual's right to free speech. The decision also demonstrated the power of judicial review under our Constitution.

JUDICIARY

In human governments, there are but two controlling
powers; the power of arms, and the power of laws. If the
latter are not enforced by a judiciary above all fear, and
above all reproach, the former must prevail; and thus lead to
the triumph of military over civil institutions.

—Joseph Story, Supreme Court Justice (1812–1845)

Accorting to the theories behind American constitutionalism, there are
three basic functions of government: judicial, executive and legislative.
For Joseph Story, an early and scholarly Supreme Court Justice, the
judiciary holds a place of special honor, and lawful government depends on it. But
it is not, in a sense, the primary function among the three. The legislative comes
first, the making of laws. Then comes the executive, which carries out, or executes,
the laws. Only then does the judicial step in, judging both the laws and their execution to make sure each reflects the deep lawfulness that we call constitutional.

The United States Constitution reflects this division of functions, or powers.
Articles 1 and 2 deal with legislative and executive powers respectively. Article 3
of the Constitution is devoted to the judiciary and opens with these words: "The
judicial power of the United States, shall be vested in one supreme Court, and in
such inferior Courts as the Congress shall from time to time ordain and establish."

Distinguishing between the legislative, executive, and judicial functions of
government predates the American Constitution and was familiar to the Greeks
and Romans. But it was an American innovation to actually separate them as
institutions. Our three branches inhabit entirely different, and competitive,
organizational structures.

Governments had done otherwise throughout history. A single institution—a monarchy, for example—might exercise two or more of the basic functions. Kings and queens once made and executed laws themselves, but they also controlled the courts that ruled on those laws. This alignment of powers made monarchs dangerously powerful, and it was this unchecked power that the American founders wanted to prevent. Alexander Hamilton in *Federalist* 78 wrote, "I agree that 'there is no liberty, if the power of judging be not separated from the legislative and executive powers.'" Then he added that "liberty can have nothing to fear from the judiciary alone, but would have every thing to fear from its union with either of the other departments."

✳   ✳   ✳

The United States federal judiciary came into existence with the Judiciary Act of 1789, which established the Supreme Court.[45] In the 230 years since, we have built a great deal on that original foundation. Today we have a three-tiered system of national courts. In the lowest tier there are 94 United States District Courts, where federal district court judges preside. These are the courts where crimes in the federal codebook, including mail fraud, hijacking, counterfeiting, and others are tried. Crimes under state laws are not tried here at the federal level, and it is worth noting that state laws cover most of the crimes covered by our criminal codes.

One tier above the District Courts are the United States Circuit Courts of Appeals. Circuit Courts are found in eleven regions around the country. These courts hear *appeals*, meaning that they review cases that have been tried previously. If, in an earlier trial, the losing party has a solid legal reason to contest the decision, they can appeal to a higher court. Thus, even within the judiciary, there is a system of checks at work to prevent the misuse of power.

Still higher than the Courts of Appeals is the United States Supreme Court. It, too, is a court of appeals, where difficult, important cases are retried. The Supreme Court only hears a small fraction of the appeals that are filed with it each year, which can number as many as 9,000. They choose cases in which their decisions might resolve difficult legal questions left unsettled by earlier trials. Some of these cases have been landmarks in American history, and their names have entered deep into our political discourse: *Dred Scott*, *Brown* v. *Board of Education*, and *Roe* v. *Wade*, for example. As its name suggests, the Supreme Court is the country's highest legal institution. When the Supreme Court makes a decision, there is no other court to appeal to.[46]

✳   ✳   ✳

The judiciary occupies a delicate place in a democracy. When Joseph Story warned that the courts must be "above all fear, and above all reproach," one threat that concerned him was the turbulence of public feeling. For the judiciary to do its work well, it must adhere to principles of justice, no matter what popular opinion demands. For this reason, the courts are insulated from the people and their will. Federal judges are appointed, for example, rather than elected, and they serve "during good Behavior," as the Constitution puts it, or effectively for life. Thus, they are not as subject to direct public approval as members of Congress or the president.

Looking at government as a whole, the judiciary acts as a counterweight in a delicate balancing act. Government must be responsive to the will of the people, which the legislative branch is especially suited to do. But as it acts, government needs an opposing force, a different perspective, to keep its actions within constitutional boundaries. This more reflective view is one that the judiciary provides.

The example of same-sex marriage illustrates the tensions within this system. Not long ago, the idea was so remote from mainstream thought that even gays and lesbians did not bother to push it as a political issue.[47] By the mid-1990s, however, the gay rights movement was gathering broad support and people began to see same-sex marriage as a real legal possibility. As the issue gained traction, Congress passed a law, the Defense of Marriage Act (DOMA), designed to preempt the legalization of same-sex marriages. It defined marriage in traditional terms, and disallowed the expansion of that definition to include same-sex relationships.

At the same time, states were also grappling with the issue. Like the federal government, several states passed laws that banned same-sex marriage. Yet in 2004, legal matters took a dramatic turn when Massachusetts, in a ruling handed down by its highest court, became the first state to recognize same-sex marriage. The ruling took effect, though it clearly violated DOMA, the national law banning the practice. Other states followed Massachusetts, until eventually, 31 recognized same sex marriage.

This left the laws across the country in a confused state. However, there was a pattern amid the confusion. Where legislatures passed laws concerning same-sex marriage, those laws generally opposed the practice.[48] Legal recognition for same-sex marriage generally came through court rulings. Thus, the more democratic *legislative* institutions tended to oppose, and the less democratic *judiciary* to support, the expansion of marriage rights.

Eventually, it was the judiciary that would win out in this confrontation. In sifting the principles at stake, the Supreme Court in the case of *Obergefell* v. *Hodges* found that legislative bans on same-sex marriage, including DOMA, were unconstitutional. More specifically, those laws violated the Fourteenth

Amendment guarantee of equal protection for all Americans before the law. With this decision, legislative bans on same-sex marriage were struck down, and such marriages were recognized as legally valid across the nation.

*   *   *

To its supporters, the same-sex marriage decision was an extraordinary step forward. With leadership from the judiciary, society discarded a long-held prejudice and drew nearer to the ideal of equality.

For some, the ruling was not just an isolated victory, but an example of how the judiciary can lead society toward justice. As legal philosopher Ronald Dworkin put it, the judiciary can make clear "how the community's practices must be reformed to serve more coherently and comprehensively a vision of social justice," adding that the courts will "lay principle over practice to show the best route to a better future... ."

Dworkin's sentiments might stir the heart, but there is a tremendous amount at stake when the judiciary lays "principle over practice" in order to reform society. Moreover, its power—manifest in the same-sex marriage case—demands scrutiny. If the judiciary can rearrange such a central institution, what other institutions and practices might come under its judgment? We might rightly ask whether there should be limits to the extension of judicial power over our society. The courts provide a tempting route toward reform, bypassing the difficulties of the legislative process. But down that route, we might find an ever-greater intrusion by government, through the judiciary, into the social life of the citizenry. We should take seriously the possibility of tension between the judgments of the courts and government of, by, and for the people.

JURY

Juries are called the bullwarks of our rights and liberties;
and no country can ever be enslaved as long as those
cases which affect their lives and property, are to be
decided in great measure, by the consent of twelve honest,
disinterested men … .

—Samuel Spencer

Juries are familiar. They are the stuff of ten thousand cop shows and crime novels, all hinging on the natural drama of the jury's work. A group of men and
women sit through a trial, then deliberate together, in seclusion, to decide
the fate of the accused. It's not only the makers of pop culture that are fascinated
by juries. For many people, serving on a jury is the most intense and rewarding
involvement with government that they will ever experience.

The familiarity of the jury, however, can mask its deeper significance. For men
such as Samuel Spencer, a thinker from the era of the American Founding, the jury
was a central institution of government, and the framers of the Constitution were
careful to include the jury in their handiwork. Article III, Section 2, reads: "The
Trial of all Crimes, except in Cases of Impeachment, shall be by Jury." The role of
the jury is also asserted in the Sixth Amendment: "In all criminal prosecutions, the
accused shall enjoy the right to a speedy and public trial, by an impartial jury of the
State and district where the crime shall have been committed."

To the Founders, the jury was a cornerstone of democratic liberty. Governments
prosecute crimes, but the jury holds authority over whether the people will actually
be punished. Thus it exercises a kind of veto over state prosecutions and, more
generally, over the government's power to impose its will on the public. If a jury
finds the accused not guilty, criminal charges are void. Nor is there any appeal from

a jury's finding of innocence. Whatever the jury's judgment, no matter the quality of its reasoning, when it finds in favor of the accused, the verdict is final. The state has no further recourse.

This is a formidable power. Among the Founders, the jury was sometimes likened to a distinct branch of the government. Within the judiciary, it was separate from, but on par with, the judges who presided over trials. The jury and the judges were related in much the same way as the House of Representatives and the Senate in Congress. "The judicial structure mirrored that of the legislature," wrote constitutional scholar Akhil Reed Amar, "with an upper house of greater stability and experience and a lower house to represent popular sentiment more directly." The jury had its own particular powers, distinct from those of the judges, but no less substantial.

*   *   *

The jury's authority placed it on a high plane of political power, which raises a natural question about the limits of that power. A primary one is this: Are juries the final word on the law, as well as on the facts in a given a case? Could jurors, for example, refuse to convict defendants if they believed the law under which the defendants were charged was unjust? A case from colonial Pennsylvania illustrates the question. A publisher named John Peter Zenger printed an article in his newspaper that mocked the Pennsylvania's new governor and suggested that he was corrupt. The article angered the colony's political leadership, and Zenger was charged with libel and put on trial.

Prosecutors had a strong case, and as most experts understood that law, Zenger was likely guilty. But during the trial his lawyer made an unusual pitch to the jury: Don't worry too much about the law as it stands, and worry instead about whether you think the accused should really be punished. The law itself might be unjust.[49]

In the end, Zenger and his lawyer won the day. Jurors found the publisher not guilty, and in doing so showed the full extent of the jury's power. It ignored the prosecution's apparently sound arguments and freed the accused from punishment by the state.

After Zenger, and through the rest of the 18th century, the jury stood near the height of its power and prestige. John Adams pondered the question of whether juries should be limited to ruling on facts alone, if the law appeared unjust, and answered in no uncertain terms: "Every man, of any feeling or Conscience, will answer no. It is not only his right, but his Duty in that Case to find the Verdict according to his own best Understanding, Judgment and Conscience, tho in direct opposition to the Direction of the Court... ."

*   *   *

Esteem for the jury, however, was at its zenith in Adams's day, and rockier times lay ahead. Over the course of the next century, the jury's powers were trimmed as the legal system grew more professionalized and more complex. A turning point in that development came in 1896 when the Supreme Court, taking a stance opposite to that of John Adams, ruled that juries could *not* put the law aside in reaching a verdict. Or, as they wrote in their decision, juries could not be "a law unto themselves."

The fault for the jury's decline in authority lay largely with the jury itself. Ideally juries will reach sound verdicts through their deliberations, producing a common-sense and democratic judgment. But when the door closes behind an impaneled jury, there is no sure way to know where their discussions will lead, and the results have not always been to the jury's credit. Crucially, different juries will also reach different conclusions in similar cases, and such inconsistency is the mortal enemy of the law. When juries fail to rule consistently across cases, defendants effectively lose their right to justice under clear, standing laws.

Justice must be not only consistent, but impartial as well. Yet here, too, juries have a checkered past, one which includes a strong streak of racism. When the African American teenager Emmett Till was murdered in 1955, two white suspects were identified and charged with the crime. Despite solid evidence against them, an all-white jury found the accused innocent after barely an hour of deliberation. One juror scoffed, "If we hadn't stopped to drink pop, it wouldn't have taken that long."

Because of these factors and others—as the law gets more technically complicated, jurors have an ever harder time making sense of it—juries have suffered a decline in prestige. In criminal proceedings, both prosecutors and defense attorneys often find it safer to plea-bargain deals, rather than go to trial. Both sides have cause to fear that juries will reach an unpredictable and strongly adverse verdict, so they opt for guaranteed and less adverse results. As of 2016, well over 90 percent of both state and federal criminal convictions come from plea bargains rather than from trials by jury.

Still, despite fading as a central institution in the American constitutional system, the jury is still alive today. With the right to a trial by jury enshrined in the Constitution, it would take a constitutional amendment to eliminate it. Yet the decline of the jury does present the country with a real loss. The jury has been among our most democratic political institutions, one in which the responsibilities of self-government, with all its challenges, are most directly experienced. In a time when politics is often a spectator sport, jury duty can re-present citizens with the fundamental elements of governing.

JUSTICE

Justice renders to everyone his due.

—Marcus Tullius Cicero

At least on the surface, *justice* is one of the easiest political terms to grasp. In a rudimentary form, we certainly recognize its violation whenever we are wronged: when something is stolen from us or when we are attacked, for example. We instinctively know injustice when we are on the receiving end of it. But justice goes a step—a very long one—beyond mere reaction to pain and a blind striking back. Justice supposes that there is a standard by which to judge the loss or the offense, a standard by which acts are inherently good or bad.

In this, the principle of justice is akin to the rules that govern a game. In the 100-meter dash, for example, all runners start from the same line, at the same time, and run the same distance. If a runner breaks the rules, the results are void; cheating in any form is off-limits.

Like the ground rules of a game, justice is blind, which is to say that it judges all acts by the same standard. Statues of Lady Justice show her this way, blindfolded and holding a scale with which to weigh right and wrong. Justice, as a foundation for our laws, plays no favorites.

*   *   *

While we have been seeking to define it for thousands of years, pinning down the essence of justice and applying it to social life has always proven difficult. For example, codes of justice differ a great deal nation by nation and era to era: what counts as a crime, how crimes are punished, what rights individuals have within society, and—importantly—how a society's rules get made and who enforces them.

No people did more than the ancient Greeks to define what justice means, seeking out its roots and thinking through its applications. Yet they embraced norms that seem thoroughly unjust to us now. For example, Aristotle wrote: "That some should rule and others be ruled is a thing not only necessary, but expedient; from the hour of their birth, some are marked out for subjection." To Aristotle and other ancient Greeks, slavery was entirely natural and no injustice.

The culture of ancient Israel has also contributed enormously to the modern understanding of justice, but its ideals differed profoundly from those of the ancient Greeks. For Israel, God's will was the source of justice, and was communicated directly to the Jews through their scriptures and prophets. The Bible, combining both Hebrew scriptures and New Testament, has been seminal in forming the conscience of Western civilization, and it continues to shape beliefs even among those who know little scripture and those who deny the existence of God.

Two examples can illustrate the differences between biblical traditions and the justice of classical Greece. Although ancient Israel was a hierarchical society, just as Greece was, justice in the Hebrew scripture carries a more egalitarian message: We all stand before God as equals. There are many places in scripture that emphasize this, including the following. Here, Israel's leaders are admonished to judge fairly:

> You shall not pervert justice; you shall not show partiality; and
> you shall not take a bribe, for a bribe blinds the eyes of the wise
> and subverts the cause of the righteous. Justice and only justice
> you shall follow... .
>
> [Deuteronomy 16:19-20]

Moreover, under God's judgment, the prophet Isaiah warns that the powerful will be accountable for how the poor are treated:

> Woe to those who decree iniquitous decrees,
>   and the writers who keep writing oppression,
> to turn aside the needy from justice
>   and to rob the poor of my people of their right,
> that widows may be their spoil,
>   and that they may make the fatherless their prey!
>
> [Isaiah 10:1-2]

Classical philosophy and biblical ideals continue to shape our thinking about what justice demands of us. Other streams of thought have also entered into the debate on how to achieve a just society. Some thinkers discern a natural sense of justice that all people feel one way or another, a natural law that reaches across all cultures.

Virtually every nation has a system of justice that acts to define and deter unjust acts. Systems of justice punish wrong-doers as a way to protect the innocent and to preserve a society's well-being, and those efforts have very real effects. Nothing poisons society quite like the consistent violation of justice.

*   *   *

Systems of justice are embedded in bigger systems of government, but we think of justice as distinct, as something rarified and separate from the rest of government. Though it is a part of that big system, we want justice to rise above the profane give-and-take of ordinary politics.

This is a wish that our government can only partially grant. Consider the institutions tasked by the Constitution with dispensing justice—with making sure that our laws are just and that they are applied fairly. This burden falls especially on the courts and their judges. The Constitution does set them apart and treats them differently than other branches of government. The judiciary is the branch most insulated from popular opinion, for example, with Supreme Court justices being unelected and serving for as long as their health holds. This policy is designed to ensure that they will be better able to do their work free from political pressure and to be more attuned to the deeper principles of the law.

Yet our justices are not members of some priesthood. They are ordinary men and women, who make their decisions within a framework of laws and ideas that come from the broader society. Judges interpret the laws, but do not write them.

Moreover, judges rise to positions of high authority by political means. Supreme Court justices, for example, are nominated by presidents and confirmed by the Senate. Through this political process, the judiciary is tethered to the will of the people. Justice in this country is not a realm of pure, abstract disinterest, but a refined version of the people's sense of what is just.

Herein lies a challenge. Through the political connection, American justice is tied to a deeply pluralist society. To the degree that our system of justice represents that public, it will be similarly divided, and even at odds with itself. We see evidence of this in our never-ending debates on many issues dealing with fundamental justice, from capital punishment to the rights of property, debates that our judges cannot solve for us.

The instinct for absolute justice never leaves us, but the American system cannot deliver that. Yet if it does not promise perfection, it does respond to injustice and offer remedies to it. Moreover, by linking justice to the will of the people, the Constitution will not impose forms of justice that are unwanted by the majority of the people themselves. This isn't everything that an abstract, perfectionist system of justice might offer, but other nations have suffered under much worse.

KING

Kings are justly called gods for that they exercise a manner or resemblance of divine power upon earth. For if you will consider the attributes to God, you shall see how they agree in the person of a king. God has power to create, or destroy, make or unmake at his pleasure, to give life, or send death, to judge all, and to be judged nor accountable to none; to raise low things and to make high things low at his pleasure, and to God are both body and soul due. And the like power have kings.

—James I, King of England, 1610

James I would have known a good deal about the royal powers. He was King of England for over 20 years, and king of Scotland before that. When people think of kings and queens, it is often in something like James's terms: their power is absolute, even god-like. Kings, and not the people, are sovereign, and their will is law.

James was king at a pivotal point in political history. In England, two institutions, king and Parliament, struggled for control over government, with Parliament on the rise and power moving its way. This was the reason behind James's anxious defense of the king's power. But the trend would continue, and time would prove unkind to the royalist side of the argument. James's own son, Charles I, would ascend to the throne only to be deposed and beheaded in 1649, a revolutionary act that shook Europe's political world to its core.

This trend places James near the tail end of a tradition that stretched back thousands of years, as historian Francis Oakley saw it. Oakley has studied the nature of kingship and its place in governance around the world. What he found is that rule by kings has been the most common form of governance as far back as records can show.

Rule by kings is a global phenomenon. Kingships, rather like those found in Europe, have been the historical norm in China and Japan, in sub-Saharan Africa, in Meso-America, throughout the Near East, and in India. Rule by king, as Oakley put it, "can lay strong claim to having been nothing less than the political commonsense of humankind."

In his studies, Oakley found something else as well. While we tend to think of kings in terms of their earthly powers, kings have also held another sort of power, which we might call priestly rather than political. So, for example, the pharaohs of ancient Egypt, seen as divine, were responsible for maintaining harmony between the natural and supernatural worlds. By carrying out the necessary rituals, which included writing out a command on papyrus and casting it onto the waters of the Nile, the pharaohs ensured that the river's life-giving floods would return every year and bring fertility to Egypt's farms.

In mediating between the divine and the earthly, kings also delivered divine commands to their people. In China, the emperor held a "mandate of Heaven," through which he was empowered to rule and to maintain order within the realm. Laws pronounced from the throne were imbued with a divine sanction. Good order in earthly matters was rooted in the sacred cosmic realities, and it was the Chinese king's responsibility to keep the former in tune with the latter.

*   *   *

This history of kingly rule is almost foreign to the American political tradition, though not entirely. Here the king appears as a kind of boogie-man, less a real figure than a near-mythical tyrant from stories of our past. As history tells us, there once was a real king who threatened our land: King George III of Britain. But that was a long time ago, and no king has bothered America much over the last 230 years.

Nor do we have any substitute when it comes to the "sacral" function of kings. Not only do we have no king, we have nothing like a national priest-leader to ensure our harmony with the cosmos. The Constitution expressly makes any such thing virtually impossible. The First Amendment opens with the words, "Congress shall make no law respecting an establishment of religion . . . ." When this law became a part of the Constitution, the United States took a long step away from the old tradition of sacred kingship, further than any nation on Earth at that time.

We might justly take pride in managing with no king and without depending on any semi-divine leader to guide us. Having lived with this absence, however, we might honestly ask just how well this is working out. And so the question: Do we face problems today that would be less vexing if we had an institution that could somehow accomplish what the priest-kings of old were supposed to do? After all, those sacral kings could hardly have been so common in history had they not fulfilled real human needs: to foster harmony among people and between them and nature, to affirm a sense of place in some larger order, and to confirm people in their sense that their lives are not meaningless. Is it the case that we no longer need such blessings?

It is hard to read the daily news without some concern. Our current political atmosphere has become so bitter that writers look to the pre-Civil War years for comparisons. Faith in our institutions is low and dropping. And it is hard to know just what to make of the epidemic of opioid abuse and suicide that plague parts of the country, which have brought something unprecedented in America: declining life expectancy. One wonders why there is such despair in a nation as prosperous and otherwise healthy as our own. We cannot look to any sacral king to solve our problems, but one wonders: What solution short of political priest-craft will actually help us in these troubled times?

LABOR

If the workers are organized, all they have to do is to put
their hands in their pockets and they have got the capitalist
class licked.

—William "Big Bill" Haywood

In political discourse, *labor* refers to the collective interest of laborers. Those laborers themselves are workers employed by large concerns, including businesses and, increasingly, government. Labor, as an interest group, is on the other side from business owners or management. "Labor" or "organized labor" can also be used as a synonym for the unions. So if one hears that a presidential candidate is bidding for support from "labor," that pitch is likely being made to one or another union.

Within recent memory, labor was a heavyweight power in America's national politics, though it is less so now.[50] Labor's strength grew as the nation's economy industrialized during the 19th century, and as enormous businesses arose. The wealth and power of those businesses, on the one hand, contrasted with the struggles of laborers on the other, and gave rise to a sense that workers needed a voice in governing that was distinct from those of other classes.

Such protection was historically scarce in the United States. The assumption was that work was done "at will." Employment was a choice, equally agreed upon by employer and worker. If either party was dissatisfied with arrangements, they could find new ones.

This understanding fit comfortably with economic doctrines that favored maximum individual freedom. However, to the degree that it assumed any real equality between employer and employee, it came to be seen as wholly unrealistic.

Modern industry concentrated enormous power on the side of management, while the workers were left to fend for themselves. In that mismatch, individual employees held little leverage to demand better wages or safer work conditions.

Workers came to understand, however, that they need not fight alone. By acting in unison with others, they could multiply their power in relation to management. This is the premise behind the drive to organize in unions. Its basic logic is neatly captured in an old union song:

> Step by step the longest march
> Can be won, can be won.
> Many stones can form an arch,
> Singly none, singly none.
> And by union what we will
> Can be accomplished still.
> Drops of water turn a mill,
> Singly none, singly none.

Without organization, labor is weakened. To realize its potential strength, labor needs to unify its membership, concentrating its force and bringing it to bear on its negotiations with management.

*   *   *

In theory, at least, interactions between labor and management could be treated as a private matter, with no government intervention. The two sides could square off in contract negotiations, with chips falling as they might. As a practical matter, however, government has been deep in the fray since the 19th century. Once, government tended to take the side of business and saw union organizing as a conspiracy against traditional property rights. Strikes, the unions' most potent weapon, were seen as illegal, and police, or even the military, were called in to break them. Over time, however, labor fought back on the legal and political fronts, and won its share of battles. Crucially, it secured the rights to organize and to strike.

Gaining power through the early and mid-20th century, the labor movement pressed for political changes we now take for granted, such as the 40-hour work week, the minimum wage, overtime pay, and more. Taken together, labor achieved something extraordinary with such victories. It pulled a remarkable number of working Americans into an expanding middle class.

In recent decades, however, labor's power has ebbed, due to various opposing forces. Not least has been the decline in manufacturing, where labor has traditionally been strong, in relation to other sectors of the economy—the service industry, for example. With a shifting economy, labor has tried to organize other sectors, with some success among government workers. But union membership has declined sharply. At high tide, nearly a third of workers belonged to a union; today it is closer to a tenth.

Another factor in the decline of labor's power has been globalization, one of the critical features of American economic and foreign policy in recent years. Globalization allows businesses relative freedom to locate factories in foreign nations where labor costs are low. Manufacturers will reap greater profits if they open plants in Southeast Asia, with its low-wage labor; and companies that choose to operate in the higher-wage United States will find themselves at a competitive disadvantage when it comes time to sell their products. Thus, globalization has further weakened the bargaining position of labor in the United States.

Labor has faced a challenging climate for decades now. But these are turbulent times, and in the current political climate, Americans are taking a fresh look at all kinds of received wisdom. Not least is the question of globalization, with the 2020 COVID-19 pandemic, for example, exacerbating concerns about depending on foreign production for so many of our goods.

Globalization, however big an issue it is, is only one aspect of a broader issue: the relative benefits of an economy in which the interests of working people carry less weight than they once did. In our changing political landscape, it may be that labor's voice will gain traction in public discourse. If Americans, anxious about the direction of the country, are willing to consider new directions in public policy, labor has an opportunity to contribute to a change in national direction.

LAME DUCK

Government officials whose terms are about to expire and whose successors have already been chosen have been labeled 'lame ducks' since the early twentieth century. The term is not a compliment.

—John Copeland Nagle

This classic American political term has roots in 18th century British financial circles. There, a lame duck was a person or business on an extended losing streak. A lame duck was a wounded party, whose financial weakness was veering toward ruin. A lame duck was on its way to being a dead duck.

Crossing the ocean and entering politics, the term retains much of its original meaning. A lame duck in politics is an official who has been wounded politically and has lost influence. It is used especially to describe elected officials who have lost a bid for reelection but remain in office until their term runs out. For example, President Jimmy Carter lost his bid for a second term in November 1980, but continued to serve in office until Ronald Reagan was inaugurated early in 1981.

In politics, success has a magnetic quality. Winners attract power, and power flows away from the weak. Thus, having lost the 1980 election, Carter held little influence during the remainder of his term. Everyone in Washington understood that change was coming, and it only made sense to wait for Reagan's inauguration before tackling any new business.

Even popular presidents, though, slide toward lame duck status as their time in office draws down. When first elected, presidents take the initiative, having won the nation's only nationwide election. Opponents, wary of the winner's proven popularity, will often allow this during the so-called "honeymoon" period. But over time, presidents often find themselves increasingly bogged down, as the opposition regains its footing and the tide of events brings its usual share of bad news. If elected to a second term, presidents also find their political power dwindling as they approach the end of their administrations. As attention shifts toward the hunt for a successor, the president's influence wanes, and as this happens, they are often called lame ducks.

President Barack Obama suffered from this phenomenon despite his general popularity. With one year left in his final term, he faced what, in other circumstances, would have been a great opportunity to add to his legacy. Supreme Court Justice Antonin Scalia died unexpectedly, giving Obama, a Democrat, the right to nominate a replacement. He did so, naming a well-regarded judge, Merrick Garland, for the seat. Had the nomination come earlier in Obama's term, Garland might well have been confirmed. The nomination, however, hit a roadblock. Senate Majority Leader Mitch McConnell, a Republican, used parliamentary tactics to stall the nomination until after Obama had left office, thus killing it.

So late in his term, Obama had little leverage to muscle his Supreme Court nominee through. There was too little time left in his term to make credible political threats against McConnell, or to make any promises to weaken McConnell's resolve. For McConnell's part, with little to gain from compromising and a great deal to gain from holding out, he had a strong incentive to maintain his partisan blockade. Which is what he did, and there was little that President Obama could do to retaliate. This type of predicament is a symptom of lame duck status.

*   *   *

The term *lame duck* can also describe a whole legislature, not just a single politician. After any Congressional election, for example, some representatives will be retiring or defeated, leaving the body with a number of lame duck members. Their presence can scramble the usual incentives that inform legislative work. Lame duck Congresses, for example, will sometimes take on politically painful chores, such as voting for raises for government employees. This is a necessary, but perennially unpopular, measure, made more viable during lame duck sessions. At least some members will bite the bullet and vote for raises. Since they will not be running for reelection, they need not fear the voters.

As handy as lame duck sessions might be for Congress, they do raise a question about the laws passed under them. Legislatures exist to represent the will of the people, but lame duck sessions dilute that will, since some members already will have been rejected by the voters.

This problem is serious enough that an amendment to the Constitution was approved in 1933 largely to kill off the practice of Congress holding lame duck sessions. It moved the date when Congress reconvenes after every election from

March 4 to January 3. The understanding was that the Congress could not meet before this new date, given the difficulties of winter travel at that time.

Of course, improvements in transportation have rendered that measure out of date, and Congress has no problem holding sessions between election day in November and January 3. So the lame duck Congress still flies, and will continue to do so, despite concerns about its democratic legitimacy.

LAW

To the thoughtful and sensitive citizen the law can present itself in a bewildering array of moods. It can appear as the highest achievement of civilization, liberating for creative use human resources otherwise dedicated to destruction. It can be seen as the foundation of human dignity and freedom, our best hope for a peaceful world. In man's capacity to perceive and legislate against his own defects we can discern his chief claim to stand clearly above the animal level. Philosophers of former ages have, indeed, not hesitated to see some kinship with the divine in man's ability to reorder his own faulty nature and, in effect, to recreate himself by the rule of reason.

—Lon Fuller

In Lon Fuller's statement, two words stand out. Together, the words frame the notion of law. One is *animal.* Too often we humans act impulsively, without regard for others and without the restraint of conscience. Whether or not it is fair to call this "animal," as Fuller does, the result is destructive.

The other term is *divine.* We have the capacity to perceive our faults, and to rise above them. We do so through reason, by which we can institute laws, thus reordering our "faulty nature." We may never perfect our society through law, but we can improve it to a degree that makes civil life feasible and frees us to achieve great things that would otherwise be impossible.

Noting the law's "kinship with the divine," Fuller raises a central challenge every lawful society faces. To be effective, law must have potent authority, even approaching the sacred. Law only works if people feel compelled to obey it.

But where does such authority come from? In many cultures, the law has been explicitly grounded in the divine, as with Moses and the Ten Commandments. In our time and place, however, we must consider the more secular processes by which law gains its force.

*   *   *

One might start with a central fact of social life, which is conflict. Disputes can be resolved in the absence of law, but through means best avoided: blood feuds, vigilantism, intimidation, and so forth. By contrast, the lawful way to resolve conflicts is by submitting them to a recognized authority, one that is responsible for making satisfactory judgments about right and wrong in such matters.

In reaching their judgment, the authorities must accomplish something both ticklish and utterly grave. The judgment must address the concerns of the parties involved in such a way that the loser, to the degree there is one, understands that some level of justice has been done. When those on the losing end feel that their rights have been violated, they will resist the judgment more or less actively. And rejection of the court's authority opens the way to the evils that law is meant to curtail: the blood feuds, and so forth.

To accomplish its goal of rendering satisfactory justice, the law must act impartially, not favoring one side or the other. It must be guided instead by principles of right and wrong that both sides will find compelling. To gain authority, law must look beneath the surface and search out the fundamental principles at stake.

In doing so, the law places a great deal of faith in reason, and does so in two ways. First, it depends on reason to identify those principles of right and wrong that can be applied to conflicts. Second, the law assumes that its reasoning will be persuasive within the broader society, enough to overcome instinctive, or "animal level," responses from those who lose the legal fights.

*   *   *

An example will help illustrate how the law works: Suppose a driver is struck from behind in traffic, resulting in physical injury. One underlying principle of our law is to hold people responsible when they cause harm. So, the injured party might sue the other driver, and if the case is straightforward, the law will uphold the injured party's claims.

Of course, the case might *not* be straightforward, and the principles involved might be less clear-cut. The driver of the second vehicle might have been driving carefully and the accident might have been caused by a mechanical malfunction in the brakes, for example. In such cases, the manufacturer might be found responsible for the accident. In any case, the work of the law is to impartially determine responsibilities among those involved and to make a judgment based on that determination.

*   *   *

The sifting process of the law—the search for principles and standards by which to make judgments—is a highly social effort. In reaching a decision, judges follow precedents set by other judges, which are understood as authoritative. These precedents accumulate over time, and following them is one key to maintaining legal consistency and authority. It prevents the law from dissolving into mere opining by willful judges.

As the law has grown over time, it has also expanded to cover wide areas of experience. There are bodies of law dealing with corporations, contracts, copyright and trademark matters, the conveyance of property, and the environment. Throughout all these areas, the law works toward similar ends. It seeks to resolve conflicts by clarifying the responsibilities of concerned parties.

After hundreds of years of growth, the law has achieved a sizable bulk. Yet it is also highly refined and exceptionally detailed. Given its immense reach, it would be impossible to sum up the effects of the law on our lives. Here is one effect though: The law sets up guidelines that simplify and discipline some of the more trouble-prone matters in our lives, from buying a home to writing a will.

Here is a single example: bankruptcy. In bankruptcy, people find themselves in debt with no plausible way of paying off creditors. This situation leaves the debtor unable to resume a normal, productive life, and the creditors without the money they are owed. In lawless times and places, bankruptcy is also rife with the potential for sparking violent conflict.

Bankruptcy law provides a way through the impasse. It allows a legitimate, socially acceptable way for debtors to pay off what they realistically can, and for creditors to recover some, though likely not all, of the money they are owed. Our bankruptcy laws have evolved through long experience, in which lawyers and judges have weighed the rights and wrongs of complex personal situations, seeking out practical and humane resolutions to the conflicts.

By doing so, the law, in bankruptcy and elsewhere, provides a great benefit to society. Energy that in the past might have gone into fighting over property is freed for more productive purposes. With this in mind, philosopher Friedrich Hayek observed: "Our familiarity with the institutions of law prevents us from seeing how subtle and complex a device [it] is. If it had been deliberately designed, it would deserve to rank among the greatest of human inventions. But it has, of course, been as little invented by any one mind as language or money or most of the practices and conventions on which social life rests."

LEGISLATION

No man with a genius for legislation has appeared in America. They are rare in the history of the world. There are orators, politicians, and eloquent men, by the thousand; but the speaker has not yet opened his mouth to speak, who is capable of settling the much-vexed questions of the day.

—Henry David Thoreau

Legislation is, first and foremost, law. Yet it is law of a particular sort. Legislation is law that is passed through specific constitutional acts, crystallizing the public will on a matter of importance at a particular time. In 1965, for instance, when many African Americans were denied the opportunity to vote, Congress passed the Voting Rights Act, a crucial piece of legislation, to secure those rights.

Though many nations look back to semi-mythical legislators as great givers of a nation's law, in modern democracies, legislation comes from legislatures. Legislatures embody and represent, at least in theory, the will of the people, and the laws that legislatures write are the primary political expressions of that will.

In the United States, legislatures are not only the primary lawmakers, but are also the most directly representative branches of the government. In the House of Representatives, for example, members are elected frequently—every two years—and from every part of the country, thus keeping the House in relatively close touch with public feeling.

Being highly representative, American legislatures were created to be responsive to the people's needs. As social problems arise, legislators at both the state and national levels can propose laws to address them. With the legislators' job being, in part, to bring the troubles of their constituents to light, no serious social problem, plausibly solvable by legislation, should go ignored for long periods of time.

While legislatures are the primary lawmakers in modern democratic governments, it should be noted that legislation is not the only source of our laws. Many American laws, for example, have deep roots in English common law. The common law has grown over the centuries, evolving as judges apply legal precedents and principles to specific cases. Our legal system was built on a common law foundation, and much of the old common law still holds authority, from the legal distinction between robbery and theft to the rights of habeas corpus.

The slow evolution of the common law contrasts with the more dramatic work of legislatures. Legislation creates new law, applied on a broad social basis, rather than case-by-case, and can be vastly more ambitious than the common law. Social security, for example, was produced by a quintessentially legislative act. Faced with poverty during the Great Depression, especially among older citizens, Congress passed the Social Security Act to relieve its burdens. The common law by its nature could never yield such an action, but legislation can.

*   *   *

The great potential power of legislation raises a question: If it is Congress's job to address difficulties the people face, why are we beset by any long-term social problems? Why don't legislators simply write the necessary legislation to bring the enormous force of the government to bear on those problems and make them go away?

There are lots of reasons why we cannot, but some of those reasons are constitutional. Our constitutions, state and national, were not designed for ambitious legislation—indeed, were designed to frustrate such ambitions—and place big hurdles in its way: bicameral legislatures, executive vetoes, and judicial review by the courts. These constitutional devices make it hard to pass legislation, especially far-reaching programs that, at least in theory, might solve big social problems. As Charles Evans Hughes, one-time Chief Justice of the Supreme Court, put it, the Constitution is "the greatest instrument ever designed to prevent things from being done."

*   *   *

With these constitutional hurdles in mind, it is worth turning the question of legislation upside down, and rather than approach it from the governing end, start with the problem on the ground. To write effective legislation, problems must be understood clearly in terms of causes and effects.

When faced with problems, legislators must determine whether they can be solved, and while some problems can, others can't. If drought strikes the Midwest, legislation that mandates rain won't help. Where problems can be addressed (if not always solved), legislators face a further task. They must analyze the problem to determine what governmental action might be useful. The legislation itself will spell out what people must do.

Sometimes the problem will have relatively clear causes, such as air pollution. When Congress grappled with writing anti-pollution laws in the late 1960s, it was able to identify the most serious pollutants (airborne lead, for instance) and where they came from. Armed with this knowledge, Congress wrote legislation that targeted pollution at its sources, especially factories and automobiles. With a clear understanding of what the legislation demanded, industries complied, and, as a result, air pollution decreased.

Not all problems have such clear-cut solutions, however. There are problems of which the causes are poorly understood, yet we demand legislation to solve them. Public education, for example, has been a source of concern for decades and a target of recurring legislative initiatives. But while many people criticize public school policies, American education is by its nature an exceedingly complex matter, with over 50 million students from all backgrounds enrolled each year. Given this complexity, it's no surprise that reforms frequently fall short.[51]

Yet no parent, and no healthy society, will stand by as the educational system fails their young, so we keep trying. One relatively recent, large-scale legislative effort at education reform came during George W. Bush's presidency: the No Child Left Behind Act of 2002—NCLB, for short.

NCLB tried a particular approach to fixing schools. It mandated a strict regime of testing to identify exactly where and when students began to fall behind in math and reading. The thinking was that by using that information, educators would know where to make extra efforts to keep students on the right path. In addition, the testing would allow government to identify schools that were lagging. For those schools, NCLB mandated that new "research-based instruction methods" be implemented, with funding provided by the federal government.

When it was enacted, NCLB had bipartisan support and plenty of good will behind it. Yet anyone who hoped for a real educational turn-around—hoped that the No Child Left Behind Act would live up to its name—was in for disappointment. Loads of tests were administered, analysts gathered mountains of data, and resources were accordingly deployed. But the test scores never budged much. By 2015, NCLB was widely deemed a failure and allowed to expire.

No Child Left Behind was well-intentioned and faithfully implemented. But it failed because, unlike the Clean Air Act, NCLB did not mandate actions that would actually result in concrete gains.

*   *   *

Today we face a number of problems of this sort, which for divergent reasons resist legislative fixes. We have, for example, been fighting a costly War on Drugs for decades, and while this may have helped—who knows how bad our drug situation might be if we hadn't fought it—the recent crisis with opioids proves that the war is far from won. We also face persistent, dense pockets of poverty in a number of rural and urban places, the decline of civil society, and other problems that fester with no clear legislative cures in sight. It would be useful if someone could map out the difficult terrain where practical legislation meets daunting problems. But for now, no such map exists and we must govern accordingly.

LIBERALISM

> I believe in a relatively equal society, supported by
> institutions that limit extremes of wealth and poverty. I
> believe in democracy, civil liberties, and the rule of law. That
> makes me a liberal, and I'm proud of it.
>
> —Paul Krugman

The heat and pressure of American politics can do to political terms what volcanoes do to minerals, melting and transforming them. The term *liberalism* is a case in point. Once liberalism was widely embraced in our politics. Equated with open-mindedness, generosity toward others, and affirmative attitudes generally, liberalism was the opposite of hardheartedness, suspicion, and bigotry. It was a quality millions aspired to, with the number of Americans identifying as "liberal" peaking in the early 1960s.

More recently, however, *liberal* has become less current, with fewer people embracing it as a political description. In the rough-and-tumble of public discourse, *liberal* has grown into a slur, at least for the likes of radio talk show host Rush Limbaugh and his enormous audience. This is why Paul Krugman felt compelled to proclaim his pride in being a liberal, and to equate liberalism with all-American ideals: democracy, civil liberties, and the rule of law.

To better understand such differing takes on the term, it helps to consider liberalism in two distinct ways. One is more traditional, more philosophical, and mostly separate from present-day polemics. This understanding will be dealt with later. The other understanding of the term is the one familiar from talk radio and the daily news. A staple of current political argument, it is the one that Krugman and Limbaugh fight over.

This more current, popular use of *liberalism* evolved within the context of political and cultural conflict over the last sixty years. Throughout those decades, Americans have fought a kind of long, cold, civil war, and popular notions of what liberalism is were forged in its bruising exchanges.

*   *   *

We might call this conflict the Reformers' War, if only for present purposes, and none of its battles would be more consequential for understanding *liberalism* than its first big one. This was the campaign for civil rights, especially as it was fought between 1954 and 1965. To be liberal on civil rights during that period was to side with African Americans against segregation and for the opening up of mainstream economic, educational, and cultural worlds to African Americans. It was to stand against deeply entrenched prejudices, and to cast one's hopes for a freer future.

It is hard to overstate the ways in which the Civil Rights movement has shaped our politics, and shaped liberalism, ever since. A generation of young Americans watched intently as the movement unfolded, and were indelibly influenced by the lessons they learned.

Here is some of what liberals would carry forward from the Civil Rights campaign. First, liberalism would be active and reformist: the status quo was not okay, and liberals would confront what they saw as complacency and self-satisfaction in the ingrained values of American public life. In addition, to bring the changes they sought, liberals would need powerful tools—ones that government would provide. Moreover, government for liberals especially meant *national* government, which alone held the potency to effect deep reform.[52] Finally, and perhaps most characteristically, liberalism would identify with the underprivileged as a matter of principle, its watchwords being fairness and tolerance.

These characteristics marked liberal positions in the many battles that followed the Civil Rights movement. Liberals opposed the Vietnam War[53] and resisted other aspects of American foreign policy. Liberals supported Lyndon Johnson's Great Society project and generally favored government efforts to benefit the disadvantaged. They rallied to the cause of environmental protection; advocated a new openness to immigration; and fought against the status quo on any number of other issues, including free speech, school prayer, gun control, and equal rights for women, Native Americans, and others.

*   *   *

One particular legacy of the Civil Rights movement merits special emphasis, that being its strong sense of moral purpose. The principled righteousness that animated the Civil Rights movement would live on among self-identified liberals as they moved from battlefield to battlefield.

Consider the career of Barney Frank, a long time Congressman from Massachusetts. If they awarded medals in the Reformers' War, Frank would have a chest full. He was a volunteer Civil Rights organizer in 1964, an anti-war activist soon after, a consistent supporter of programs to serve the disadvantaged, and, as one of the first openly gay members of Congress, a national leader of the LGBT rights movement. Frank saw all his efforts as united by an underlying purpose. "I chose a political career . . . because nothing was more important to me than doing all I could to reduce the suffering inflicted on vulnerable people by unfair societal arrangements." Liberalism fights on its principles, fairness and tolerance above all, and many individual liberals derive their strong sense of political purpose from this identity.

*   *   *

As noted above, the contemporary, popular meaning of *liberalism* has an older, more philosophical counterpart, one which we might call "classical liberalism." While older, however, this liberalism is not ancient. In fact, philosopher John Gray calls liberalism "the political theory of modernity," beginning to take shape in the 17th century. The essence of modern political life, he believes, can be found in the ideals of liberalism. Gray fleshes out this notion when he adds something critical: Liberalism could only have fully developed "in the post-traditional society of Europe after the dissolution of medieval Christendom."

Here one finds a key to the deeper philosophical meaning of liberalism. It is best understood in relation to the belief system it displaced. In very brief terms, medieval government was understood to reflect a coherent, cosmological order, modeled on the divine: God created the world as part of His plan, and government, like all the rest of creation, had its rightful order and place in the grand scheme of things. The aim of government was to uphold this divinely modeled order, and rights, duties, and laws reflected it. The place of kings, for example, differed from that of the aristocracy, which differed from that of the clergy, which differed from that of the peasantry. Each class had its niche, enshrined in law.

Europe's medieval order was shaken during the tumultuous 16th and 17th centuries, and was effectively destroyed in many countries. Civil wars, including highly destructive religious wars in the heart of Europe, tore at society's fabric, leaving Europe's traditional systems of government shattered.

Out of this dissolution of the medieval order, the liberal alternative emerged, and one of its chief characteristics was a kind of metaphysical modesty. Under liberalism, government would no longer be seen as reflecting a divine order. Nor would the old hierarchies—kings, aristocrats, the Church—hold their traditional powers and privileges. To a large degree, liberalism meant liberty from these historical structures and their power.

In place of the old order, liberalism asserted new ideals, including the following:

- Individualism, or the primacy of the individual over and above collective identities
- Egalitarianism, or the equality of all people under the law
- Universalism, or the idea that people share a common humanity more fundamental than distinctions of culture, nationality, or race
- Meliorism, by which society is seen as improvable through rational planning

In each case, these tenets of liberalism were at odds with the old view. Individualism and egalitarianism, for example, both defied notions of a traditional hierarchical order. Meliorist beliefs ran contrary to the tradition that society was by nature part of a fixed, providential order.

Under the inspiration of liberal thought, government took on certain characteristics. Liberalism tended to foster free speech, free association, freedom of conscience, and free-market economies. Liberal government was also much less in the business of enforcing a traditional religious order than governments had been. The United States Constitution, one of the great landmarks of classical liberalism, expressly prohibited any established national church, for example, something that France emulated soon after, as would other nations in time.

*   *   *

Eschewing an established religion, however, does not mean that the question of order disappears under liberal government. No government, no society, can survive without some shared sense of what to value and what to condemn. But liberalism is by definition open about what that order entails and will not impose an answer. One must then ask where order will come from under liberalism and what sort of shared social values can exist where individualism and egalitarianism are the key ideals of the day.

The United States Constitution provides a practical solution: The will of the people, flowing through the institutions of government, will yield the laws that sustain order. There is no need for privileged institutions, such as the Church, to impose it; order will come from the people themselves. In a sense, this is what government of, by, and for the people means, and relying on the common sense of the people has yielded a political order that has allowed the country to thrive in many ways.

However, the dependence of liberal constitutionalism on whatever order arises from the common sense of the people can run into difficulties. For starters, liberal societies tend to be highly dynamic. Their freedoms bring profound social change. But profound change is naturally in tension with any order, which by definition will have a degree of stability and coherent structure.

Moreover, classical liberalism has an inherent logic that works to undermine systems of order. Liberalism embraces freedom of thought and of conscience, and the questioning of accepted beliefs and practices. Skeptical minds, thriving under this liberalism, cannot help demanding explanations for our customs and laws. Over the last sixty years, such skeptical questioning has led to all kinds of changes in our governing: Why do we have segregation? Why do we have prayer in public schools? Why shouldn't women have equal rights with men?

Nor does liberalism put any limit on the questioning, so on the margins of our current public discourse people ask: Why should we use government to support the poor? Why do we have national borders? Why do we value human life any more than the life of animals? No questions are out of bounds.

Questions flourish in the fertile ground of classical liberalism and grow freely. Compelling answers, however, struggle to survive, not least because every answer is subject to further skeptical questioning: the ever-ready "Why?" and its natural follow-up "Says who?" To govern itself, society needs to muster enough order and authority to give some direction to its political life, direction that people find satisfying. But classical liberalism on its own finds it hard to do that mustering.

*   *   *

In terms of current public discourse, look for the more traditional and philosophical meaning of *liberalism* to rise in use. Deep currents of discontent are roiling our political life, deep enough that some thoughtful observers have begun to question the future of the liberal tradition as a whole. Of particular concern is exactly the question of whether liberal political institutions can produce, or even allow, any order that will sustain society.

By challenging systems of order and hierarchies of value, the inner logic of liberalism makes it difficult to define public goals that transcend individual desires. Under economic liberalism, it is difficult to articulate compelling goals other than maximal individual gain. Under social liberalism, it is difficult to defend a culture of self-discipline and decency in the face of popular trends rushing in the opposite direction.

It might be that liberal government depends on an order it cannot generate on its own, that it, indeed, undermines its own promise even as it fulfills it.

"Liberalism has failed because liberalism has succeeded," one of its critics, Patrick Deneen, has written. In his view, liberalism's success makes it difficult to address major challenges, since liberal beliefs make it difficult to articulate common goods. Failures in the face of multiple social challenges lead to a "loss of confidence and even belief in legitimacy among the citizenry, that accumulates not as separable and discreet problems to be solved within the liberal framework, but as deeply interconnected crises of legitimacy and a portent of liberalism's end times."

If our current political distempers deepen, similar concerns about the viability of the long liberal tradition, even including the American constitutional system, will grow.

LIBERTARIANISM

> Little else is requisite to carry a State to the highest degree of opulence from the lowest barbarism, but peace, easy taxes, and a tolerable administration of justice, all the rest being brought about by the natural course of things.
>
> —Adam Smith

In American politics, libertarianism is one of a small handful of core ideologies with sharply defined ideals that appeal to substantial numbers of citizens—this despite the fact that relatively few identify as libertarians. As to those core ideals, libertarians seek maximum personal freedom and minimal state intrusion into personal or social affairs, whether that means work, leisure, culture, or, to the doctrinaire, much of anything else.

The libertarian stance has two aspects, the first being rather abstract. This is a strong commitment to personal rights. Libertarians embrace freedom and equality in pure forms, and tend not to recognize the government's right to impose its will on the people in the name of some higher good.

The second aspect is more practical. Libertarians see government as ineffective, or even harmful, in nearly all of its efforts. To the libertarian, individuals understand their own interests better than the state possibly can and act more effectively toward beneficial ends. Taken in the aggregate, the actions of free individuals will add up to the optimal happiness for society, far better than if the government imposes its own will on the decisions that private parties make.

Libertarian ideals can be seen most clearly when applied to specific problems. Consider the example of worker safety. Libertarians point out that there are real options, apart from government regulation, to reduce injury and death in the workplace. One option is the threat of legal action if working conditions are hazardous. Workers naturally seek their own well-being and will use the law to ensure it. Employers just as naturally want to avoid liability for harm to workers. Together, these incentives drove improvements in worker safety long before the arrival of the Occupational Health and Safety Administration in 1971, and wholly apart from government regulations.

Moreover, libertarians believe that similar dynamics can help solve other thorny problems, from poverty to environmental protection. Self-interest, individual responsibility, and personal effort are the real forces that drive improvement in all walks of life. Government derails, rather than helps, those improving forces.

Distrust of state action shapes another, crucial feature of libertarian thought. Libertarians have shown a frequent disgust for war as the ultimate in government misadventure. The 20th century libertarian Murray Rothbard wrote, "For centuries the state has enslaved people into its armed battalions and called it 'conscription' in the 'national service.'" War, to such a thinker, is the most massively destructive and expensive of government projects. It is also the antithesis of creative personal effort (which is the lodestone of libertarian values).

Given the libertarian's deep suspicion of government, a question arises. If the state is so inept, even dangerous, is there anything it actually should do? One can be brief here. Libertarians support state action to support the public good, but define that concept very strictly. It includes goals that cannot be achieved except through government action, including national defense (despite libertarian critiques of war). And public goods are those in which the whole public has an equal stake. For a mainstream libertarian, a classic example of government's inescapable responsibility is providing a sound judicial system to enforce laws evenhandedly. (Affirmative action, on the other hand, is out of the question, favoring as it does some people over others and empowering the government to enforce that favoritism.)

*   *   *

Libertarians have a more complicated relationship with what we might call cultural goods, as opposed to those public goods that government must provide. These goods include education, the well-being of the arts and literature, and any number of other areas where the line between the purely personal and the public can be hard to pinpoint: drug use and sexual mores, for example.

For libertarians, individual rights in such matters remain in the forefront. "Libertarian social analysis begins with the individual," writes David Boaz. "Each individual is responsible for his or her own survival and flourishing. Only individuals can assume responsibility for the consequences of their actions." In keeping with this stance, libertarians often oppose the war on drugs, for example.

It is not for the state to tell free adults how to live, nor to impose any social ideal on the public.

At the same time, many libertarians chafe at having their views equated with libertinism. There are, in fact, conservative libertarians who value all kinds of traditional virtues: good manners, faithfulness in marriage, sobriety, tidy streets, and much more. However much libertarians insist on individualism, such notions of good order can be compatible with their ideals.

Consider one context in which some libertarians surely value traditional order: the academy. There, high scholarly standards have evolved over the course of hundreds of years without government help. In a complex, ongoing, highly social effort, scholars have hashed out among themselves what good scholarship consists of. They haven't arrived at a perfect system, but continue to refine it. They have generated what libertarians call "spontaneous order," by which scholars evaluate the quality of each other's work in various disciplines.

If a libertarian embraces order in such a case, it might seem a betrayal of the iconoclastic bent of the libertarian soul. However, it might not actually be so. While libertarians often celebrate the rebel and lone wolf, there is something more fundamental at stake in the formation of spontaneous order: personal choice. If one chooses to submit to the disciplines of traditional scholarship, it is a decision freely made. People have every right to obey whatever authority they find compelling.

But the state as an authority stands apart. As Murray Rothbard notes, the state depends on coercion to sustain itself, and only the state can legally use violence against other members of society. The powers of the state place it in a category of its own, and libertarians insist that it be treated as unique.

Thus, as the libertarian Charles Murray says, the state should not be in the business of imposing any preferred values on society. "Government is the one entity in society that must be absolutely forbidden to discriminate. Whereas citizens and private institutions have the freedom to follow their tastes and beliefs, the government is permitted neither tastes nor beliefs."

LIBERTY / FREEDOM

> Now the corrupted nature in men is such that it would like
> to live freely, without God, without law, without any fear.
> One sees godless, wanton people, tyrants, Cyclops, and
> Centaurs living thus, and they give to this desolate existence
> the honourable name of freedom. But there is no freedom
> when there is no order... .
>
> —Philip Melanchthon

No words, no ideals, are closer to the heart of the American project than *liberty* and *freedom*. They define the goals of our constitutional order and have a place of honor in our most treasured documents. The Declaration of Independence speaks of "Life, Liberty, and the Pursuit of Happiness," for example. The Gettysburg Address describes ours as a "nation conceived in liberty" and calls for "a new birth of freedom" in the wake of the Civil War and its vast sacrifices.

The two terms cover much the same ground and are often used interchangeably. The fundamental concept behind both was captured by philosopher Isaiah Berlin: "I am normally said to be free to the degree to which no man or body of men interferes with my activity." Yet *liberty* and *freedom* are complex terms and have meant somewhat different things at different times. Berlin notes that over two hundred differing "senses," or connotations, of *freedom* have been understood over the centuries.

Word histories can illuminate some of the different shades of meaning in play. The roots of *liberty* are in Latin and the history of Rome. In Latin, *libertas* was a matter of status under the law. In its fullest form it was a state reserved for mature male citizens. To have liberty, in this ancient sense, was to hold a position of authority not only over one's own life, but also over the lives of dependents under one's care. These included slaves, who were property and had no liberty of their own, as well as family members. The patriarch's authority was such that he had the legal right of life and death over his own children. If a son, say, should step too far out of line, the patriarch could legitimately kill him (at least in certain historical times and places).

This liberty was as much a matter of responsibility as of free choice, and the patriarch's responsibilities rippled out from him in concentric circles. He was first responsible for himself, but also responsible for those under his power. If a slave or a child destroyed property belonging to another family, it fell to the patriarch to make compensation.

Beyond the family, responsibility extends further. Liberty assumes that free citizens share responsibility for the well-being of the broader society. And here is an essential difference between liberty and license. License—acting on selfish impulses and appetites to serve oneself—undermines well-being on a personal level, but also on the social. A licentious society is one that cannot maintain its liberties, because licentiousness leads to disorder, and disorder is not an option. Social order is a necessity, and if it does not come from free citizens, it will come from political overlords.

As political philosopher Allan Bloom wrote, there is a long history of philosophic belief that "republics required the greatest self-imposed restraints, whereas tyrannies and other decadent regimes could often afford the greatest individual liberties." According to this view, liberty, order, and responsibility stand on one side, with license, disorder, and irresponsibility ranged in opposition and eventually leading to authoritarian government.

*   *   *

Often, when we speak of *freedom,* we have something slightly different from Roman liberty in mind. Having freedom generally suggests being allowed to grow and flourish without impediments. For early immigrants coming to America, freedom often meant leaving behind class structures or other social constraints to enjoy life without them in the United States.

Freedom was also the keynote of the American Civil Rights movement, where that word had a higher profile than *liberty.* It was, for example, freedom that was invoked at the end of Martin Luther King, Jr.'s "I Have a Dream" speech: "'Free at last! Free at last! Thank God Almighty, we are free at last!'" For Civil Rights supporters, freedom meant breaking down the barriers that kept African Americans from achieving the highest goals they might aspire to. It meant opening the doors to business, government, the academy, and the worlds of the arts and sports as well.

To be free is, in part, to be able to strive, according to one's will, toward one's own goals. To feel free is to sense an openness in the present and future in which we can grow, think, work, and play as we choose.

*   *   *

Of course, freedom is complicated by the fact that no society can survive with everyone acting without restraint. So we have laws to discourage murder, robbery, and other crimes, to protect people's rights and well-being. But we also have the various customs and conventions that people learn as part of a community: court-ship and marriage, education, manners, the Golden Rule. Our lives are necessarily social, and society, if it is to exist, will have its rules.

On the face of it, those rules limit freedom. Yet customs and conventions can be seen in a different light as well. They provide channels that can lead to growth and fulfillment. Education, for example, provides an opening that can lead to a rewarding life. We feel free when the channels are clear and we are confident in our ability to move through them; confident, too, that they will lead us somewhere that will satisfy our yearnings. We feel the opposite—frustration—when those channels are blocked or confused, and our growth is stifled.

Yet in our own highly individualistic times we have a conflicted relationship with social conventions. At least for some people, the rules chafe and feel like infringements on our freedom. To them, a more satisfying sense of freedom comes from flaunting conventions than in living through them.

As a matter of law, this individualism has played a part in any number of Supreme Court rulings on a range of "culture war" issues, including free speech, school prayer, same-sex marriage, and others. In many cases, the Court has taken a strong stance on behalf of liberal individualism and against long-held social customs. Justice Anthony Kennedy captured this individualist ethos in a 1992 Supreme Court decision: "At the heart of liberty is the right to define one's own concept of existence, of meaning, of the universe, and of the mystery of human life."

For many people, these are inspiring words, full of the promise that each of us is our own master, even to the point of defining "one's own concept of existence." But the uplift should not hide the audacity of Kennedy's opinion. According to it, our understanding of the universe and our place in it come solely from our own imaginations, and freedom amounts to the individual's right to act according to whatever we discover there.

Yet, despite Kennedy's claim that we have the right to "define our concept of existence," we still live in a world we do not create ourselves, and that world has its own stubborn realities. Consider the cheerless example of pornography. Within living memory, we have had modestly effective restraints, legal and conventional, on the production and sale of obscene materials. These restraints reflected a broadly held understanding that pornography was unhealthy not just for individuals, but for society as a whole.

Down the road, those restraints have loosened, to understate the matter wildly, as changes in the laws, community standards, and technology have reshaped the cultural landscape. This may be all to the good, as the Kennedy ethos would have it. The individual today is largely free to use pornography, according to his or her conscience or inclination. And many in the broader community are glad that the government is not charged with monitoring the public and enforcing much in the way of anti-obscenity codes.

But the realities of pornography do not begin and end here. While the individual is free to indulge in it, he or she will not be free from its effects. And it is implausible that substantial exposure to porn, which strikes with such neurological force, leaves developing minds untouched. And those minds, altered to whatever degree, will in the course of things come into intimate contact with others.

Unless they do not. We should at least consider the possibility that exposure to pornography is one factor, among others to be sure, in the increased difficulty American adults have in forming close bonds with others. Marriage rates have dropped steadily in recent years, reaching their lowest point since 1870, with more adults living alone for long stretches of their lives. One cannot blame a single cause for a doubtlessly complex phenomenon, but according to a National Institute of Health report, pornography has been linked to various problems in sexual well-being and intimacy in relationships.

*   *   *

In the case of pornography and elsewhere, we have spent much of the last several decades deconstructing all sorts of conventions that punished certain behaviors and fostered others. In the abstract, our freedoms have grown as the guardrails have come down. But in more concrete ways, our sense of freedom might be diminished. Freedom without some sense of direction lacks substance. And if freedom is linked to flourishing, and flourishing is by nature social, the purely autonomous self might be at a loss in the anti-conventional world. "Freedom is like the magnetic needle of a compass," as Polish thinker Maciel Zieba wrote, "always pointing to something beyond itself."

LOBBY

No mention of 'lobbies' is to be found in the Constitution, nor does any statute declare them to be a governmental unit. Nevertheless they have over the course of time come to function as an active part of the American government in operation.

—James Burnham

To many Americans, lobbying is a grave and growing threat to good governance. It is also, as James Burnham understood, a practice deeply integrated into the operations of American government. So deeply entwined are the two that our government might have trouble operating if the lobbies suddenly disappeared.

The term itself comes from Great Britain and British politics. There, in the lobby of the House of Commons, journalists and other interested parties would stop lawmakers to chat, gossip, and, in some cases, ask for legislative favors.[54] In the United States, the term has come to refer to such favors. Lobbying covers all the efforts made by outside parties to influence government, especially in the writing of laws.

One can easily understand the motivation behind lobbying. When the government passes a law, its effects have real impact. Businesses can be crushed, or business opportunities opened. Private interests naturally want to shape the outcome for their own benefit.

What the public fears in this is that when lobbyists do their work the common good will be sacrificed on the altar of special interests. Ordinary citizens rightly worry that when laws are being written, shady fixers will be pleading for breaks that will be buried in a bill's complexities. Or, conversely, that lobbyists might derail legislation that would serve the broader society, but at the expense of the lobbyists' particular interests.

Those concerned about these dangers can only be horrified by the size of the lobbying industry. It is a huge and lucrative business. There are well over 10,000 lobbyists registered with the federal government. All of the biggest industries have lobbying arms, as do unions, foreign governments, environmental groups, and all kinds of other interests. Some famously potent lobbies include the National Rifle Association, the American Association of Retired Persons, the American Medical Association, and the American Israel Public Affairs Committee, an organization devoted to strong ties between the United States and Israel.

It makes sense to be wary of lobbies, yet here is something not often said aloud: They can be useful. One of the great dangers of legislating a nation as complex as the United States is acting with insufficient information. Legislators will often be stretched beyond reasonable limits if they try on their own to understand all the consequences and implications of the bills they vote on.

Lobbyists can and do help. Where members of Congress have little chance to master the ins and outs of, say, regulating the financial industry, it is the lobbyist's job to do so, and to provide legislators with in-depth views of likely effects of their legislation. At their best, lobbyists can help lawmakers craft laws that actually achieve the lawmakers' desired effects.

This aspect of lobbying flies in the face of popular opinion, but the more positive uses of lobbying should not be discounted. As one former U.S. Representative, Morris Udall, wrote, "[T]he major Washington lobbies are backed up by research staffs, specialists in various fields, speech writers, and public relations experts. Most are eager to provide drafts of speeches and information for Congressmen whose legislative interests are similar to theirs, in effect serving as an extension of a member's staff." Much lobbying takes place whereby lobbyists share goals with lawmakers, and are not seducing them to some legislative dark side.

*   *   *

However, whatever positive purposes the lobbies may serve, the potential for serious abuse remains. Lobbyists do not work for the public at large, but for the interests they represent. Nor could they stay in business if they did not produce the desired results—legislation that serves those interests—and their business is thriving.

To diminish the danger of lobbyists corrupting the legislative process, Congress has passed a series of laws, starting with the 1946 Federal Regulation of Lobbying Act. This law required, among other things, that professional lobbyists register with Congressional officials, the better to keep their actions under watch.

Fifty years down the road, a new law, the Lobbying Disclosure Act of 1995, was passed to strengthen the earlier one. It, in turn, was amended and reinforced by the Honest Leadership and Open Government Act of 2007. These laws had the effect of restricting gifts that lobbyists can make to lawmakers and curtailing the use of lobbyists' donations for campaign purposes. As the new laws make clear, for a lobbyist to make a campaign donation to a member of Congress in return for a particular legislative vote is considered bribery and could be prosecuted.

When pushed, however, efforts to restrict lobbying run into an opposing legal barrier. That is the First Amendment, with its protections of free speech, and, especially, the right to "petition government for a redress of grievances." As the Supreme Court has interpreted these elements of the First Amendment, lobbying generally is a protected activity, just like other forms of political advocacy.

Legal, too, are the natural fruits of lobbying: policies that advance specific interests. For example, high tariffs to protect American industry, which lobbyists argued for, were a longtime staple of national trade policy. Subsidies to sugarcane or corn growers, also supported by heavy lobbying, have likewise been prominent among national laws. So, too, have tax credits that support home-ownership, renewable energy, retirement savings, and various other goals. Lobbyists have had their hands in such policies for generations, and for better or worse will continue to be a fixture of American politics for the foreseeable future.

Majority Leader / Minority Leader

Chosen by the members of the majority party, the majority leader technically is not an officer of the House but of his political party. Nonetheless, it is inconceivable that the House could function without him.

—Carl Albert, House Majority Leader (1962–1971)

When the term *majority leader* crops up in the news, that news is always about Congress. The position is a congressional one, with a single majority leader in each house, the House of Representatives and the Senate.

But while the position of majority leader is congressional, it is not exactly an office of Congress. The position is never mentioned in the Constitution and was not created until early in the 20th century. There is no official charter that establishes it, no external authority that says, "leadership in Congress will be vested in a Majority Leader."

Instead, majority leaders are creations of the parties within Congress, Democratic and Republican. The majority referred to in the title is whichever party holds the majority of seats in either the House of Representatives or the Senate, and that party's chosen head is the majority leader. The party in the minority also chooses a chief, who is called the minority leader.

According to the rules of Congress, the majority party controls the legislative agenda in each house, and it is here that majority leaders wield their power. They have a great deal to say about what legislation will be considered and when it will appear on the legislative calendar. Majority leaders work closely with the rest of the leadership team—whips, committee chairs, and, in the case of the House of Representatives, the Speaker of the House—to coordinate the movement of bills, from committee mark-up to the "floor" votes that either pass or kill legislation. They have been likened to traffic cops, controlling the flow of legislative traffic, and no legislation gets through either house of Congress without the majority leader's blessing.

*   *   *

The job of the majority leader is complicated, and majority leaders must wear several different hats. To start, they represent their constituents back home. Like any other member of Congress, they must do this effectively or they run the risk of losing their seat, and, thus, their leadership position as well.

Majority leaders, however, have a second constituency to consider: their fellow party members in the House or the Senate. It is these fellow members who elect majority leaders to that position in the first place, and to retain it majority leaders need to serve the needs of those other party members. Thus, majority leaders will press a legislative agenda that suits the aims of party members and helps them politically. If leaders fail in this, one-time supporters can turn into opponents and drive them from the position, just like any other voting constituency.

To achieve their party's legislative goals, the majority leader must also look beyond Congress. They will, for example, confer with presidents when planning what legislation to pursue. Presidents, after all, hold veto power over Congress's work, so their views must be taken into account. If the majority leader and the president share legislative goals, cooperating can maximize their effectiveness.

When a majority leader and a president are from the same party, they will generally work together. But their interests can never be exactly the same, since they represent different branches of the government. This points to another responsibility of the majority leader, that of protector of his or her institution.

Consider the case of Alben Barkley. A Democrat from Tennessee, Barkley was Senate majority leader from 1937 to 1948. During much of that time, fellow Democrat Franklin D. Roosevelt was president. The two saw eye-to-eye on most things, and Barkley was generally ready to meet Roosevelt more than halfway in pushing for the president's programs. But Roosevelt was an exceptionally ambitious politician, and at times he pressed Barkley hard to overcome any opposition that arose in the Senate. Finally, in 1944, the president pushed too hard.

The issue in question was a tax bill. In the midst of war, Roosevelt wanted to raise extra taxes from certain industries to cover the government's extraordinary costs. As Barkley warned, however, the president's plan was distinctly unpopular in the Senate. Despite the warning, Roosevelt persisted in his demands and refused to compromise.

This put the two institutions, the presidency and the Senate, on a collision course, though both were led by Democrats. When the matter came to a head, it was Roosevelt who lost. Deeply accustomed to political victories, the president reacted sharply when the Senate passed a bill without his tax increases. Roosevelt not only vetoed the bill, but added a biting message that accused Congress of bowing to the demands of special interests.

Then it was Barkley's blood pressure that rose. No less livid than the president, he launched a blistering counter-attack. In a Senate speech, Barkley denounced the president's message, calling it "a calculated and deliberate assault upon the legislative integrity of every Member of Congress." To punctuate his words, the majority leader then resigned his position. Surprised by this rebellion from the usually compliant Barkley, Roosevelt commented, "Alben must be suffering shell shock."

Shell shocked or not, Barkley's resolve in the face of the president's attack electrified the Senate. As a formality, the Democratic caucus accepted his resignation, but then promptly re-elected him majority leader by a unanimous vote. Jubilant senators rushed out of their chamber to spread the word, and as they pushed their way through crowded halls, one cried, "Make way for liberty!" Barkley's defense of the integrity of the Senate marked a turning point in his own career, but more importantly, renewed the independent spirit of the Senate as a whole.

Thus, another hat for the majority leader to wear: As a high-ranking and highly public member of either the House or the Senate, the majority leader has a responsibility to protect the honor and prestige of those institutions. Any decline in the respect of those institutions can be placed at least partly at the majority leader's feet.

MARXISM

You cannot just sample Marxism ... you must be converted to it.

—Gyorgi Lukacs

The term *Marxism* appears infrequently in daily political discourse. Marxist notions, however, do, and for this reason it is worth exploring the term. In politics, Marxism is a species of thought descended from the German philosopher Karl Marx. Along with Charles Darwin, Sigmund Freud, and Friedrich Nietzsche, Marx was one of the nineteenth century's "bearded god-killers," men whose philosophies undermined long-held beliefs about human nature and the nature of society.[55] Even today, 150 years after his death, Marx's work continues to disturb the peace. "No thinker in the nineteenth century," claimed philosopher Isaiah Berlin, "has had so direct, deliberate and powerful an influence upon mankind as Karl Marx."

As Marx developed his philosophy, scientific thought provided a model. Just as physicists had found a single force—gravity—driving all kinds of motion, from the orbit of the Moon to falling rain, so Marx searched for an underlying law that moved human history. Under the surface, he wondered, what makes societies tick? Why, for example, do civilizations grow, change, and decay?

Marx claimed to find an answer. He argued that what is really at work in human history, under all its varied appearances, is in essence economic: work and the use of resources to provide for our material wants. Moreover, history demonstrates the way that economic development has always led to the division of society into classes, and to conflict among those classes. "The history of all society up to now is the history of class struggles," he wrote. As soon as agriculture developed, for example, a ruling class formed and began to exploit those beneath it. Thus, what should have been a great blessing for humankind—the ability to produce surplus food—led to an evil by which the few thrived by riding the backs of the many.

Early advances in agriculture produced something else, as well: a cultural revolution. For example, the growing complexity of society made laws necessary, along with a leadership class who would write and administer them. Written by rulers, those laws served their own interests, legitimizing their power. This dynamic was also behind all sorts of other cultural phenomena, from religious beliefs to educational practices. They all justified, celebrated, and reinforced the system that gave them life: exploitation of the workers.

What was true in early agricultural societies remains true through the ages. Ruling classes always promote their own interests, no matter how economic systems evolve. "What else does the history of ideas demonstrate than that the products of the intellect are refashioned along with the material ones? The ruling ideas of an age were always but the ideas of the ruling class."

It's here that Marx's thought proves most beguiling. Once one accepts his premise, it provides a remarkably versatile tool for analyzing virtually all customs and institutions. In the hands of believers, Marxism is like an X-ray machine that reveals deep structures in society that are otherwise hidden. Marxism sees all and judges all. This power—revelatory, one might say—gives Marxism a religious kick, and explains why an adherent like Gyorgi Lukacs compares the acceptance of Marxism to a conversion experience.

*   *   *

In politics, Marx's most concrete legacy was in the self-consciously Marxist governments in, among other places, Soviet Russia. But Marx's legacy has had an important, though less direct, impact elsewhere, as his ideas filtered out into the broader political environment. Out there, Marxist ideas "continue to survive, mutate, and reproduce in the wild," as law professor Glenn Reynolds put it.[56]

Those ideas have certain characteristics, stamped by Marxism's DNA, as it were. Marxist thought, for example, systematically devalues social traditions and institutions. When liberal democracies proclaim the "unalienable rights" of their people, for instance, Marxists claim that they are really defending a system that enriches the few (owners) at the expense of many (exploited workers). Those unalienable rights do not exist by nature. They have no existence apart from the wishful thinking (and political power) of the people who prefer to believe in them.

In this devaluation of core cultural ideals, Marxism has a leveling thrust. It has little interest in judging any given society by its own standards, nor by its prized achievements. So, where many Americans might take pride in the country's accomplishments, the Marxist stands at a critical distance and aims to deflate. For Marxists, the key question is not how impressive a culture's attainments may be. Rather, the fundamental one is always, who is oppressing or exploiting whom? And Marx's descendants can be impressively diligent in their searches. If Jane Austen's novels carry hidden messages supporting British colonialism, or the architecture of the Brooklyn Bridge implicitly reinforces the oppression of the working class, Marxist sleuthing will find it out.

This essential spirit—critical of broadly held values, on alert for any sign of oppression—can also be found at work in contemporary politics, broadly conceived. Marxist perspectives have substantial influence in the academy, notably in the application of "Critical Theory" to the law. Where traditional theories of law embrace the ideal of law as impartial, Critical Theory assumes otherwise. Its adherents expose (as they see it) the ways in which traditional law imposes unfair standards on oppressed minorities, racial or other. As law students steeped in its doctrines have graduated and taken their places in the legal system or other positions of social influence, they have spread the lessons of Critical Theory abroad with at least some effects on the law and on the broader culture.

It is unclear whether this approach actually makes for a more lawful, or better ordered, society. Nor, for that matter, is it clear whether that matters in the broader Marxist project of reversing oppression everywhere. Whatever benefits come from the familiar, practical application of the law may be beside the point, as Marxists prepare for future revolutions.

Perhaps Marxist critiques *can* work to our social benefit. It might be that Marxism, like strong medicine taken in careful doses, will prove healthful so long as we protect our vitals from its effects. But we ought to be under no illusions: the descendants of Marx aren't doctors, and it is the vitals they are aiming for.

Meritocracy

The sorting out of individuals according to ability is very nearly the most delicate and difficult process our society has to face.

—John W. Gardner

Unlike its etymological cousins *democracy* and *aristocracy*, *meritocracy* is not an ancient word. It was coined in the 1950s by a British sociologist, Michael Young, in titling his book, *The Rise of the Meritocracy*. Young did, however, draw on ancient languages to come up with the term: *merit*, from the Latin verb "to earn," and *-cracy*, from the Greek word for "rule."

Young needed a new word to describe a phenomenon germinating at the time in his homeland, the development of a ruling class that would hold power on the basis of merit. They would be people who had earned positions of leadership through proven talent and hard work, unlike Britain's traditional aristocracy, whose leadership was a matter of inheritance.

When Michael Young coined the term *meritocracy*, the British government was engaged in an effort to break the grip of that country's age-old class system. A key mechanism in that effort was a testing program in the schools that would identify promising students at an early age, no matter what social class they came from. Once identified, those students could be channeled into programs that would prepare them for leadership in various walks of life. In this way, testing served as an escalator for bright young people, lifting many out of the lower classes. Seen against the backdrop of Britain's traditional class divisions, the new meritocracy was conceived as a giant step toward democratization.

*   *   *

A good deal of what the British attempted in their drive toward meritocracy they learned from the United States. It included the idea of testing the young to identify intellectual potential. When the British started in earnest with this during the 1950s, the United States had been at it for decades. One keystone in American testing, the SAT, was first administered in the 1920s. Designed to measure the academic potential of students toward the end of high school, its results have long been used by colleges to assess the academic potential of students, and to sort the best—for their purposes—from the rest.

To its supporters (though not to its detractors), the SAT is egalitarian, since it does not discriminate except according to the student's performance on the test. Its administrators had no way of knowing "whether the youngster was in rags or in tweeds, and they couldn't hear the accents of the slum," as one author put it. "The test revealed intellectual gifts at every level of the population." And tens of thousands of talented students rode the SAT, or similar tests, to acceptance in good colleges and universities and, beyond, to fruitful careers.

The benefits of testing to such individuals are apparent, but the SAT's supporters thought the test served a crucial social need, as well. As society grows more complex, it needs ever-greater levels of expertise in the workforce, and improving our ability to find and develop those capabilities is a necessity. "Throughout the ages, human societies have always been extravagantly wasteful of talent," wrote John W. Gardner, one-time member of Lyndon Johnson's cabinet and a firm supporter of meritocratic education. "Today, as a result of far-reaching social and technological developments, we are forced to search for talent and to use it effectively. Among the historic changes that have marked our era, this may in the long run prove to be one of the most profound."

*   *   *

We are in the process of learning how right Mr. Gardner was about that. Our modern meritocratic system has been in place for decades, and through all those years its principles have been shaping our society. Elite colleges and universities have grown increasingly selective, for example. Like super-magnets, they attract some of the world's best minds, students and teachers alike. And in these elite institutions, those sharp students are prepared for leadership roles in all sorts of fields.

When employers in business, law, government, or the sciences look for exceptional talent, the graduating classes of the elite universities provide splendid hunting grounds. The most prestigious among them will seek out, and attract, the very best of that highly endowed cohort.

The result is a system in which talent and power grow together and are highly distilled. Social scientist Charles Murray calls the most powerful of this leadership class "the narrow elite" and puts their number at as few as 10,000. This narrow elite holds the commanding heights in various fields. "Some of them wield political power, others wield economic power, and still others wield the power of the media," Murray wrote. In their different spheres, this elite will determine how the Constitution is interpreted and enforced. It will organize the nation's financial life. It will set health care policy in the national government. It will determine what you will read, see, or hear in our most high-profile media. It will also be rewarded handsomely for its efforts.

*   *   *

Something about this result does not sit well. Meritocracy today rubs against the American grain, and it is worth asking why. After all, we celebrate the liberty to pursue happiness as we see fit, and we embrace individual initiative. Americans have always loved stories of a young man or woman who come out of nowhere to make good.

So why should today's meritocracy cause unease? The answer lies partly in its basic function. Just as it opens doors for the apparently talented, meritocracy closes doors for others. This can hardly help but breed resentment. Surely those who do not rise in the meritocratic sorting still have plenty to offer society, and know as much themselves.

The current meritocracy presents another problem, one that appears to be deepening. As the system continuously sorts out its winners, it draws an elite toward centers of power—Washington, New York, Silicon Valley—where its members form something of a new class. They marry fellow elites, socialize with them, and go to remarkable lengths to make sure their own children follow similar paths. To a degree, they are self-segregating in a movement that economist Robert Reich calls "the secession of the successful." If this trend deepens, our elite will increasingly live apart from the broader society. Carried toward its natural conclusion, this sorting process threatens to harden into a caste system.

Anything like that endpoint may be distant, of course. But the forces of meritocracy are real and have their effects. They include a worrisome psychological component, one that concerned Michael Young decades ago. The meritocracy not only rewards a subset of the population very well, it also emphasizes that they have earned and fully deserve their rewards, including the power that comes with their social leadership. In this way, meritocracy nourishes a sense of entitlement among its winners. This entitlement is made dangerous as they, self-segregating, have less contact with, and perhaps less sympathy for, those who will live under their leadership.

While fostering a sense of entitlement among the "winners," the meritocracy may have a damaging effect on those who do not excel. Among them it can encourage the notion that failure is also deserved. At its worst, meritocratic principles foster passivity in the face of a sense that one's prospects are determined by a cold-blooded fate—and by an elite that "losers" might easily come to resent.

Thus, meritocracy is a double-edged sword. A flowering of democratic culture in one sense, it also threatens to poison the wellsprings of democratic society.

MILITARY

I must study Politicks and War that my sons may have
liberty to study Mathematicks and Philosophy. My sons
ought to study Mathematicks and Philosophy, Geography,
natural History, Naval Architecture, navigation, Commerce
and Agriculture, in order to give their Children a right to
study Painting, Poetry, Architecture, Statuary, Tapestry and
Porcelaine.

—John Adams, President (1797–1801)

It is a useful, if disheartening, fact that so many of the world's nations came
into existence as a result of fighting. Dig into their histories, and one finds
conquests, wars for independence, or civil wars in the origins of seemingly all.
Warfare has been a primary element in political life from the start, and even today
virtually every nation has some sort of military force to defend borders, maintain
domestic peace, or respond to national emergencies.

The role that militaries play in national life, however, varies greatly, country
by country. In some societies, the military dominates to such a degree that it
stamps the society with its character. Nazi Germany and Imperial Japan in the
mid-20th century come to mind, fostering a highly militarized ethos throughout
their societies.

It is otherwise in today's democratic societies, including Germany and Japan,
where that degree of militarization seems alien. It has been a signal achievement
of liberal governance to separate the military from the civilian in politics and to
subordinate the former to the latter. Rather than a militarized ethos marking the
whole society, liberal government allows the flourishing of the widest range of
talents, interests and virtues. This is the society that John Adams, quoted above,

strove to build through his political career.

The United States Constitution, itself a landmark of liberal government, makes the subordination of the military clear. It does so through two key devices. First, it makes the president commander in chief of the armed forces. Second, it gives Congress the power of the purse over the military. Thus, the military's top officers answer to the president, a civilian; and the flow of money, without which the military cannot operate, is controlled by the legislature.

The United States military understands its subordinate position and reinforces it through its own rules and customs. This starts as soon as new recruits enter the service, whereupon they take the Oath of Enlistment. In the oath, they swear to "support and defend the Constitution" and "to bear true faith and allegiance to the same."

Beyond the Oath, the Department of Defense has service-wide rules to foster a depoliticized military. These rules distinguish between political activities that are allowable for active service members and those that are out of bounds. For example, men and women in the service can vote and take part in organized political activities, but cannot present themselves as representing the military when they do so. They can attend rallies or fundraisers, but not in uniform. They cannot speak at such rallies if the rallies are clearly partisan. Active service members can put political bumper stickers on their cars, but may not display large, partisan signs on their property.

There are more of these rules. Generally their goal is to distance the military from any overt political role or partisan affiliation. The power of the military must serve the will of the people as a whole, and never be seen as serving its own preferred ends.

*   *   *

The necessary presence of militaries in liberal democracies makes for something of a puzzle. They must exist and must hold some position in the government. Yet the military must also stand apart from the rest of liberal society.

It stands apart because in essence the military is not liberal. The virtues of liberalism—open-mindedness, the free exercise of one's gifts, generosity of spirit—are not those of the military.

The military depends for effectiveness on other, often opposing qualities: rigorous discipline, strong authority, and the voluntary sacrifice of the individual will to the demands of national defense. Take these away, and the military loses its effectiveness.

Moreover, the military could become dangerous without its essential order and discipline. Any place where the young, especially young men, have access to weapons and are schooled in violence is a place where discipline had better be strong. Whether in combat, in training, or even in off-hours, good order defuses potential disasters, the ingredients of which are present at most times.

The unique disciplinary demands of military life are reflected in its system of justice, which runs parallel to, but is nearly separate from, that of the civilian system. The military, for example, punishes offenses unknown to civilian law, such as insubordination or improper fraternization. In addition, the military holds its own trials for misconduct, and has its own jails and prisons.

For much of our history, the military has been left relatively free to handle its justice as it has seen fit, and more generally to maintain its distinct culture and ethos. Civilian authorities have tended to grant the military leeway in arranging its internal affairs, acknowledging the unique demands of its mission. The military, while subordinate, has also historically been substantially self-contained.

*   *   *

Yet the military has never been hermetically sealed from the broader society, nor immune from political force exerted from the civilian side. An interesting case of this came in the wake of the 1992 election of Bill Clinton as president. Clinton, attuned to cultural changes that were reshaping American society, thought the time was right to reform military policies concerning homosexuality. Traditionally, military leadership viewed homosexuality as a serious threat to unit cohesion and internal discipline, and strictly sanctioned it. But as the gay rights movement gathered momentum in the broader society, its advocates, including the president, began to press for reform of the military's rules.

Clinton, however, ran into strong opposition when he raised the subject of reform, including that of the military's leadership.[57] Navigating that opposition, Clinton settled for a halfway measure, imposing the "Don't ask, don't tell" (DADT) policy on the military by executive order. In essence, this called for the armed forces to stop actively screening out homosexuals and bisexuals who volunteered to serve, while maintaining its traditional understanding that homosexuality was incompatible with service.

The story did not end there, however. Over the next several years, active-duty gays, lesbians, and bisexuals began to file suit in the federal court system to protect themselves from the military's ongoing pressure against active homosexuality in the ranks. The resulting court decisions chipped away at DADT. By 2011, Congress too addressed the issue, passing legislation aimed at guaranteeing homosexuals equal protection within the armed services. Under pressure themselves, military leaders made the necessary adjustment and implemented new, more neutral policies toward homosexuality in the services.

Following this complicated path, the country found its way to a constitutionally satisfactory result. The major institutions of our national political life were all involved: the presidency, the courts, and the legislature. Through their interworking, the subordination of the military to civilian authority was renewed.

The confrontation over DADT, however, raises questions about the military's future. In a time of dramatic social change, in what ways will it be able retain its own distinct culture? And in what ways will the changing civilian culture press its values on the military?

With the potential for future conflict in mind, it is worth restating the old, tacit arrangement between civilian and military, if only because we tend to forget why some customs exist in the first place. The military and civilian worlds exist in tension that cannot be resolved. Civilian control of the military must be definite. But the military and its culture must remain distinct if it is to do its job. We are a liberal society that depends, to some degree, on an illiberal institution to insure our own survival.

NATION / NATIONALISM

A man must have a nationality as he must have a nose and two ears; a deficiency in any of these particulars is not inconceivable and does from time to time occur, but only as a result of some disaster, and it is itself a disaster of a kind.

—Ernest Gellner

There are two ways to think of the term *nation* and what nations are. One is the nation simply as an institution of government. To be without a nation in this sense would mean somehow living apart from the 150 or so national governments that cover virtually all of the inhabited world. The nation has become the basic building block of the world's political order and is the source of citizenship for most of the world's people.

However, when Ernest Gellner wrote that not having a nationality is seen as a "disaster" akin to not having a nose or ears, he had something deeper in mind than the merely institutional. He was thinking of the nation as a primary community to which we belong and a crucial source of personal identity. In this sense, nations are not merely institutional, but have specific histories, languages, customs, and lands, and to belong to a nation is to inherit these legacies as one's own. In this sense, too, a nation might not have its own institutional existence. The Kurds, Tibetans, and Basques all have a national identity without having their own state.

The roots of the word *nation* itself are useful here. Those roots go back to the Latin verb *nasci*, meaning "to be born," and by extension a nation is the land in which we are born. One could add that by providing much of the culture we inherit, nations serve as nurseries for our character. Nations themselves are like organisms, born and developing from particular origins. When a nation is threatened, one recognizes the danger posed to its people, not only as individuals but as members of a distinct group with its own coherent, social existence.

Without any nationality, we would be disconnected from that shared life, which is why Ernest Gellner describes it as a disaster. Being a member of a nation completes us, so the thought goes, giving us an identity that the solitary individual—if such a thing exists—cannot claim.

Gellner himself, it should be noted, did not celebrate nationalism. Though he understood its force in political life, he devoted much of his life to overturning the concept of national identity as a unifying ideal. He came of age in mid-20ᵗʰ century Austria, amid the devastation of World War II and the Holocaust, and saw nationalism as a prime factor in bringing those disasters about. Thus he opposed nationalism and all political systems that divided peoples and closed one group off from another.

Fighting against nationalism in the 20ᵗʰ century, however, was all uphill. No political force did more to shape the world during that time than nationalist feeling. In a rearview mirror, we recognize it in the aggressions of Germany and Japan that led to World War II. We see it too in the responses of other nations to their attacks. Nationalism added immensely to the intensity of that war.

We see the continued strength of nationalism around the world today as well, for example, in the independence movements of the Basques in Europe and the Uighurs in Central Asia. There are resurgent nationalist movements in many places, not just among subjugated ethnic groups. In Hungary, Germany, India, and other countries, potent nationalist movements are on the rise, powered in some cases by reactions against recent waves of immigration.

There are certainly plenty of people opposed to nationalism, and its appeal is far from universal. But if we think of the different social orders that might claim human loyalty, from clans and tribes to such supranational "communities" as the European Union or the United Nations, the nation appears to have a uniquely strong grip on public imagination around the world.

*   *   *

This seems true, at least partly so, of the United States as well. To outsiders, Americans often appear unusually patriotic, with visitors remarking on how common the national flag and other patriotic displays are here.

Even by the high standards of the past, however, nationalism appears to be on the ascent in the United States. Stimulated by such challenges as globalization and historically high rates of immigration, Americans are hearing more political arguments and slogans delivered in a distinctly nationalist vein—"Make America Great Again," for instance. Economic nationalists have been revising the American commitment to international free-trade, pursuing policies that instead enhance protection to American businesses and workers against foreign competition.

But nationalist feeling in a country as large and diverse as the United States will always have a different basis from that found in smaller, more homogenous countries. This is not a land in which a single ethnic group—with the major exception of Native Americans—has struggled to retain its own thousand-year-old cultural identity alongside that of a neighboring people. The United States lacks some of the "blood and soil" orientation found in, say, the Balkans, or various other parts of the world.[58]

Something else is also at work here that tempers the nationalist impulse. It is found in the First Amendment, which reads in part: "Congress shall make no law respecting the establishment of religion, or prohibiting the free exercise thereof…." With those words, the Constitution broke from a long tradition. According to that tradition, it was assumed that nations would naturally have a single, unifying religion, established as part of the state. That unity of church and state gave national governments a claim to undivided sovereignty, ruling over souls as well as bodies.

Like every nation, the United States depends on the devotion of its citizens. Unlike many, it draws a line on that devotion. Its citizens can, and many do, feel a higher loyalty than that owed to the state. This is a nation that, while it might be loved, is, by the logic of the Constitution itself, never to be worshipped.

PARLIAMENT/PARLIAMENTARIAN

Nowadays, the physical instrument of leadership (both in the military and the political spheres) is no longer a blow from a sword but quite prosaic sound waves and drops of ink—written and spoken words.

—Max Weber (1918)

Governments around the world and over time have been amazingly diverse. But the political historian S. E. Finer thought that all those different systems of governance could be boiled down to a very few basic types. Most fundamental were the two he called "palace" and "forum." In palace governance, decisions are made behind the scenes, within the palace, as it were, where power is concentrated in the hands of the few. Once made, decisions are handed down for all to live by.

Forum governance is nearly the opposite. Power is not concentrated behind the scenes, nor are its decisions imposed as if they were mandates from heaven. Decisions are made in the open, in public forums, argued over by the people themselves, or at least by their representatives.

The central institution of forum governing, at least in the modern era, is the representative legislature, and among all the world's legislatures there is one that has a special place of honor: the British Parliament, or, as it has been called, the "Mother of Parliaments." Britain's Parliament is a bicameral body, with its House of Commons and House of Lords. Between the two, all the nation's people are represented in the legislating—that is, lawmaking—process, at least in theory. Thus, the laws of Parliament reflect the interests of all the British people.

The nature of Parliament also means that the British people grew to expect representation, to have some say, in effect, in the making of laws. This expectation has been carried wherever British political ideals have been transplanted, especially through colonization. Historian Finer likened the spread of British parliamentary ideals to a "contagion," racing abroad like fire. Beginning in the 17th century, parliaments were established in Canada, Australia, India, South Africa, Kenya, Uganda, Ghana, New Zealand, Jamaica, Fiji, and numerous other countries.

Although the United States has no parliament in name, the basic parliamentary idea took very firm root here, too. From the earliest years colonists founded representative assemblies that made the rules that ordered their various societies. The House of Burgesses in the Virginia colony was the first, opening in 1619, but others followed in time. Finally, with the Constitution in 1787, the new United States capped this history by forming a national government with a representational, bicameral legislature—Congress—at its heart.

*   *   *

What makes government necessary is trouble. With problems come questions about how to respond. Palace politics has its characteristic ways: power politics behind closed doors, then edicts for the people.

Parliamentary systems differ, and the key difference is implied in the word *parliament* itself. The word is rooted in the French verb *parler*, "to speak." The earliest parliaments in England were places where regional leaders came together to discuss, or parley, about political problems.

Legislatures derived from Parliament still revolve around this elemental function: open discussion. As with the British Parliament, all basic interests of a nation are represented in these forums, where problems are discussed and remedies are proposed. Through deliberation and a vote, the assembly settles on a policy that represents, as well as possible, the varied interests of the nation.

Talk is the lifeblood of parliamentary government, always including disagreement. One benefit of its process is that through their disagreements, parliaments institutionalize self-criticism. Unlike authoritarian governments, where disagreements are hidden, parliamentary legislatures function best when they raise disputes and air them openly.

One-time American legislator T. V. Smith noted something crucial about the way parliamentary legislatures confront difficult challenges. The effect of gathering itself is crucial. It is nearly impossible for one person to *really* see an issue from other perspectives. That only happens when people with differing views speak for themselves. Parliamentary governments provide the forum for exactly that to happen: representatives with diverse points of view, but equal standing, make their case before their peers and on behalf of their constituents.

*   *   *

To allow open debate, while also allowing legislatures to accomplish their basic job, rules have developed over time. In the United States we call them parliamentary procedures, and each house in Congress has an official *parliamentarian*. His or her job is to make sure the rules are followed, as bills are maneuvered through the complicated legislative process. The ultimate goal of parliamentary procedures is not perfection of the legislation itself, but useful deliberation. Discussion and debate should improve the quality of bills as they are considered, and should weed out the worst that are considered.

But something else is at stake in parliamentary processes. To pass a bill in a diverse, representative legislature, supporters must assemble a majority to vote the bill into law. To do so, members will not only try to persuade others, but must accommodate other points of view. Through discussion, debate, and compromise, legislators build consensus among themselves. In fact, as representatives, they are doing so indirectly for all citizens. Consensus within the legislature translates into broad support of the governed, and practical, sustainable, if unspectacular, government in the land. This, more than the perfection of the legislation itself, is the hallmark of parliamentary governance, and it can only be produced through its defining feature: talk.

PARTY

The Rancour of that fiend the Spirit of Party had never appeared to me, in so odious and dreadful a Light…. It destroyed all sense and Understanding, all Equity and Humanity, all Memory and regard to truth, all Virtue, Honor, Decorum, and Veracity. Never in my life was I so grieved and disgusted with my species.

—John Adams, President (1797–1801)

For many of the Founders of the United States, including John Adams, the whole idea of political parties inspired a feeling somewhere between concern and horror. (Note that *party* in the political sense has nothing to do with the get-togethers people enjoy on, say, birthdays or New Year's. The Founders were okay with those.) In politics, *party* means division. It is related to "parting," like parting one's hair or parting ways with a friend. Parties are evidence of disunion, of one side separated from and opposing another.

Early in its history, the United States was a small, powerless nation facing long odds for survival. Internal division in the face of threats might easily have made a quick end to what has been called "the American experiment." So unity seemed vital to leaders such as John Adams and George Washington, who warned in his farewell address that political parties threaten "to become potent engines by which cunning, ambitious, unprincipled men will be enabled to subvert the power of the people and to usurp for themselves the reins of government…."

However much they feared parties, Washington and the other Founders could do little to keep them from actually forming. In fact, some of the most prominent Founders played key roles in building our earliest parties, doing so even under the nose of President Washington. Within Washington's cabinet, its two leading figures squared off in political warfare, each vying to set the country on his favored course. Secretary of the Treasury Alexander Hamilton wanted the president to pursue a program of economic development, led by a strong, active national government. Opposing Hamilton was Secretary of State Thomas Jefferson, who wished the young country to retain its largely agricultural basis, and wanted the balance of political power to remain with the states rather than with the national government.

Presented with these differing visions for the country, the politicians of the era found themselves choosing sides. Those who backed Hamilton's program came to be called Federalists, and those who stood with Jefferson, Democratic Republicans.

One can understand why Adams and Washington feared the spirit of party, but they were contending with deep currents in human nature. One is the powerful human tendency to disagree. Another is the tendency when disagreeing to join with others to gain leverage against opponents. This partisan propensity is unstoppable in a legislature where votes are cast to pass legislation and where majorities win the votes. Bonding together to win is nature at work, and members of Congress did so from the start, foreshadowing the rise of our modern political parties.

*   *   *

The growth of our parties since the Founding has been spectacular. Where the earliest American parties barely existed as formal organizations, today's Democratic and Republican parties are huge, highly structured, and well funded, with national offices as well as hundreds of state and local chapters. Party membership runs from ordinary citizens to the top elected officials in the nation. For the Democrats, the total number comes to around 45 million; for the Republicans, around 33 million. Both parties have specially organized wings for the young, for women, and for citizens living abroad.

The major parties also employ large professional staffs that include highly trained pollsters, election organizers, fundraisers, and policy specialists. All this expertise is organized around the effort to elect party members to offices nationwide, and the parties are highly active in seeking out candidates to run at all levels, funding them and advising their campaigns. Once elected, those officials will be expected to act in coordination with the party and its leadership. Party leaders are never amused by mavericks and have tools at their disposal to punish the overly independent, such as withholding party resources from future campaigns.[59]

Unity gives a party power, which in turn can be shared by individual members. Almost all the leading figures in American politics are members of one or another major party, and most are careful to demonstrate their loyalty to these political homes.

Although parties are powerful political operations, they are separate from the basic institutions of our government. The Constitution, for instance, makes no mention of them. Parties have instead grown up alongside the structures of government, deeply entwined with those institutions, yet distinct. At the same time, it is hard to imagine contemporary government without the major parties. Much of what government accomplishes, good or bad, is accomplished through party channels and might not be possible without them.

*   *   *

The most important thing parties accomplish, though, has little to do with any specific policy. To see this other accomplishment clearly, start with a basic fact about the United States: This is a very big, very diverse nation; and in our politics, we must do something exceedingly difficult. We must create, from all that diverse opinion, enough of a unified will to give our government direction. With a population over 330 million people, there are plenty who have their own preferences as to what government should or should not do. Yet we cannot have, for example, a thousand different foreign policies or ten thousand national budgets. Managing just one is plenty difficult.

So somehow, we need to fuse diverse views into a very few viable political options that can serve as a platform for governing. The parties, despite their questionable reputation, carry a heavy burden in bringing this about. Doing so actually comes naturally for them. To accomplish their own goals, parties will articulate a message and publicize it, in order to attract support. In this way, the parties spell out specific, practical political options for the voters to choose from.

With party programs presented to them, voters then rally to one or another, or to none at all. But the parties give them a plausible set of policies to respond to, freeing individuals from the burden of thinking up their own.

The dynamic here, however, is not simply a top-down presentation of options by the parties to the public. It is more a complex feedback loop. If parties are to survive, they must take stock of whether voters like their message. This can involve some hard self-examination at times. When parties lose decisive elections, for example, their leaders often find themselves at war behind closed doors, sorting out how to re-present their message.

These fights often follow a pattern. One faction says the party must emphasize its central message, the better to motivate its core supporters. Meanwhile, another faction says the party must reach out beyond its core and appeal to a broader public. With a true-believing hard core squaring off against centrist "softies," party infighting can be bitter.

The parties get little credit for these internal brawls. The party's supporters hang their heads during the fight, while partisan opponents watch and gloat over their misfortune. This reaction is misguided, though. With their infighting, the parties are responding to public opinion, sensing its moods, and deciding how best to appeal to it. Only by doing so can they present a persuasive program and thus provide voters a practical way to put their electoral power to use. The parties, in effect, create actual political power from the formless potential of popular will. Through internal fights and other means, parties build the coalitions that make governance possible.

PLURALISM

> If it becomes national policy to make the public values of
> Kokomo or Salt Lake City indistinguishable from those
> of San Francisco or New Orleans, we have as a nation
> abandoned the social experiment symbolized by the phrase
> 'E Pluribus Unum.'
>
> —Peter Berger and Richard John Neuhaus

The Latin motto *E pluribus unum* is worth translating correctly; some prominent politicians have gotten it backwards.[60] It means "Out of many, one." That is, a unified nation, the *unum*, can come from a diverse population, the *pluribus*. Yet how should we do this? Should the nation's diversity yield to the demand for unity, or should we live with less unity and embrace our differences? Whatever else it is, American pluralism is a balancing act.

Pluralism is also an elemental fact of life in the United States and in most modern nations. Immigration is at historically high levels, and national populations reflect this. As of 2017, for example, nearly 45 million residents in the United States were born in foreign countries, roughly one out of every seven. Similar levels are found in Sweden and the United Kingdom—roughly 14 percent foreign born—and immigration has brought tens of millions of foreign-born residents to other nations in Europe. Around the world in 2015, almost a quarter billion people were living beyond the borders of their home country.

Ethnic and racial pluralism, however, is only part of the pluralism story. It also concerns differences of beliefs and convictions—differences of culture, in other words. Apart from race and ethnicity, cultural differences can be plenty sharp. White secularists might well have have stronger political disagreements with white Evangelicals than with secular immigrants from India.

*   *   *

Pluralism presents political and constitutional quandaries, ones that the American
Founders had to face squarely. They wanted the will of the people to guide national
government, but knew that regional differences would make that difficult to manage. What the people of New York wanted would differ from what Rhode Islanders
wanted, and both from what North Carolinians wanted. So one fundamental task
for the Constitution was to provide a process that *creates* a sovereign national will,
conjuring it out of the varied opinions of a pluralist people.

This is what the American Constitution does. At the national level, legislators
from around the country gather in Congress, representing the opinions of their
constituencies. In Washington, they are, metaphorically at least, locked in a room
to battle it out over what laws will or will not pass.

Those representatives reflect the diversity of the people as a whole. In the House
of Representatives today, for example, members include Muslims, Mormons,
Evangelical Christians, mainstream Protestants, Catholics, Jews, and atheists. There
are lawyers, members of the military, business owners, and ex-athletes, including
one woman who fought professionally in the mixed martial arts world. Whatever
laws can pass the gauntlet of review by this exceptionally diverse group will amount
to the sovereign will. From many, one, as the motto says.

*   *   *

It is easy to lose sight of what a remarkable achievement this is. Governing is difficult under any circumstances, but it is a particular challenge in the United States,
which has a diversity unmatched by any nation in history. To create a system of
government in which all elements of such a pluralistic society have some voice, and
none are legally subjugated, is an achievement for the ages.

But it is not an achievement that we necessarily find fulfilling. Pressing the
political hopes of such a diverse people through the meat grinder of constitutional
processes cannot produce policies that satisfy everyone. Generally, in fact, it will
produce compromises that hardly anyone really likes, at least profoundly. The
system is democratic, but it is no crowd pleaser.

We ought, by now, to expect that. The Constitution was never designed to
serve our wishes, but rather to protect our liberties. But we find it frustrating not
to demand more from the system. We want our political life to reflect our own
values. Where we can use power to bring others into line with those values, we do.

Herein lies the significance of the various Christian baker and florist controversies
that have erupted in recent years. The pattern goes something like this: LGBT
customers ask Christian store-owners to supply a product that celebrates same-sex

marriage. Those owners refuse on the grounds of religious conscience: they see same-sex marriage as a violation of God's will. In response, the customers file a lawsuit, seeing their own civil rights as compromised. The rights claimed by the parties involved cannot be reconciled. Nor, in our current mood, will those claims be put aside. We are not inclined these days to live and let live.

Pluralism means real, deep disagreement, of a sort that cannot be wished away. Theologian Aidan Nichols made a useful, if challenging, point about this. If our deeper beliefs can be reconciled, then society is not really "radically pluralist." But if our differences really are in conflict, "then the human environment in which we live is not a society at all, but an uneasy collection of potentially alternative societies."

"Uneasy" is a good adjective to describe the present-day United States. Yet we should take consolation from the facts on the ground. Americans live side-by-side, day in and day out, generally with remarkable good will toward one another, a fact that news headlines rarely reflect. The challenges posed by pluralism are real and will test us in coming decades. But, given that contemporary democracies are the most diverse in history, we can at least say this: No nation has done better at navigating such pluralism than we are doing today.

POLICE

The police are the public and the public are the police; the
police being only members of the public who are paid to give
full time attention to duties which are incumbent on every
citizen in the interests of community welfare and existence.

—Robert Peel

Taking *police* as a verb, we can say with confidence that societies have been policing themselves since the beginning of organized government. Every society will have its norms, rules, and taboos. And every society, as far as we know, will have its renegades. Hence the need for policing—that is, for enforcing society's rules and restraining those who would damage its fabric. In this broad sense, *police* is always a political term. It has to do with the self-protection of the *polis*—the people and their state.

While some form of policing must have been present since the earliest nations and states, police as a distinct, official force have been less of a historical fixture. We know what they look like. We recognize the uniforms, badges, and marked cars. Yet organized, uniformed police forces are actually relatively new.

In America, for example, the earliest ancestors of today's police were a miscellany of local, often part-time, officials, far too irregular to be considered a real force or profession. They included night-watchmen, constables, sheriffs, deputies, and posses. Their work had an improvised, decentralized character. To the degree that it was organized, it was by village, town, or city. However improvised it may have been, though, policing was always necessary and always present in some form.

The American police story of the last 350 years has been one of dramatic evolution. Over time, police have become far more organized, professional, and disciplined by the law. But it has taken a long while. For example, it was not until the mid-19th century that city cops wore uniforms for the first time, or that the first state police forces were founded. National police forces followed not much later, with the Federal Bureau of Investigation (FBI) dating to 1908.

Despite all the change, however, some things have remained the same since the early years. Our police forces are still remarkably decentralized, with more than 20,000 distinct police agencies around the country, many being locally based.[61] And the essential job of the police has remained the same as well. That job relates to a legal concept, known as *police power*, a common enough term in constitutional law, though one rarely mentioned in the news. According to *Encyclopedia Britannica,* police responsibilities focus on "the promotion and maintenance of the health, safety, morals, and general welfare of the public." The basic job of the police is to step in where these values are threatened and protect against their violation.

*   *   *

It is said that one defining characteristic of legitimate government is that it has a monopoly on the use of deadly force within its territory, and in many countries the police are the primary holders of that monopoly.[62] Being on the front line in enforcing public order, police are armed and authorized to use physical force when necessary in the line of duty. In this regard, they are in a category of their own. Our police have legal rights in this regard that ordinary civilians do not.

Yet Americans have never entirely subscribed to the doctrine of the state's monopoly on force. We have always seen the government as a creation of the people. And if anyone holds a monopoly on force, it is the people themselves, who yield some, but not all, of that power to the state.

Our relationship to the police is marked by this fact. We have, for example, held more firmly to the right to bear arms than many other nations. We also have a robust tradition of the right to self-defense. In addition, we have long had large numbers of private security agents, who number over a million in the United States today.

Despite these factors, we do delegate a great deal of power to the state and the police because we understand that social order is safer in official than in exclusively private hands.

However, delegating that power to official hands is no simple matter, because the public is not of one mind on policing. People disagree about how much power the police should have and how that power should be used. Consider the Black Lives Matter movement. According to its advocates, police have often used far too much deadly force against members of minority communities. Agree or not, every person must recognize the potential for danger here: Police power must be used impartially, and always for the safety of the public as a whole.

Thus, the police are subject to strict rules and oversight, and those rules are determined through politics. For example, elected officials, especially mayors, have a responsibility to oversee police behavior, administered through their appointed police commissioners. And citizens can use the courts to defend themselves against police abuse. Thus, through various political and judicial functions, the public exercises control over the police.

In recent years, municipal rules allowed New York City police great leeway to stop and frisk young men on the streets in search of weapons. But many saw "stop and frisk" as a violation of civil liberties. With class-action lawsuits against that procedure and a change in elected political leadership, the rules were changed, and the use of "stop and frisk" greatly reduced there.

There is no fixed point in this balancing act, however. As long as police are accountable to the public and the people themselves differ on how to define the abuse of police power, we will continue to adjust and readjust the rules that govern police and their actions.

POLITICS

The great Question which in all Ages has distorted Mankind and brought on them the greatest part of those mischief's which have ruin'd Cities, depopulated Countries, and disordered the Peace of the World, has been, Not whether there be Power in the World, nor whence it came, but who should have it.

—John Locke

W ords often lead double lives. On the one hand they have their strict definitions. On the other hand, they can carry connotations based on popular opinion. The word *politics*, for example, carries strong and negative innuendoes. It often suggests posturing, double-dealing, and self-indulgence, as in "They're playing politics again in Washington!" or, "God how I hate politics—it's all a bunch of lies."

Yet the ancient Greeks hardly thought of politics with this negative spin, and since they invented the term we might benefit from recalling the way they did think of it. The word is derived from the word *polis,* or "city-state," the basic political unit of the ancient Greeks. The polis had a central significance in their social thought, since they believed that community itself was fundamental to satisfying human life. As Aristotle wrote, "Man is by nature a political animal."

Greater than a neighborhood or a village, the polis was big enough to serve all human needs. It was a center for learning, commerce, military might, and the arts. The polis was a crucial environment, a seedbed for all human achievement, and for this reason its health was paramount. Here is Aristotle again: "[I]f all communities aim at some good, the state or political community, which is the highest of all, and which embraces all the rest, aims at good in a higher degree than any other, and at the highest good."

In its strict meaning, politics is about the guidance of the polis, about "the business of attending to the community's overall well-being," as legal scholar Anthony Kronman put it. That includes seeing to its survival, of course, but also its flourishing. To the Greeks, guiding the polis demanded the highest capabilities a leader could bring to the job: the wisdom to understand what the polis needed, as well as the greatness of spirit necessary to lead others. Where we so often associate politics with cheap tricks, dishonesty, and personal smallness, it was for the ancient Greeks the scene of the highest dramas a people could face, and the supreme test of their capabilities.

*   *   *

In daily discourse, though, when we want a term that captures this nobler aspect of political life, we might use *statesmanship* rather than *politics*. For us, before it is about high leadership, politics is about the nitty-gritty struggle through which we hash out questions of who will lead and how society will solve its pressing problems.

In practice, this means competition. No community is so unified in its interests, goals, and values that it can come to any simple consensus about those basic political issues. There are always contenders for leadership, for example, and as they vie for leadership, they must appeal to different, conflicting interests for support.

Those interests vary a great deal. People are always concerned about their own well-being and that of their families, so pocketbook issues always matter. But think, too, of all the broader concerns that mark today's political landscape. Out in the public are people who believe that the biggest challenge we face is social inequality, others who think it is foreign threats, or cultural disorder, or climate change, or racial discrimination. There are deep and differing notions of what is good or bad for society and its individual members. These varied opinions can never add up to a consistent, unified political will, and the conflicts embedded there are the starting point for politics. Politics is a matter of leaders gathering enough power from competing interests to guide the community forward.

Though at times we joke about politics, it is worth recalling that in the broad scope of history, this effort to gather and use power has often been an unspeakably brutal matter. It is politics of a sort when tyrants—the Stalins and Hitlers and Maos—seize power and rule through violence and terror.

In a constitutional state, however, the struggle for power is channeled into lawful processes. The processes, at least in a democracy, are messy. Cobbling together laws that can pass the scrutiny of the people, with all their varied interests, is always a matter of trimming and coalition building. No one alone gets to determine what policies a given state will follow. As Otto von Bismarck, the 19th century German statesman, famously put it, "[P]olitics is the art of the possible, the attainable—the art of the second best."

We employ this "art" to solve problems and to prepare for an unpredictable future. In one sense, however, we are fated to fail: as problems fade, others take their place, in a never-ending sequence.

There is an often-used metaphor that puts this in perspective. Governing is something like sailing a ship, with the governor as helmsman. However, the ship of state sails with no final destination. To govern well means navigating all the storms that societies face, staying afloat as best a state can. But with no final destination, there is no harbor over the horizon, no time when all the politics are done and settled. The ship of state sails on, until it can sail no further.

POPULISM

Vox populi, vox dei. (The voice of the people is the voice of God.)

—Traditional

In recent years, populism seems to be on the rise, and use of the term has been more frequent lately than at any time in decades. Donald Trump's 2016 election, for example, is often described as a populist eruption, but the current populist wave is also international in scope. The roiling politics in Great Britain, with Brexit, as well as the current leadership in Hungary, India, Brazil, and elsewhere can all be seen as evidence of populism on the rise.

What ties them together? Populism is not quite an ideology, and Brazil's populist leaders would doubtless differ from those of India on the specifics of policy. Populism is more like a wave of political emotion. The term is, of course, related to words such as *popular* and *people (populus* in Latin), and populism is, broadly speaking, the belief that government must satisfy the will and interests of ordinary people, first and foremost.

Yet populism is never simply that. It does not really exist without that antithesis of the ordinary people: the "elite." When populists speak of "the people," they mean the disempowered, the salt of the earth, the average guy, and always in contrast to the powerful, the rich, the intellectuals, and the trendsetters.

Moreover, populism in politics rides waves of resentment. The "people" in populism are the people aggrieved, frustrated, and resentful. One might hear of a politician tapping into "a cauldron of populist anger," but never of a politician appealing to "the reservoir of populist contentment." Populists are always mad as hell, and they're not going to take it any more.

It is hard to stay angry forever, and this is one reason populism is not a constant in our politics. It rises and falls. We had a major populist movement in the late 19th century, fueled by the anger of farmers against railroads, banks, and a government they saw as corrupt. Now a new wave of populism has risen in recent years. Both here and abroad, populist sentiment is fueled by frustration with mainstream political leadership. Often that frustration centers on immigration policy, with populists lining up against relatively open national borders. But there are plenty of other issues that raise populist hackles, including free international trade and globalization.

Since populism is not so much a set of policies as a public mood or mindset, politicians of both the right and the left may tap into its power. But while populism can serve the purposes of the left or the right, it is often harder for the left to capture its force. Populism sees itself, for starters, as a movement of ordinary people. As self-conscious commoners, populists are not inclined toward the upending of the social order, however much they demand political change. Populists are often defensive of social traditions and fearful of changes that threaten their sense of place within an orderly society. There is often an embrace of nostalgia in the populist ranks, an example of which can be found in Donald Trump's 2016 campaign slogan: "Make America Great Again."

*   *   *

In American politics, holding tight to the established order means holding tight to the Constitution, and populists here often see themselves as defenders of the spirit of the Constitution. It would surely play poorly to attack it on talk radio, for example.

Yet it is worth asking how well the populist sensibility, or "take" on things, actually meshes with the Constitution. This is no simple matter. There is plenty in the Constitution for populists to embrace, especially the fundamental fact that power, under it, ultimately rests with the people. Their will drives government; in fact, the legitimacy of the Constitution itself is based on the will of the people, as emphasized by its opening words: "We the People . . . ."

At the same time, there is a great deal in the Constitution that is tailor-made to frustrate the populist. Populism depends on a fundamental, us-versus-them polarity. It sees "the people" as a natural political force, one that must stay unified to accomplish its ends.

The Constitution, however, works against such unity in government. It divides power, among the branches of the government, for example, and pits competing interests against one another. Crucially, it does so in the legislative branch, where the will of the people reigns, and where populism might be expected to flourish.

But there power is divided between the two houses of Congress, and in the more representative House, we find power divided again among its 435 members. Because each House member represents one particular geographical district, the Constitution diffuses legislative power among all the varied interests found across the nation. When populist anger flows into Congress, its force is often splintered into prickly factions, as diverse as the people themselves.

Recent history provides an example. When Barack Obama was president, populist critics mercilessly attacked his signature legislation, the Affordable Care Act. To hear those critics, the ACA was the most destructive legislation in living memory. If the opportunity ever presented itself, populist politicians assured their supporters, they would toss it out in an instant.

For better or worse, that opportunity did in fact come their way in 2016. Populist champion Donald Trump took the presidency that year, as Republicans, often of a populist stripe, won majorities in both houses of Congress. Thus all the political stars came into alignment, and if they wanted to undo the Affordable Care Act, little stood in their way.

Despite several tries, however, the Republicans found it impossible to repeal the ACA. On the surface, they had all the power they needed, but supposed populist unity came unglued under the pressure of actually legislating in Congress. The interests of those populists, combined with all the other members of the legislature, proved more diverse than populist pretensions could account for.

Something similar often happens when populist feeling meets the realities of legislating. When faced with the details of writing and passing laws, one sees that the apparent unity masks natural disagreements. The Constitution does not paper over the nation's diverse interests; it draws them into government and gives them a voice in Congress.

This is not to say that populism plays no constructive role in American government. Yet populist anger is difficult to translate into effective legislation: laws that actually benefit the very diverse people in whose names they are written.

PRESIDENT

> Though the powers of the office have sometimes been grossly abused, though the presidency has become almost impossible to manage, and though the caliber of the people who have served as chief executive has declined erratically but persistently from the day George Washington left office, the presidency has been responsible for less harm and more good, in the nation and the world, than perhaps any other secular institution in history.
>
> —Forrest McDonald

Whether Forrest McDonald was right or wrong in making this arresting claim about the American presidency, one thing is certain. He could never have made it persuasively about any other American political institution—not Congress, nor the Supreme Court, nor any other. The presidency is without doubt the preeminent institution in American political life.

Which is interesting, in light of attitudes toward it at the time of the Founding. When the Constitution was written, there was real reluctance to include such a strong, unified executive office in the governmental scheme. The colonists had just had their experiences with such an executive, King George III of Great Britain, and had little appetite to repeat the experience.

So to create a new government that included a powerful executive leader was a hard sell when the Constitution was written. This concern was reflected in the choice of the term *president* itself, which was favored over other candidates, such as *governor*. At the time of the Founding, the word *president* suggested passivity as much as power. In its etymological midsection, one finds the root Latin verb, *sedere*, "to sit," with its decidedly inactive connotations. Presidents preside over gatherings without taking part in the scrum of advocacy. At the Constitutional Convention, for example, George Washington was president, lending the convention his great dignity, but he stood above the arguments taking place there.

As a symbolic matter, choosing the term *president* was useful for placating opponents of a strong executive. But the framers of the Constitution had to grapple with more substantive matters, too. They had to state in concrete terms the rules that would define the presidency, and this meant confronting the core challenge of the Founding: how to give the national government the power necessary to survive and prosper, while keeping that power in check.

Many of the Founders saw the executive office as a key to this challenge. "Energy in the executive is a leading character in the definition of good government," Alexander Hamilton insisted. And, in arguing against an executive council (as one option to the presidency), James Wilson wrote, "By appointing a single magistrate we secure strength, vigor, energy, and responsibility in the executive department." Yet in the face of those arguments, opponents expressed their dismay. Patrick Henry, for example, warned that the presidency, as conceived by the Constitution, was "an awful squint toward monarchy."

What the Constitution actually says about the presidency is mostly found in Article 2, and the president's job description is found there: "The executive Power shall be vested in a President . . ." and "he shall take Care that the Laws be faithfully executed." In other words, the laws come from Congress, and it is the president's job to see that they are carried out.

Beyond that, the Constitution offers a handful of specifics about the president's powers. One is that the president is commander in chief, or the ultimate head of the nation's military. The president also has the power to make treaties with other nations, subject to confirmation by the Senate: the president has always been the nation's acknowledged leader in foreign relations. Similarly, the president appoints ambassadors, Supreme Court justices, and other judges in the federal courts, as well as heads of the Cabinet-level departments (again with the Senate's approval).

The president is also granted the power to veto legislation coming out of Congress. This is not, strictly speaking, an executive function, but instead involves the president in legislative matters. With the threat of a veto, Congress has to take into account the president's view of pending legislation.

Beyond these specifics, however, the Constitution is mostly silent about presidential powers. Since the Founding, presidents have pressed to expand those powers, the exact limits of which have been a matter of serious contention from the start.

*   *   *

Fast forward 230 years, and a great deal has changed both in the country and in the presidency. Not only has the United States grown enormously, but it has survived the most profound challenges imaginable, from world wars to great depressions, confronting the legacy of deep racial inequality, terrorist attacks, natural disasters and more.

To deal with massive challenges, one must have commensurate powers. But the United States government was designed to diffuse power in its branches, and not to deal efficiently with the industrial-scale problems of the 20th century. It had to adapt in order to bring sufficient power to bear on them, and one primary adaptation was the growth of the presidency's power.

We see evidence of this in Theodore Roosevelt's career. With rapid industrial growth, Roosevelt saw a need for government to limit the power of some corporations and to regulate business in ways government never had before. He put together a legislative program, which included laws to accomplish these goals, and called it "the Square Deal." Roosevelt then used the presidential "bully pulpit" to spread the word.

This Square Deal was fertile in its way, being the father of all the presidential programs that would follow, including Franklin D. Roosevelt's "New Deal," John F. Kennedy's "New Frontier," and Lyndon Johnson's "Great Society." The rise of such programs in the 20th century points to an important fact of our governance: presidents have largely captured the legislative initiative from Congress. They, more than ever before, determine the main directions of our lawmaking and what challenges we will address through legislation.

In retrospect, this growth in the president's legislative power seems all but inevitable. As a single leader, elected in a national vote, the president is in a unique position to spell out a programmatic legislation to meet national challenges. Congress, representing constituents of districts and states with widely divergent interests, faces a nearly impossible task in coming together to identify problems and articulate solutions in the same way.

*   *   *

Of course, presidents are not all-powerful, and traditional checks and balances are still in place. Congress still has a great deal to say about what bills become law. And the judiciary still judges the constitutionality of presidential actions.

In addition, the federal bureaucracy often acts as an institutional anchor. Made up of millions of employees in the executive departments, the "administrative state" tends to hold fast as presidents try to steer government in new directions. Fighting this bureaucracy, Franklin D. Roosevelt once said, was like punching a feather bed. "You punch it with your right and you punch it with your left until

you are finally exhausted, and then you find the damn bed just as it was before you
started punching."

Yet there is no doubt about the president's commanding position in American
government. While institutional safeguards remain, the political logic of our
times aims toward a powerful presidency. We are highly invested in government
generally, and in what we expect and demand from it; we are especially invested in
the national government; and above all other institutions, we invest a tremendous
faith in the position of the presidency. Whether this level of faith in a single office
is politically healthy or not is another matter.

PRIMARY

Imagine that a convention of clowns met to design an
amusing, crazy-quilt schedule to nominate presidential
candidates. The resulting system would probably look much
as ours does today. The incoherent organization of primaries
. . . and the candidates' mad dash attempts to move around
the map, would be funny if the goal—electing the leader of
the free world—weren't so serious.

—Larry Sabato

A primary is an election of a particular sort. As the name suggests, primaries
are *early* elections—*primus* in Latin means "first" or "early." They are held
before general elections and to determine which candidates survive to run
in those later contests. Primaries are intraparty affairs, in which Democrats run
against Democrats and Republicans against Republicans. The winners then square
off against other each other in the general election.

Primaries are held for various positions, including governorships, mayoralties,
and House and Senate seats. But presidential primaries are the most prominent
ones in our political landscape. They are also unique. Unlike others, presidential
primaries are not single events, but a series of separate, statewide elections over
the course of a long season. The presidential primaries traditionally start with the
New Hampshire primary in February of a given election year. Then the two major
parties hold primaries in more than thirty states during the late winter and spring
of that year.[63]

As presidential candidates move through a primary season, they accumulate
support by winning those statewide elections. When a candidate wins a primary,
he or she gains delegates from that state who will later support that candidate at the

national party conventions. In a big vote of all delegates from across the country, the convention determines who will be the party's presidential nominee in the coming general election.

By competing in the primaries, presidential candidates prove their electability. They are tested in campaigns across the country and scrutinized intensively by voters, opponents, and the press. By surviving the ordeal, candidates prove their broad appeal, a necessity for the general election campaign. Presidential primaries amount to trial by fire, by which the parties find out who will be their best and toughest candidate in the run for the nation's highest office.

*   *   *

We are so used to primary elections that we can hardly imagine the political world without them. However, primaries arrived relatively late to the political scene. For much of our history, party insiders decided who would run for the presidency. These party leaders famously made their decisions in "smoke-filled rooms," with little input from grassroots party members.

Not until the early 1900s did reformers first call for primary elections. Primaries, these reformers hoped, would democratize the nomination process. They would open the nomination to any candidates who had the strength, will, and resources to run, taking the decision out of the hands of party gatekeepers. Most important, the primaries would give the party faithful their say as to which candidate would get the nod.

In the hundred-plus years since the first ones, primaries have grown enormously in importance. At first, only a few states held them and public interest in primaries was low. Over time, however, more states joined in as the primaries became a major national phenomenon. No one in recent memory has been elected president without performing well in them, so the primaries are seen as a key to winning the office.

Early advocates of primary elections hoped that they would democratize our politics, opening doors to fresh competition. Recent elections show that those hopes have been fulfilled. Several presidents have used the primaries to launch campaigns that would have been impossible in an earlier era. In 2008, for example, Barack Obama, a one-term senator at the time, used the primaries to challenge and defeat the favorite of his party's leadership, Democratic stalwart Hillary Clinton.

Of course, an especially striking example of the primary's subversive power came in 2016. On the Republican side, a number of contenders entered the presidential race, including prominent governors and senators. In addition, businessman and TV personality Donald Trump, a thorough political outsider, joined the field.

Trump had run for the presidency before, but without making any mark. Nor was he expected to have an impact in 2016, and Republican party leaders heartily wished as much. They saw Trump as a renegade and beyond their influence.

However, the primaries were designed to sidestep exactly such leaders, and Trump made full use of that power. His campaign caught fire in the spring of 2016 with a string of primary wins that shocked political observers. During these months, Republican leaders made plain their disdain for Trump, but without any visible effect on the voters. The primary system opens doors, and the Republican establishment was unable to keep Trump from charging through.

As to whether the openness of the primary system is a good thing in the long run, we might well wonder. With an office as demanding as the presidency at stake, is it a good thing to provide an entry point to any candidate with super-abundant bravado and cash? Given the crucial place of the primaries in our political system, and with the precedent of Donald Trump's success, we might well wonder who will mount successful insurgent campaigns in the future. There is no absolute reason to assume that he or she will be better for the country than a candidate chosen by knowledgeable insiders.

PRIVACY

The right to be let alone is indeed the beginning of all
freedom.

—William O. Douglas, Supreme Court Justice (1939–1970)

Since politics concerns what is public, it seems odd to think of privacy as a
political term. Yet it is. Where we draw the line between private and public,
or political, has a great deal to do with our personal freedoms, for example.
It also has a lot to do with how the broader society can foster its norms and values,
without which social life is difficult to maintain. Where the private begins and the
political leaves off is one of the critical questions in any society.

Everyone grasps the basic meaning of privacy. It concerns those parts of our
life that are intimate to us. Matters that are private are not meant for sharing with
people outside chosen circles of confidence. We rightly feel defensive about private
matters, not wanting intrusions there. We see, too, a relationship between privacy
and liberty. Freedom means making our choices for reasons of our own, and we
bridle at the thought of our decisions being subject to public judgment. Privacy is a
right, by this understanding, closely tied to what the Declaration of Independence
calls the pursuit of happiness.

Interestingly, though, the Founders spoke little about privacy, and the term
never appears in the Constitution. As a specific right, privacy was not much of an
issue in the United States until the late 19th century. That was when a prominent
lawyer and socialite from Boston named Samuel Warren grew frustrated by the
way reporters were crashing social events and publishing stories and photos of what
they found.

Fighting back, Warren joined forces with a fellow lawyer, Louis Brandeis, who was destined to become one of the most important figures in modern American legal history. Together the two men published an article in the *Harvard Law Review* titled "The Right to Privacy," expounding for the first time the idea that citizens had a right to be left alone.

In the article, Warren and Brandeis drew attention to two converging trends in society at that time, both of which are still prominent in our own. One was the rising intrusiveness of the media, boosted by new technologies. At the time, those technologies included mass printing and the emergence of photography; in the meantime, we've added radio, TV, and more recently the Internet and social media.

The other trend Warren and Brandeis noted was less tangible. The law had always addressed the physical aspects of our lives, protecting against bodily harm, for example, or the theft of goods. Over time, however, the broader culture grew increasingly appreciative of what Warren and Brandeis called "man's spiritual nature, . . . his feelings and his intellect." As society grew more aware of this dimension of human life, Warren and Brandeis demanded legal protection for it alongside the protections already in place for the physical. The legal world, Warren and Brandeis argued, needed to catch up with this new appreciation and build into our law codes something never explicit previously: protection for "the sacred precincts of private and domestic life."

*   *   *

Having proposed this new direction for the law, Warren and Brandeis would not live long enough to see it come to fruition. By the 1960s, however, the right to privacy had become a central concern in our national politics and a cornerstone of crucial Supreme Court decisions.

For example, Erwin Griswold, Solicitor General of the United States, used the right to privacy as the basis of his 1964 Supreme Court argument, in which he called for the voiding of a Connecticut law that banned the sale of contraceptives there. The Supreme Court agreed with Griswold, despite the fact that the Constitution makes no specific mention of a right to privacy, and the Connecticut law was struck down.

Arguing for the Court, Justice William O. Douglas found that, while the right to privacy was not explicit in the Constitution, it was implicit there, especially in the First, Third, Fourth, Fifth, and Ninth Amendments. The right to privacy was insured by "penumbras," as Douglas put it, emanating from those parts of the Bill of Rights. For example, the Fourth Amendment protection against unwarranted "search and seizure" makes little sense without some implied private space to which people have a particular right and the state does not. In writing the amendment, the Founders assumed the reality of privacy, even if they did not spell out this assumption.

The Supreme Court would go on to use the right to privacy as a basis for other major decisions, including the very prominent *Roe* v. *Wade* ruling, which struck down state laws banning abortion (though the Court's ruling left states free to restrict abortion within certain bounds). Personal decisions about such an intimate matter were deemed essentially private, to be left to the judgment of those directly involved, and not to be made illegal by the public at large.

* * *

In thinking about privacy, it helps to consider the meaning of the related term *public*. The two words are, of course, opposites in some sense. But the opposition is not simple. Things that are public are not just not-private, but somehow belong to everyone; what is public is the concern of the people as a whole, and perhaps also of the people's agent, the government.

There are, however, entities that are not public but private, yet at the same time social and not individual. Businesses, charities, private schools, and churches, for example, fall into this category, as does the family.

It might also be useful to keep these social, but private, entities in mind when we think of the highly personal issues where privacy rights have been invoked by the courts. In grappling with such issues, the courts have shown a strongly individualistic tendency. So, for example, the Supreme Court ruled in a 1976 case that women have no responsibility to tell their spouses when deciding to have an abortion. Women have a right to make that decision privately, without the consent, or even the knowledge, of their husbands. The circle of privacy here is drawn very tightly, indeed to the strictly individual.

There were undoubtedly good reasons for this decision, but there is also something unrealistic about pure individualism as it relates to the way people actually make decisions. When the Supreme Court defines privacy as being strictly individual, it implies two poles of authority. One is the empowered individual, of course; the other is the state itself, which defines and enforces the right to privacy.

Left out are any other sources of authority. Yet none of us is a simple, isolated island of conscience, and we depend, knowingly or not, on external authorities to develop our sense of right and wrong. These authorities might include family, friends, teachers, religions, and others. They are private, not public, but social and not merely individual.

By failing to recognize these authorities, the courts reinforce assumptions that might be unhealthy. One is the notion that individuals ought to think of themselves as insular in decision-making. Another is that the decisions individuals make affect only themselves and that society has no stake in them. These tendencies to see the individual as insulated from the broader community are surely out of step with some very basic realities.

Progressivism

If progressivism is to be constructive rather than merely
restorative, it must be prepared to replace the old order with
a new social bond... .

—Herbert Croly

The term *progressivism* is, in part, self-explanatory. It is an ideology that
embraces change, the promise of progress, with confidence. It emphasizes
our potential for social improvement. Moreover, it not only places faith in
the future; it refuses to glorify the past or the present. Immune to nostalgia, progressives actively seek change in part because they see so much need for it. They are
disinclined to indulge society's shortcomings.

Progressives believe strongly in our ability to grasp social problems and solve
them. They tend to place great faith in the uses of rational planning, especially when
put in the hands of experts. This faith colors progressive thought on government,
which is activist as a rule.

There is plenty here to contrast with conservatism, progressivism's natural
counterpart. Where progressives see society as malleable and in desperate need
of reform, conservatives demur. For starters, conservatives are attuned to society's
complexities and are more likely to appreciate the difficulties of reform. Moreover,
conservatives see traditions and customs as the fruit of long experience and not
the unfortunate accidents of history. To the conservative, traditions carry a kind
of wisdom unmatchable by rational planning. Much of what we have today is the
result of those traditions and can easily be lost if we tinker with them.

Of course to progressives, losing traditions—if they impede social
improvement—is the point.

*   *   *

The distinctions between progressives and conservatives are clear enough, but it is harder to see the differences between progressives and liberals. The two terms are used almost interchangeably in daily talk, and the self-identified progressives and liberals will agree on a great deal. If they survey contemporary American society, both will identify plenty of problems that need solving, and they will be mostly the same ones: economic inequality, educational failure, systemic racism and sexism, gun violence, and environmental degradation.

And where liberals and progressives diagnose the same diseases, they likewise agree on the cures. Government exists to solve problems, so we should use it: tax the rich and redistribute wealth, invest heavily in education, control guns, subsidize renewable energy, and so on. In all this, one finds little daylight between progressives and liberals.

But the similarities hide deep historical differences. Liberalism's emphasis has, for most of its life, been on the defense of personal liberties. Liberals have fought against class privileges, favored economic freedom, and fought for free speech, free thought, and free conscience. The United States was liberal in this sense from the start.

Progressivism's origins are more recent. It arose in the late 19th century, summoned into existence by the great changes reshaping the nation at that time, including industrialism, urbanization, and mass immigration. Any of these taken alone would have presented immense challenges, but together they amounted to a seismic upheaval, one that affected society "more fundamentally than any political revolution known to history," as the early progressive hero Louis Brandeis put it.

This was the crucible in which progressivism was forged. With those immense changes, millions of people felt themselves to be at the mercy of dangerous forces set loose by the evolving economy, from unsafe work conditions to exploitative labor contracts, unsanitary housing, tainted food, and, emphatically, political dispossession. Traditional liberties seemed to have produced something monstrous, along with all the wealth that came with industrialism.

Given the scope of these troubles, government appeared to many as the public's only plausible protector. But it was a government ill-formed to take on that responsibility. Defending the common good in the new industrial environment meant giving government new tools to wage its war. Thus, progressives supported various political innovations to tip the balance of power away from private interests and toward the government. These included the national income tax, anti-trust laws, and the increased power of the presidency.

One other progressive innovation from this late 19th century needs mention here: the founding of the regulatory bureaucracy. Made up of various independent and executive branch agencies, this bureaucracy has over time gathered great power to regulate behavior in nearly every facet of our public life, from deal-making on Wall Street to workplace safety, the environment, fair employment, food and drug safety, and much more. This vast regulatory apparatus, designed to empower experts in various fields to act on behalf of the common good, is the quintessentially progressive element of our government.

Strengthening government in these ways horrified many who held to a traditional, liberal understanding of American constitutionalism. But progressives were not overly concerned about that. In their view, government must adapt to changing times or grow obsolete.

Theodore Roosevelt put it this way: "There was once a time in history when the limitation of governmental power meant increasing liberty for the people. In the present day, the limitation of governmental power, of governmental action, means the enslavement of the people by the great corporations who can only be held in check through the extension of governmental power."

*   *   *

The contours of progressivism today remain much as they were 120 years ago, when the movement was born. Progressives are still zealous in pursuit of social improvement. And today's progressives still hold faith in our capacities to rationally address whatever problems we confront.

Yet today's progressives face a historical moment very different from that of their predecessors. Where the early progressives faced the challenges of their day with verve, many progressives today feel a certain exhaustion as we confront our own. Too often, despite decades of effort, the problems seem to be winning, as with economic inequality or educational underachievement. Policy failures do not necessarily cause progressives to lose their self-assurance, a trait that nearly defines them. But the confidence of progressives in their fellow citizens is perhaps less certain.

Persistent problems also highlight the apparent weaknesses of our political institutions, and this raises a familiar question for progressives. Can our current political system meet the big challenges we face, or does government need still newer tools, more potent weapons, to combat our social woes? And what do we do when traditional institutions, including Congress, the free press, and presidential elections, yield such discouraging results?

In coming years, look for progressives to wrestle with these questions. And look for some to double-down on the long-term transmission of power from private hands to the governments' in the campaign for social improvement.

PROPERTY

In no country in the world is the love of property more active or more anxious than in the United States; nowhere does the majority display less inclination for those principles which threaten to alter, in whatever manner, the laws of property.

—Alexis de Tocqueville

The concept of property, with its rights and uses, is at the center of every political system and of most political controversies. This is so because property is the stuff of life. We live and act largely through property, and to control it is, to some degree, to control our fate. Property is, as philosopher Michael Oakeshott wrote, a form of power.

Property has a primal quality, in that the urge to hold property appears to be almost universal. A great legal historian, Harold Berman, noted that he learned his first lessons about property in the nursery, as we all do. "A child says, 'It's my toy,'" Berman explained. "That's property law."

Some of the basic aspects of property appear in Berman's example. Especially this: property is thoroughly entwined with the notion of *rights*. The object is ours, we believe, and we have a right to use it as we please. This assumed right is also exclusive: we have it, and others do not.

This claim to ownership is utterly familiar, not just for children but for most of us. Being so common, we might wonder where ownership comes from and on what grounds we can claim something as our own. What, in other words, are the roots of property and its rights?

The philosopher John Locke took a stab at explaining this. Locke started by supposing a time prior to formal government and any formal law. In that state of nature, the resources of the world were available to all, the property of none. From this common bounty, he reasoned, a person creates property by making something out of the resources at hand. When one has taken some resource from the natural world, and "mixed his own Labour with, and joyned to it something that is his own…thereby [he] makes it his property."

Property, to Locke, is not just the inert stuff we hold. It is created by human effort. The first claim to any property comes from this effort, and property is legitimately owned because of that creative act.

Once created, property can be passed on to others, with all its rights intact. It can be legitimately sold, given away, or left to descendents. One of the jobs of the law is to clarify those processes, and one of the jobs of government is to protect the rights of those who hold property.

The rights of property, if we accept Locke's line of thought, cannot be separated from another touchstone of government: liberty. The choices we make in life inevitably involve property. We might, for example, use our labor—our time, effort and imagination—to build a business. That business will be our legal property, as will its profits. Liberty is in part a matter of having control over, and responsibility for, the decisions involved: what to do with our personal resources, and what to do with the fruits of our effort.

In all this, property never loses touch with the creative impulse. It is generated by creative acts, but also provides an avenue for creative expression. For this reason, the widespread ownership of property is one of the goals of liberal democracies. G. K. Chesterton noted, in his good-natured way, the connections between property, imagination, and politics. The average man, he wrote, might not be a sculptor, "but he can cut earth into the shape of a garden; … the average man cannot paint the sunset whose colours he admires. But he can paint his own house with what colours he chooses; and though he paints it pea green with pink spots, he is still an artist; because that is his choice. Property is merely the art of democracy."

*   *   *

As Alexis de Tocqueville understood, Americans have had a long love affair with property, going back deep into the colonial era. At that time, America reversed a basic economic reality found in Europe. Instead of Europe's scarce land and abundant labor, America had abundant, hence cheap, land and scarce, hence well-paid, labor. For those willing to cross the ocean, this reversal made America a land of opportunity for settlers, where they could own property in a way that would have been nearly impossible in Europe. What those settlers said of colonial Pennsylvania could have been said of much of America. It was the "best poor man's country," and one of the few places on Earth where those without property could accumulate it and reap its benefits.[64] Fidelity to property has been in the bloodstream of American life and politics ever since.

This devotion to property has been reflected in American law throughout our history. Preservation of property rights inspired the writing of the Constitution, for example, and the cause of property is written into its fabric. The Fifth Amendment is just one example, insuring that citizens shall not be "deprived of life, liberty, or property, without due process of law . . . ."

Despite the long history of their protection, however, it should be noted that property rights were not then, and never have been, absolute. Long established legal traditions also limited property rights where those rights were in conflict with certain broader public goods.

Consider, for example, the power of eminent domain, which has deep roots in English law and history. When the public interest is at stake, government has the right to take private property from people, as, for instance, when a piece of real estate is needed to build a public road.

More broadly, we could add the concept of "police power" as the source of legitimate encroachments on property rights. According to traditional understandings of this power, government has a right to restrict behaviors damaging to the public's "health, safety, or morals." Local and state governments can legitimately outlaw houses of prostitution, for example, or limit which venues can sell alcoholic beverages, or designate residential and business districts, and by doing so will inevitably infringe upon property rights.

The Founders understood and accepted such impositions, while seeking to limit their expansion. But the Constitution is flexible. While it lists and limits the powers of the federal government, it also empowers the government to "provide for the general welfare of the United States," providing something of an escape hatch from those self-imposed limits.

One key question for American citizens has always been what that "general welfare" consists of, and how to identify which government actions serve some necessary public interest and which illegitimately impose on citizens' liberties. What, if any, are the hard and fast rules that we can apply?

*   *   *

If such hard and fast rules exist, we are still searching for them. For the nation's first 150 years, the Supreme Court enforced a relatively strict understanding of what constituted the general welfare, beyond which legislation could not go. In time, however, the pressure to rethink the strict standards grew. The industrializing economy of the late 19th and early 20th centuries, for example, presented unprecedented social challenges, with the rise of tremendous private wealth and powerful corporations, along with deep concentrations of poverty.

Seeing concentrated wealth and power side-by-side with profound deprivation delivered something of a shock to the American political system. Part of that shock came from the fear that the benefits of property, so central to American political ideals, might no longer be within reach for whole classes of people. Meanwhile, the power that came with property was growing dangerously concentrated among the wealthiest citizens and the great corporations.

The result of this concern was the rise of what has been called "social" legislation. In practice, this meant using state power to improve the lot of the poor and to curb the power of the wealthy, whatever the effect on traditional property rights might be. The surge in reformist social legislation included certain key elements: a national income tax; anti-trust laws to break up big monopolies; the rise of minimum wage and maximum hour laws; and eventually, the rise of welfare state programs after 1932.

To some property holders these laws felt like an assault on their fundamental rights. Seen from another angle, though, the reforms were necessary to protect a broad range of Americans in their enjoyment of property, preserving it from the insecurities growing out of the industrial economy.

After the burst of reforms of the early and mid-20th century, the movement toward more activist social legislation slowed but never really abated. We have continued to pass laws that extend the concept of general welfare and impose constraints on private property rights. Environmental laws, for example, reflect a broad public concern that private actions can have a detrimental effect on the public good and so should be regulated. By their nature, those laws reduce the free use of property.

Civil rights legislation has had a similar effect. No business today can refuse to serve African Americans in any "public accommodation," as they once could. For the sake of a public good—the equal treatment of all Americans—we have passed laws that limit the owners' use of such property.

This rise in social legislation over the last hundred and more years has dramatically altered the landscape of property rights. It has also altered the framework in which we think about government and our expectations about what it can and should do, about where its responsibilities extend and where individual rights begin.

As we continue thinking about the lines that separate the public from the private, we should be clear-eyed about the place of property rights. Supreme Court Justice Potter Stewart once offered the country a reminder about our traditional beliefs: "A fundamental interdependence exists between the personal right to liberty and the personal right in property. Neither could have meaning without the other."

REFERENDUM

The Referendum is today accepted as the most important part of the mechanism of real democracy by all but machine politicians and those who would exploit rather than serve the people.

—*The Farmers' Open Forum,* August 1916

Americans pride themselves on their democratic ideals, but any simple love of democracy will be out of sync with our fundamental institutions. By constitutional design, the will of the people is generally *not* translated directly into law. It flows through our governing institutions. But the Framers of our constitutions, state and national, feared public opinion when it ran at full force. To protect against the damage the democratic will could do, American constitutions channel that will into a complex network of competing institutions, where it is tamed and put to controlled use.

By doing so, our constitutions, national and state, tend to frustrate those who seek a more responsive, active government. When times are good, this frustration is minimal, but when we face grave challenges, it mounts. That was the situation near the end of the 19th century, when industrialization, urbanization, mass immigration, and other challenges confronted the United States.

It was during the early industrial era that the modern referendum was born. The referendum is a form of election in which the people vote directly for or against a proposed law. To its supporters, the referendum provides a way to bypass failing legislative institutions and is especially useful when government is dominated by great corporate powers: big oil, steel, finance, and other interests.

Referendums take a number of forms. In some cases, laws written by a legislature are submitted to the people for their approval; if the people vote in favor, the proposition goes on to become law. In other cases, individuals or groups outside of government can propose laws that go to a popular vote without screening by any legislature. This subset of referendums is called the *initiative,* since outsiders initiate the legislation.

Still other referendums are nonbinding. When used this way, the people's vote in favor of a proposed statute does not automatically become law. Instead, the proposed law might go to a legislature for further consideration and, if legislators see fit, passage. While those legislatures are not bound to enact the proposed law, they would do well to reckon with the results. Nonbinding referendums indicate where the people's wishes lie, a fact that legislators ignore at their peril.

It is worth noting that the same forces that produced the referendum also gave birth to another device of direct democracy, the *recall.* With it, remorseful voters can recall governors or other officials after electing them to office, doing so through a special election. The recall has used been used sparingly, but has played a role in fairly recent politics. One California governor, Gray Davis, lost a recall vote in 2002, and was replaced by actor Arnold Schwarzenegger.

*   *   *

The referendum, like the initiative and the recall, is found in state and local governments in the United States, but not at the national level. In fact, each of these measures runs contrary to the spirit of the Constitution. The Framers had substantial experience with popular government and were clear-eyed about its defects. So they included in the Constitution features, such as the bicameral legislature, that checked the thrust of popular will.

By squeezing the demand for new law through the tortuous process of voting in both the House of Representatives and the Senate, the Founders assured that legislation would be debated, reviewed, and likely revised before passage. The hope was that this elaborate process would screen out bad laws and improve those that survive. Its slow indirection is a feature, not a bug, in constitutional eyes.

Not so with the referendum, whose supporters believe that the people's will needs less buffering and more simple implementation. In contrast to traditional legislative processes, referendums are direct and geared toward straightforward majority rule. Once written, propositions go to an up or down vote. There is less compromise built into the process than in standard legislation, and less responsiveness to minority concerns. And, of course, once written, a proposition's fate is put directly into the hands of the people, bringing risks that the Founders feared in direct democracy. They preferred that legislation be approved by representatives of the people instead, who would be unusually capable men (and now women) whose views would be broadened through contact with fellow legislators.

Yet, however much the referendum violates the spirit of traditional lawmaking, the two need not be seen as incompatible. States can use the referendum as an occasional corrective to ordinary politics. If the bulk of a state's laws are passed by the usual means, the referendum can inject a more directly democratic element when frustration with that system's results develop. As Theodore Roosevelt said, "No man would say that it was best to conduct all legislation by direct vote of the people . . . but, on the other hand, no one whose mental arteries have not long since hardened can doubt that the proposed changes [referendums] are needed when the legislators refuse to carry out the will of the people."

REGULATION

The study of regulation in the United States demonstrates that American political culture and our political institutions are not nearly as hostile to activist government as we are usually led to believe.

—R. Shep Melnick

For such a commonplace word, *regulation* has an extraordinary pedigree, with roots that go deep into Indo-European linguistic history. In its primordial sense, the *reg* in *regulation* signified a simple straight line or movement in a line. From that root, the Romans got the word *regula,* a straight rod that could be used like a ruler.

One can see how that original meaning could be put to use in government, the goal of which is to bring order or rule to an otherwise disordered world. That Indo-European root, *reg,* reappears frequently in words with political meanings: *reign, regime, rex* (king), the military *regiment,* the German *reich,* and even the Sanskrit *raj,* as well as the familiar *regulation.*

In the broadest sense, much of what government does is to regulate people and their actions, to keep them from getting too far out of line. Yet in current discourse when we speak of government regulations, we have something more specific in mind. We distinguish, for example, between legislation and regulation. In comparison to legislation—the laws produced by legislatures—regulation is finer-grained. We use legislation to accomplish big things, such as desegregating public spaces through the Civil Rights Act. Regulations, by contrast, are used to protect against unsanitary food preparation, undertrained doctors, inadequate septic systems, and all sorts of other potential problems that confront us in daily life.

Such regulations are a constant presence in modern America and come at us from all sides. Governments at the national, state, and local levels all produce regulations in bulk. Legislatures pass regulatory laws, and all regulation depends ultimately on legislative sanction. The key sources of government regulation, however, are not legislatures but specialized agencies, such as those of the executive branch departments of the federal government. In essence, legislatures delegate authority to these agencies to enact regulations that have the force of law but are not, strictly speaking, laws themselves.

As noted above, regulations depend ultimately on the sanction of legislatures, and legislatures have a responsibility to oversee the regulators to make sure their rules do not escape legitimate bounds. But the delegation of authority to the agencies gives them a substantial degree of leeway to write regulations in their given fields.

The regulations produced by these agencies take various forms. They produce straightforward rules by the tens of thousands, and those rules concern everything from the number of fish that can be harvested from our coastal fisheries to the security protocols for airplane pilots. There are zoning regulations, as well: one generally cannot build an oil refinery in a residential neighborhood, nor a shooting range next to an elementary school. And there are building codes: structures of all kinds, from trailer homes to hydro-electric dams, must meet specifications for safety and strength; and the specifications for earthquake-prone California will differ from those of snow-prone western New York state.

We also regulate the economy through licensing. Broadcasting on radio or TV requires a license, as does selling firearms, serving alcohol in restaurants, and, in many places, working as a hair stylist. Similarly, to become a teacher, a doctor, or a lawyer, one needs a certificate that proves one's professional training, which in turn must come from a school with proper accreditation. All of this licensing is a form of regulation.

Since much of our regulation is produced by specialized agencies rather than by slow, painstaking legislative processes, regulation is relatively supple and can be applied more easily than statute law. It provides a way for government to bring competent authority to bear on the myriad challenges that arise in the modern economy. Legislators might understand that the nuclear power industry, for example, needs rules and guidelines if it is not to generate disasters along with electricity, but they are in no position to understand in detail what the rules ought to be. The Nuclear Regulatory Agency, on the other hand, is in precisely that position, and so it is given authority to produce regulations for that industry.

*   *   *

It is worth noting that it is virtually impossible to go back far enough in our history to find a time when we lived without regulations. Colonial Massachusetts, for example, had dress codes, and early Jamestown imposed mandatory religious services on its inhabitants.

But the modern regulatory state stands apart. One early landmark was the founding of the Interstate Commerce Commission in 1887. The ICC was formed to address the problem of "predatory" pricing by the railroads. The original ICC was made up of just five members, tasked with the enormous job of monitoring railroad rates across the country and insuring that all were fair and reasonable.

This commission was tiny, but like the proverbial mustard seed, it was destined for terrific growth and impressive fertility. Among the descendants of this first regulatory commission are dozens of "alphabet soup" agencies, including the SEC, the FDA, the FTC,[65] and many others, all of which are tasked with monitoring and regulating various sectors of the modern economy.

Over time, the regulatory state has grown in surges. The New Deal and the Great Society era, for example, each brought massive new growth in federal regulation, and in both cases regulations came in response to our evolving sense of what needed regulating. For example, the Environmental Protection Agency, the EPA, was founded in 1970 in response to growing ecological concerns, pollution being seen as a major threat by the late 1960s.

In addition, the surge of regulation that came with the Great Society of the mid-1960s and following years, added new elements to existing layers. For example, new regulations included a strong anti-discriminatory emphasis. Their targets included workplace discrimination on the basis of race, sex or physical disability. Together, all these regulations have brought sweeping changes to the United States, not just by addressing specific problems, but also by creating a climate in which citizens expect to find regulations woven into the fabric of daily life. We have grown used to a much higher level of regulatory interference in our lives than previous generations of Americans.

*   *   *

There is a notion abroad that the United States government intervenes so little on behalf of the common good, that it is all but absent. European progressives, for example, sometimes express this belief: the law of the jungle reigns in America, and the devil take the hindmost.

If we consider the growth of the regulatory state, we see this is not really the case. What is true is that our constitution makes it difficult to pass highly ambitious, comprehensive legislation, such as national health care.

What American government can do, much more easily, is to use regulation as a tool to protect the common good. Legislators delegate a great deal of rule-making power to regulators, giving them a relatively free hand to write the rules they think necessary. This delegation of power frees regulatory agencies from the difficulties of the legislative process as they do their work. It also frees them from direct responsibility to the people, the essence of the legislator's job.

With this channel open, the zeal of American reformers has poured into the regulatory system. In their incursions into the private sphere, as political scientist R. Shep Melnick notes, American regulations are remarkable for their "scope and rigidity." By comparison with regulations found in Europe and Japan, the regulatory state here is "more stringent, legalistic, adversarial, and punitive . . . ."

For these reasons, the regulators generate considerable resentment. But it is hard to know how to do better. The complexities of the modern economy are so densely woven that even experts have difficulty understanding the challenges they present to society as a whole, and thus to government. Consider the financial meltdown of 2008, which hardly anyone predicted, and the causes of which still seem hard to grasp. In its wake, Congress passed a 2,300 page law, the Dodd-Frank Act, to impose new regulations on the financial industry. But making sense of this enormous document is difficult, and applying it to a terrifically complicated financial industry is an immensely daunting task. If that task must be done, who but the regulatory agencies can be up to it?

Legislators appear to be right in delegating power to the more technically proficient regulatory agencies. In some sense, our demand for regulation outstrips the capacities of our legislative system to administer and oversee it.

REPRESENTATION

> By what rules shall you chuse [sic] your Representatives?
> . . . The principle difficulty lies, and the greatest care should
> be employed in constituting this Representative Assembly.
> It should be in miniature, an exact portrait of the people at
> large. It should think, feel, reason, and act like them.
>
> —John Adams, President (1797–1801)

American government depends on representation to fulfill its most basic promise. As the Preamble to the Constitution reminds us, the nation is founded on the will of "we, the people." And it is through representatives, chosen by the people, that the popular will is conveyed to government's institutions. By relying on representation, American citizens are assured that government will act in accordance with, and not against, our will.

The device of representation distinguishes modern republics from the more direct democracies of antiquity. In ancient Athens, for example, the fundamental political institution was the citizens' assembly, which included any citizen who chose to attend.[66] In these assemblies, the gathered crowd voted yes or no on legislation, often by a show of hands. Given that all citizens were eligible to take part, ancient democracies governed relatively small areas, typically one city and its immediate surroundings.

Through representation, however, republics can expand far beyond the size of the ancient city-states and still retain their democratic basis. With relatively little trouble, elected representatives travel to distant political capitals to take their part in governing. In contrast with direct democracies, representative republics not only extend over large areas; they can also govern millions rather than thousands of people.

In the eyes of James Madison, this expansion brought a great benefit. In a large republic, a central government would bring together representatives from across a diverse land, who would give voice to highly varied interests. By contrast, the ancient democracies were dominated by the narrower interests found in a single city-state. With the infighting that is inevitable to politics, a dominant faction would naturally arise in a small democracy, and that faction would tend to dominate and abuse its opponents.

Madison believed that larger republics are less prone to this dynamic. "Extend the sphere," wrote Madison, "and you take in a greater variety of parties and interests; you make it less probable that a majority of the whole will have a common motive to invade the rights of other citizens." Elsewhere, Madison compared factionalism to a fire, which cannot spread if political interests are varied enough. Thus, as he wrote in *Federalist* 10, with a large, diverse populace "we behold a Republican remedy for the diseases most incident to Republican government."

*   *   *

There was another threat that Madison feared nearly as much as factionalism, one he also thought an extensive republic could mitigate. This other threat was the mediocrity of the leaders who rose to power in smaller democracies, a problem Madison was familiar with from serving in the state legislature of Virginia.[67]

When people vote, they generally do so out of self-interest and often without regard for the common good. But in electing representatives, the narrowness of the individual viewpoint is transformed. Representatives, elected by a substantial number of people, can hardly help but see policy in broader terms than the individuals who elect them.

And if the district that elects the representative is large, the viewpoint is made even broader. Moreover, in a big, populous nation, the pool from which elected leaders are chosen will be larger, and the number of genuinely distinguished candidates for office will be greater. With relatively large voting districts, Madison believed that a better quality of representative would naturally rise to power. When these relatively accomplished representatives gathered to deliberate on legislation, the effect would be "to refine and enlarge" all their views, producing policies "superior to local prejudices, and to schemes of injustice."

In this, Madison hoped that representatives in a large republic would not be *too* representative. Rather than strictly reflecting the wishes of their constituents, representatives ought, according to his view, serve more as trustees. Once elected, representatives would act as they saw best, taking into account the interests of the whole republic as well as those of their immediate constituents. "[I]t may well happen that the public voice, pronounced by representatives of the people, will be more consonant to the public good than if pronounced by the people themselves."

*   *   *

Perhaps Madison's take on representation is right, and it might be that our representative government provides us with about as good a form of self-rule as we can expect. There is, however, a wrinkle deep in the fabric of representative government that we should not lose sight of. It concerns the right of the people to govern themselves, and their right to govern others also.

In American constitutionalism, the rightful power of government ultimately comes from the people, and representation is the means by which that power is granted to those who govern. The legitimacy of our government depends on this delegation.

All Americans share in this right to have a say in how they are governed. Yet when representatives are sent off to govern, they will speak for those who did not vote for them as well as those who did. Given this brute fact of our democracy, we need to ask what happens to the right to self-government of those on the losing end. After all, no elected official can fully represent the views of all his or her constituents. And when representatives hammer out legislation, the result will always frustrate some substantial percentage of their constituents. While John Adams might have called for representatives who "think, feel, reason, and act" like the people, such a thing is impossible. All the wishes of all the people cannot be represented in government.

For this reason, there is inevitable tension between the power granted to representatives and the right of *all* people to self-government. Moreover, there are real dangers here. If we are to honor the rights of all to "life, liberty, and the pursuit of happiness," we cannot have a government that forces its values on people. We believe that representatives "must not impose on the people their partial opinions of how to live," as political scientist Harvey Mansfield put it, "and they must prevent a part of the people, whether a majority or a minority, from imposing on another part of the people."

This is a difficult discipline, however, and one that implies necessary limits on government. Both representatives and the people who elect them must abide by those limits. Voters must, in effect, settle for a government that does not go all the way in advancing their own values on the polity as a whole.

In a time when we tend to demand more from government rather than less, and the question of imposing limits on government is hardly ever raised, this is a discipline that seems distinctly foreign to our politics.

REPUBLIC

Men are equal in republican government; they are equal in
despotic government; in the former it is because they are
everything; in the latter it is because they are nothing.

—Baron de Montesquieu

Among the achievements of the Founding, there is this: that the Founders
managed to produce a republic, despite the fact that there was no blueprint to build one like it, and indeed little certainty as to what a republic
actually was. John Adams, one of the most learned men of that generation, wondered about this in a letter to fellow Founder Roger Sherman. He asked, "[W]hat
is your definition of a republic? Mine is this: *A government whose sovereignty is vested
in more than one person.*" If so, however, even a state ruled by some all-powerful
council of aristocrats might fit that definition, so Adams's understanding hardly
conforms to what we think of as a republic today.

During the debates over the Constitution prior to ratification, James Madison
offered another definition of *republic*, and it is worth spelling out. Significantly, he
distinguished republican government from democracy. He said, "[I]n a democracy,
the people meet and exercise the government in person; in a republic they assemble
and administer it by their representatives and agents. A democracy consequently
will be confined to a small spot. A republic may be extended over a large region."
No one had previously thought to define it this way. Given Madison's central
role in getting the Constitution written and ratified, his definition would seem as
authoritative as any American's.

*   *   *

The strict institutional definition of *republic,* however, matters less than the term's spiritual connotations. Its origins, which are Latin, help here. *Republic* comes from *res,* or "things" and *publica,* or "public." In a republic, the government is a public thing, belonging to all the people. A republican government reflects the will of the people and is grounded in their active support. Moreover, the purpose of governing in a republic is the flourishing of the whole society. This contrasts with an aristocracy, where government reflects the will of an upper class, and where the flourishing of the best—the *aristoi,* in Greek—is more the measure of political success.

The political history of Rome underscores this definition. That history includes the long era of the Republic, followed by its fall and the succession of the Roman Empire. For Rome's historians, the Republic was a period of special greatness, and Rome's strength grew out of its republican values. As those historians told the story, the Republic was a time of rural hardiness and simple virtues, marked by deep attachments to family, the household gods, and the *patria,* or fatherland. Later Roman moralists loved to contrast the virtues of this period with the vices of the Empire: its materialism, selfishness, and impiety.

This lament might sound familiar, as it has strong echoes in our own history. We too have made a transition from a simpler, more rural past to an era of imperial wealth, and we too worry about the loss of old virtues. Even in the 1780s Patrick Henry feared that we were on our way "from a simple to a splendid government," and looked back on a time when Americans were devoted to ancestral liberties. "But now," he wrote, "the American spirit is about to convert this country into a powerful and mighty empire. ... Such a government is incompatible with the genius of republicanism." So there were Americans who rued our decline even before the Constitution had been ratified and before our first president had taken office.

*   *   *

Perhaps there is more to such moralizing than mere nostalgia. We might well ask whether a nation such as ours depends on republican virtues to thrive. That is, whether we can live well as a nation without cultivating a veneration for civic traditions and embracing the sacrifices our shared life requires of us.

To understand the question better, we should contrast the republican view with *liberalism.* In a philosophical sense, liberalism emphasizes individualism and celebrates freedom from external authorities. It resists tradition and values the private sphere as much as the public: the *res privata,* we might say, as much as the *res publica.*

This liberalism has also been a cornerstone of American government since the Founding. The freedoms granted to personal initiative have given birth to remarkable achievements of all kinds, from business to the arts. Unlike the Roman moralists, we must attribute the success of the American system as much to our liberties as to public spirit, familial piety, and similar republican virtues.

There is more to be said, however. The two views, republican and liberal, stand in contrast. But they have also been compatible in practice. After all, we have had a liberal republic for 230 years. Perhaps the freedoms found in liberal society depend on the cohesiveness provided by republican values. If so, we should be careful in dispensing with them.

*   *   *

We might also consider our republican health from one final angle, in light of an older definition of the term. It comes from St. Augustine, a North African who lived under the vast umbrella of Roman imperial rule. Augustine defined a republic as a people "bound together by a common agreement as to the objects of love." Augustine was fully aware of the traditions of the old Roman republic, and its devotions to family and fatherland. He was also intimately involved with the growth of the Church, which had its own "objects of love" and formed something like a separate republic within the decaying Roman Empire.

With Augustine's definition in mind, we might take stock of America's health as a republic. Republics depend on two fundamentals, according to Augustine: unity and love. As to unity, the great size and diversity of the United States presents a difficulty. Affluent Manhattanites have their own devotions: their values, aspirations, religious and political affiliations, and so forth. Their devotions differ from those of, say, African Americans in the deep South, from suburbanites around Midwestern cities, and from our many immigrant communities. Likewise, the culture of our academic archipelago differs from that of our military bases, and both differ from the similarly scattered subculture of our prisons. We are a profoundly diverse nation, and though we celebrate diversity on bumper stickers, we should understand that deep diversity poses a natural challenge to the shared devotions of any republic.

As for Augustine's other republican fundamental, love, we will find cause for concern any time we check on the news. Yet love is a strong force in its own right and often binds us in unseen ways. We may love each other more than we realize, as we see in times of emergency.

Still, we live in a time of obvious social discord. That being the case, we would do well to remember words spoken by one hero of our republic in another time of deep division. "We are not enemies, but friends," Abraham Lincoln said in his first inaugural address. "Though passion may have strained it must not break the bonds of our affection. The mystic chords of memory, stretching from every battlefield and patriot grave to every living heart and hearthstone all over this broad land, will yet swell with the chorus of the Union, when again touched, as surely they will be, by the better angels of our nature."

REVOLUTION

In a time of revolution there are but two powers, the sword and the people.

—Walter Bagehot

In terms of etymology, the word *revolution* describes the action of rolling, or turning around a center. Revolutions entail a rolling or turning over of established institutions, or, in politics specifically, the overthrow of an established government. In the wake of the overthrow, political revolutions also entail the rise of a new government, an action that completes the rolling over at the heart of the matter.

In the case of the American Revolution, for example, British rule was overthrown and, once independence was won, the American colonists formed their own government. Previously, the British Parliament held political power over the colonies, but from the Revolution on, Americans would rule themselves and chart their own course. (Fittingly, the British Army Band is said to have played "The World Turned Upside Down" after the battle that assured the Revolution was won.)

The word *revolution* has unexpected nuances, however. It came to politics directly from the science of astronomy. There the notion of revolution applied to the movement of the stars, which were observed to travel across the heavens in set patterns. Having completed their circuits, they revolved again, continuing endlessly in their path. The cycles of the stars and galaxies were perfectly regular in their courses, and any deviation meant catastrophe had struck.

In politics, something similar was once believed about governing. There was a proper order to be followed, and if states broke with this order, it could only bring trouble. In such cases, revolution could return those states back to their right and natural pattern. In fact, the first application of *revolution* to a political upheaval came in the 1680s, with the Glorious Revolution, which was not at all what we would call a revolution today. It was instead a return to a stable, accepted monarchy in Britain, after decades of civil strife.

It was only later that *revolution* came to suggest a political break with the past, and an escape from the old order. The tipping point came late in the 18th century, and among the key events was the American Revolution itself. With it, the old meaning of the term—a return to proper order—and the emerging sense of movement toward an open-ended future existed in precarious balance.

To many American revolutionaries, British rulers had broken with tradition and were infringing on the colonists' customary rights in new and illegitimate ways—taxing them without representation, for instance. In their eyes, revolution held the promise of a return—a re-turn of the wheel—back to rightful order.

But Patriot leaders also understood that declaring independence and forming a new nation was a radical and unprecedented step. No nation had previously been founded in the way the United States would be, with a written constitution and government based on the will of the people.

*   *   *

The novel side of the American Revolution, ripe with the promise of change, inspired revolutionary movements elsewhere. But in some cases the balance that had marked American independence tipped decisively away from notions of traditional order.

Consider the French Revolution. As in America, this was a political upheaval, with an old regime overthrown and replaced. But the French Revolution struck deeply at traditional social institutions as well. Many of its leaders loathed those institutions, and made their overthrow as much a part of the Revolution as the political overturning. They fought against the Church and its teachings, for example, nearly as much as against the monarchy.

But liberating people from so much traditional authority leaves a revolutionary society with some stark choices. One, which is only theoretically possible, is to do without authority altogether and live with anarchy. The other is to reconstruct authority and somehow invest it in new institutions.

Which is exceptionally difficult. The new institutions need to be compelling to function, and revolutionaries are faced with the problem of making them so. But what will be the source of this new authority, once tradition and habit are undone? Revolutionary thinkers might come up with all sorts of answers, from the will of the people to the dictates of one particular party. But the freedom to think abstractly about the problem of authority is a far cry from actually finding a workable solution to it.

In any case, historical experience suggests that the real question has little to do with preferable choices. It is instead which strongmen will step in to take power and what sort of order they will impose. This is what happened in the wake of the French Revolution with the rise of Napoleon, during the Russian Revolution with the rise of Lenin, in the course of the Chinese Revolution with Mao Zedong, and in various other cases. In the midst of political upheaval, the ruthless are free to rise. What authoritative power could block them, when the old authorities have been thrown down and new ones have not yet taken form?

Revolutions inevitably present people with difficult choices, much at odds with the liberationist rhetoric that surrounds the overthrow of established government. Societies need order, and order inevitably constrains us. Whatever our wishes, we are not free to conjure out of thin air an order that will do otherwise. "All revolutionists, the moment they undertake actual responsibilities, become in some sort conservative," wrote one historian.[68] This is why modern revolutions, which flourish in an atmosphere of utopian expectation, so often frustrate the hopes that give them life.

RIGHTS

Americans are still fascinated by the idea of individual rights,
which is the zodiac sign under which their country was born.

—Ronald Dworkin

The notion of rights, as Ronald Dworkin understood, is central to
American political life, and has been since the Declaration of Independence. From the first Fourth of July, when the Declaration was formally
adopted, to the present day, Americans have embraced the idea that we hold with
"certain unalienable rights, that among these are Life, Liberty and the pursuit of
Happiness." Moreover, the very purpose of government is their protection: "to
secure these rights, Governments are instituted among men." And if a government fails in this primary task, it is "the Right of the People to alter or to abolish
it." The concept is so central to the Declaration of Independence, and to the
founding of the nation, that it is impossible to imagine either one without rights
being in the forefront.

*   *   *

Rights are claims we can make upon others, either legally or morally. When
we assert a right, if it is a legitimate right, others are obligated to yield to us.
Rights serve as a shield to protect the interests of individuals or groups who claim
them, generally against threats from other parties. To take an example from the
Declaration of Independence, we all have a right to life, which is to say that we
each have a right to continue living. As a corresponding obligation, others must
respect that right—that is, refrain from killing us. Rights are always social in this

respect. One does not assert them in a void; one asserts a right in relation to others.

To say that we have a right to something also implies that there is some code or law that is broken when that right is violated. When a person is robbed, for example, and is deprived of the right to enjoy his or her property, a basic state of justice is breeched. We feel certain of the reality of that violated code. But we understand the state of justice by intuition as much as by reason. There is no perfect, universally accepted way to define rights and their application. Nor do all people understand justice and rights in the same way. Since beliefs about rights differ, people disagree a great deal about how our laws should reflect them.

Consider the right of self-defense. When threatened with bodily harm, a person has the right defend him- or herself with deadly force, if necessary. Suppose a woman comes home to find a robber in the midst of stealing her valuables. The robber is armed with a knife, and when surprised, attacks the homeowner. If she draws a gun, she is clearly within her rights to use it, and if the attacker is killed, she can hardly be charged with any misdeed.

But life is complex and often presents us with less clear-cut situations. Suppose that the woman is attacked and shoots the robber, but only wounds him. Suppose further that, in a state of angry agitation, she fatally shoots the disabled robber a few moments later. Is that final shot a matter of self-defense, or is it an unlawful killing?

Opinions will differ. The sifting of rights—in this case, hers to self-defense, and his to life—will not necessarily lead to a perfect result. The sifting is also the lifeblood of the law and a project that has no real end.

*   *   *

Whatever confusion there is in applying them to specific cases, Americans have long embraced their rights with something like religious fervor. In recent decades we have even intensified our claims to them and expanded the range of rights we demand. In fact, we have lived through a "rights revolution," as many observers have put it. This revolution includes the Civil Rights Movement, in which African Americans sought full protection of their rights as citizens under the law. It also includes similar movements among women, Native Americans, Hispanic Americans, and, more recently, LGBTQ individuals.

But the rights revolution goes far beyond these examples. It includes expanded demands for privacy rights, consumer rights, the right to good education, a right to medical care, and environmental rights. The last of these include not only the right of all people to live in a safe, clean environment, but even the granting of rights to features of the land, such as rivers, that they be protected from degradation by human activity.

Taken together, this explosion in rights claims is remarkable. As philosopher Richard Flathman put it, the claim to rights has become "positively ubiquitous," cropping up constantly "in political speeches, in the law, in the media, and indeed in the workplace and marketplace."

We are so attached to the notion of rights that it seems perverse to argue against them. It is worth considering, however, whether at some point the expansion of rights and the intrusion of rights talk into every facet of life is actually beneficial. For example, given that obligations are incurred whenever rights are claimed, the expansion of accepted rights in recent decades means that our society has accumulated a very substantial burden of obligations to fulfill. While individuals might find the assertion of their rights liberating, the profusion of rights can actually reduce freedom for society as a whole.[69]

There are also subtler costs involved when rights become the main lens through which we view our political and legal life. It is in the nature of rights, for example, that they focus attention on confrontational aspects of our problems. This might be clarifying and useful in some cases, as it was in the Civil Rights Movement.

Yet simplification and confrontation are not necessarily proper approaches when facing many challenges. If problems are multifaceted, viewing them in terms of rights and obligations can be misleading or even destructive. We often speak of a right to education, and if understood as a right to access or availability of education, it is surely a keystone of modern social life. But education is such a complex, collaborative matter that any absolute claim to it as a right seems misbegotten.

Which leaves a question. If the assertion of rights is less than fruitful as a way to approach complex challenges, what are the options? In the wake of the rights revolution, Americans will have to think creatively about that question if we are to make headway on the problems we face today and the challenges that the future surely holds. Rights are crucial, but they are not everything.

SENATE

> This house is a sanctuary; a citadel of law, of order, and of liberty; and it is here—it is here, in this exalted refuge; here, if anywhere, will resistance be made to the storms of political phrenzy and the silent arts of corruption; and if the Constitution be destined ever to perish by the sacrilegious hands of the demagogue or the usurper, which God avert, its expiring agonies will be witnessed on this floor.
>
> —Aaron Burr, Vice President (1801–1805)

These words come from a farewell speech Aaron Burr made in 1805 as he left the Vice Presidency and his office as President of the Senate. In the speech, Burr paid tribute to the Senate as a "sanctuary," free from political corruption. There is rich irony here. While Burr was defending the Senate as a citadel of law and a bastion against corruption, he was at the heart of a great "political phrenzy" himself, having recently killed the great Alexander Hamilton in a duel. To Hamilton, Burr was the sort of corrupt schemer who presented the gravest of threats to democracy. If Hamilton was right, Burr was exactly the demagogue and usurper that Burr warned against in his farewell.

Whatever Burr was, however, he was no fool, and his tribute to the Senate made perfect sense to those who were present that day. Indeed, many senators were overcome by Burr's words, openly weeping by the end of the speech. They understood and embraced Burr's vision of the Senate's unique role in protecting the nation's government from corruption. Without it, many in the Founding era feared, the federal government might drift away toward tyranny. The Senate was to be, in James Madison's words, "the great anchor of the Government."

*   *   *

The Senate was created by the Constitution, which calls for a bicameral legislature—that is, a legislature made up of two separate bodies. The Constitution calls
for the Senate to be made up of two members from each state, giving a total of 100
senators today. Since each state has equal representation, states with small populations wield relatively greater power in the Senate than in the House of Representatives, where membership is proportional to population. Fearing the potential
power of big states over the small, the Framers constituted the Senate as one of the
government's bulwarks against the tyranny of the majority.

Though the Senate is part of the legislature and no laws can pass without going
through it, Article II, Section 2 of the Constitution also gives the Senate powers
that are more in line with the executive branch and function. The Constitution
mandates that the Senate vote on treaties negotiated by the president, which must
pass by two-thirds to take effect. The Senate also has a role in confirming men and
women nominated to serve as judges in the federal courts, as ambassadors, and in
certain other high-level offices.

*   *   *

Today, we might lose sight of the Senate's distinctive role and think of it as roughly
the same as the House of Representatives. However, the senators who listened to
Aaron Burr's farewell would have had a thorough understanding of what a senate
is, likely knowing something about the term's long history. The word, taken directly
from ancient Rome, is related to various others with the same Latin root, such as
senior, seniority, and *senile*. The Roman Senate was a body made up of elders, patri-
archal leaders of prominent families, who were assumed to embody certain virtues
necessary for the guidance of a republic. One of our own senators, Robert Byrd of
West Virginia, spoke to this point, describing the ideal senator as "…not the swiftest
of the swift, nor the strongest of the strong, but the wisest of the wise. That is the
reason they were to be old men. They were to have had the experience of a lifetime,
with lessons learned from the hard school of experience for their guidance."

Many governments over the 2500 years since the founding of Rome have
included such bodies in their governments. The House of Lords has played a similar
role in British government. Almost all of our own state governments also include a
senate; only Nebraska does without one. In every case, the notion of a senate suggests
certain qualities: ideally, senates bring a steadying influence to the governing of
institutions, a voice of experience, as Byrd said, from men and women who will
speak for long-term interests rather than short-term gain. Embodying the wisdom
of experience, senators should be above the daily fray of governance, independent of

the shifting currents of political passions.

The Constitution's provisions for the Senate reflect this understanding. For example, it limits senators to people 30 years of age and over, thereby ensuring some worldly experience. For the House of Representatives, by contrast, the lower limit is 25 years of age.

The Constitution also calls for longer terms in the Senate—six years—than in the House of Representatives, whose members are elected every two years. Longer terms in office give senators more time between elections, loosening the grip of electoral politics on their judgment. Buffered from direct democratic pressure, the Senate should be better able to make difficult, unpopular decisions when the times demand them.

*   *   *

Doing its job puts the Senate in a tough spot. Its mission in our government is, in part, to do the unpopular thing. On a big scale, the Senate is the part of our government that is meant to slow the pace of lawmaking, to be a sticking point where legislation can be held in place for closer scrutiny. This is the logic behind the Senate's quirky rules.

The most familiar of these rules are those that allow filibusters. A filibuster happens when a senator takes the floor as part of a debate and, in effect, refuses to yield. According to Senate rules, the speaker can go on indefinitely, and can only be stopped by a three-fifths vote for "cloture," at least for ordinary legislative business. Just the threat of an endless filibuster can force a bill to be pulled from consideration.

One other Senate rule accomplishes something similar. This rule allows senators to attach non-germane amendments to bills under debate. So a senator who dislikes a bill can add amendments that have nothing to do with it. By introducing unrelated content, a senator can slow the progress of the bill, perhaps to the point of killing it altogether.

Rules allowing filibusters and non-germane amendments give individuals or small groups of senators crucial power over the Senate's work. As one historian put it, "The Senate is a shrine to the rights of the political minority and its rules confer considerable power on it to thwart the will of the majority."

A former congressman, John Culver, put it more acidly: "If you just want to be unpleasant and have a temper tantrum, and if you just want to be excessively self-obsessed, you can have a field day in the Senate. You can break all the toys in the sandbox if that's what you want. ... The rules of the Senate are congenial to permitting the least consequential member to shut the place down if he's smart enough or willful enough to do it."

*   *   *

Yet those willful members rarely bring the Senate to a halt. Senators like to show their constituents that they too can get things done. The Senate also has a long history of personal clubbiness, and it is a rare senator who will anger colleagues by constantly tying up business.

So the Senate gets on with its work and legislates. Indeed, if one looks at the massive growth in laws passed in recent decades, one might ask whether the Senate has been meeting its responsibilities in protecting the republic from too much and too intrusive governing. When one recent hero of the Senate died, he was widely praised for authoring or co-sponsoring over 550 laws passed during his long career.[70] It may be that each of those was necessary and each has had, on balance, a positive effect on this country. But the heavy output from this one senator suggests, at the very least, that the Senate has not been over-performing in its role as a brake on legislative excess.

Socialism

And so the earth that was made a common treasury for all to live comfortably upon, is become, through man's unrighteous actions one over another, to be a place wherein one torments another.

—from *The True Levelers' Standard Advanced*

In 2016, a major American political figure performed a feat many thought suicidal. Bernie Sanders announced his run for the presidency as a self-proclaimed socialist. In doing so, he firmly grabbed one of the third rails of American politics. According to the common wisdom of not long ago, embracing socialism meant instant, smoldering political doom for a national candidate. Yet Sanders, who had been a committed socialist throughout his long career, did more than just survive; he attracted fervent support and millions of votes.

Something about his candidacy seemed discordant, however. Sanders ran as a Democrat. This raised questions. Was Sanders less socialist than he claimed? Or, was the Democratic Party more socialist than generally understood? Many Democrats, after all, were surprisingly comfortable with Sanders as their standard-bearer. This alone suggests that socialism is not some alien concept in American politics, but that it is, perhaps, more ingrained here than is often understood.

The word's history might clarify matters. The term *socialism* isn't especially old. Its first use came in the early 19th century in Europe, when modern industrialization was taking off and shaking nations like an earthquake.

The early industrial era, with its swelling slums, its "dark Satanic mills," and its impoverished workers, was the context that gave rise to socialism. The industrial economy created enormous wealth, but also had one salient feature that early socialists focused on. The profits of industrialism went into private hands—but at enormous social cost. The disparity between huge private gains and equally great suffering drove the development of socialist thought.

The responses of the first socialists varied. Some drew up plans for small utopian societies, founded on novel programs of work and distribution of its profits. Classical socialism, however, took a different path. For its thinkers, the solutions to workers' problems lay not in experiments on the margins of society, but in wholesale social change. Revolutions would be required that would do away with the legal and political structures that supported the industrial economy.

If society was to be reordered from top to bottom, property rights, the basis of the economic order, would need to be drastically altered, or done away with altogether. In a just society, economic goods would be distributed according to need, rather than according to the traditional rules of ownership.

For mainstream socialists, only one plausible agent could manage such a profound reordering: the state. So, as socialist thought matured during the 19th century, the state took center stage in its plans. Economist Friedrich Hayek summed it up: "The common aim of all socialist movements was the nationalization of the 'means of production, distribution and exchange,' so that all economic activity might be directed according to a comprehensive plan toward some ideal of social justice."

There were other, less drastic, ways to deal with economic inequality: the ways chosen by the United States, among other nations. The measures they took—welfare programs, progressive taxation, minimum wage, and other regulations—were reformist rather than revolutionary. Yet those measures can be called socialist (and certainly were, and are) by critics. The broader society, acting on behalf of the less fortunate, imposed policies that infringed on traditional property rights. However, these reform efforts were made within a system that maintained a basic fidelity to private economic freedoms. The reforms eroded the rights of property, but without destroying them.

*   *   *

To understand socialism, especially in its classical form, it is important to consider what it is that gets socialized under its rule. It is not just a matter of shifting economic goods from rich to poor. For example, at a deeper level socialism socializes decision-making. It removes the authority to decide what, where, and how to produce goods from private parties and places it with the state.[71]

To 19th century socialists, this idea was immensely appealing. They could hardly imagine that government planners would do a worse job at organizing the economy than the people at large. They mocked capitalism for its wasteful, irrational results: wild swings between growth and depression, the overproduction of some goods, and the failure to produce enough for the poor. The obvious answer was to shift economic decision-making from the millions of uncoordinated, self-interested parties in the general market and deliver it to the state. There, the economy would be subject to rational planning and coordination across economic sectors.

This confidence in socialist planning was put to the test during the 20th century, with generally distressing results. Economies, as we came to see more clearly over time, are immensely complex organisms that run on fantastic amounts of information. In a market economy, decision-making is widely dispersed, and information flows freely throughout the system. People, including business owners, make decisions constantly about what to produce or consume, what must be spent, and what can be saved. This diffuse system of decision-making seemed a recipe for chaos to socialists, but it proves to be a relatively efficient way to process vast amounts of information and allocate resources. When planning is centralized, the enormous load of information proves nearly impossible to digest.

In addition to decision-making, socialism also socializes responsibility by having the state bear the burden for economic trouble. Free markets generally place responsibilities for the outcome of decisions on those who make them. If one's decisions work well, one enjoys the rewards. When they don't, for whatever reasons, one endures the penalties. This can be a cruel system, but self-interest prods people toward actions that strengthen the economy.

To the degree that socialism breaks down the connections between private choices and economic rewards, it dampens those incentives. While it promises to ease the lot of those who suffer, socialist economies, missing this incentive, have had less innovative, more sluggish economies as a result, and in some cases full economic breakdown. This, of course, has ill effects across the economic board, among the poor at least as much as among the rich.

*   *   *

In addition to decision-making and responsibility, socialism socializes something else as well: political power. To plan or reshape economies, to any degree, depends on applying concentrated political force.

But concentrating power this way is something that the American constitutional system was designed, in large part, to prevent. It limits governmental power to begin with and disperses it throughout its various branches and levels. Finally, it grounds that power on the most diffuse possible source: the will of the people themselves.

Thus, socialism faces a serious problem in the United States. It requires concentrated power in a system designed to deny that, and democratic support from a people whose traditions and ethos run mostly another way.

For the 20th century's harder socialists, constitutional niceties did not matter much, and power, however gotten, was all. There is, however, a democratic socialism, which seeks power through persuasion rather than imposition (although power it must have). In effect, it aims to socialize the people themselves, encouraging them to think socially first, and less in terms of one's own welfare. As democratic socialist Michael Walzer put it, "[S]ocialists have argued that mere private life, however enhanced by state action, cannot sustain a significant human culture." Our human calling, a socialist believes, is not to live for the narrower circles of attachment—self, family, neighborhood—but to recognize a present and future shared with the broadest possible community of people.

SOVEREIGNTY

> In every government there necessarily exists a power from which there is no appeal, and which for that reason may be termed absolute and uncontroulable. The person or assembly in whom this power resides, is called the sovereign or supreme power of the state. With us the Sovereignty of the union is in the People.
>
> —Charles Cotesworth Pinckney

Like the Roman deity Janus, national sovereignty has two faces. One looks out to other countries; the other looks within, to the heart of a nation. In ordinary political discourse, it is the outward-looking sovereignty that one comes across most often, and the context is international relations. There we speak of sovereign nations, which are nations with an independent government, one with enough power to control its own territory, free from internal threat or control from abroad. The United Kingdom is a sovereign nation; Tibet, dominated by China, is not.

National sovereignty is a key to international relations. For example, recognized sovereign nations sign treaties with others. Sovereignty implies that the governments of such nations are legitimate and actually hold the power they claim. If one party to a treaty is more puppet than sovereign, the agreement may be worthless.

There is a brute reality behind the notion of national sovereignty. Power is key, and even governments that have only the slimmest claim to the loyalty of their people may be sovereign. For example, governments led by tyrants—Gaddafi in Libya, for example—might well be recognized as sovereign if they clearly control their country.

In international relations, that control gives other countries a party to negotiate with, one to hold accountable for national actions. Negotiating with a tyrant such as Gaddafi might have been unpleasant, but it was preferable to ignoring Libya instead. Gaddafi's corruption mattered less to other nations than the fact of his rule and the necessity of dealing with Libya on trade, immigration, and other issues. They needed results, and Gaddafi was the leader to produce them.

*   *   *

Turning inward from external relations, the concept of sovereignty relates to that question of internal power, within a nation. One of the first modern philosophers to explore sovereignty in depth, Thomas Hobbes (1588–1679), listed what he called its "marks." He included the power to make and repeal laws, to make decisions about war and peace, and to judge all disputes. He added something less tangible as well. The sovereign, he wrote, is "the Soule of the Common-wealth." His point was that whoever holds sovereign power must embody a nation's spirit.

Hobbes wrote about *the* sovereign, because he believed that sovereign power must be unified. Dividing the sovereign power, Hobbes insisted, "is absolutely fatal to commonwealths." Some single power must have a final word in matters of law, war, and justice to make governing possible. To allow competing centers of power to flourish is to risk civil strife.

Hobbes was emphatic about this point, for good reason. He lived through the long years of the English Civil War, during which England's king, Charles I, was executed, leaving that country without its traditional leader. With no sovereign power uniting them, the English were undone, as warring parties fought their way across the land, sowing destruction as they went.

Hobbes's fear of chaos was such that he dismissed the dangers of despotism when political power was strongly centralized. Tyranny "signifyeth nothing more, nor lesse, than the name of Sovereignty," he wrote, and "a Toleration of the professed hatred of Tyranny, is a Toleration of hatred to the Common-wealth in general."

*   *   *

The American Founders could hardly have disagreed more. They not only attacked tyranny constantly in their writings, but founded a nation on its near opposite: the sovereignty of the people. The real power of this government would come from the will of the people, they insisted. And by framing such a government they complicated our political life immeasurably.

The doctrine of popular sovereignty presents many challenges, but the most obvious is practical. If sovereignty lies with the people, how is their will—divided among millions of people—translated into functional government?

The Founders' answer was highly complicated. The will of the people is delegated to representatives, in not only one government, but several: national, state, and local. At each level, power is further divided into different, competing branches: legislative, executive, and judicial. (Hobbes, champion of the unified sovereign, would have dropped dead at the thought.)

But the challenges presented by popular sovereignty do not stop there. If the people are sovereign, what happens when they disagree among themselves, which they always do, and sometimes violently? We have mechanisms to deal with disagreement. We have elections, for instance, where majorities win, and winners determine what government does. Victory in them creates a certain temporary, practical sovereignty.

This being the case with elections, however, we might spare a thought for political minorities, whose sense of sharing in the sovereign power must suffer with each defeat. Of course, they are "the people" too. We should spare a thought, as well, for the government, which is put in the uneasy position of imposing unwanted policies on some of the people all of the time.

*   *   *

The imposition of unwanted policies is unavoidable in American government. One plausible way to ameliorate the problem of governing in the face of disagreement is to govern less. Less active government leaves more room for people to act according to their own will, to be sovereign in their own spheres, as it were.

But when a broad majority demands active government, it must get its way. Which leaves us on difficult terrain, in times such as the present, when divisions run deep and so much of our social life is politicized. Among the people, in the "Soule of the Common-wealth," dissension reigns. We have today what Hobbes feared: a divided sovereign power, at odds with itself.

SPEAKER OF THE HOUSE

The House of Representatives shall chuse their speaker.

—The United States Constitution

The office of Speaker of the House, while not ancient, has a long history, one that goes back before the founding of the United States. It is British in origin, and under the British constitution the Speaker of the House was the leader of the House of Commons. Historically, it was the Speaker who spoke for, or represented, that institution to the rest of the British government—to the King or Queen, for instance—and to the country as a whole.

The office was carried to the American colonies and in time put to use in the framing of the Constitution, specifically Article 1, Section 2. The Speaker is the leader of the House of Representatives, chosen by its members. As leader, the Speaker sits atop one of the key institutions in the national government. No legislation can become law without passing a vote in the House, and the Speaker has a great deal to say about what legislation will be considered for passage, and when. The importance of the office is recognized in the Presidential Succession Act of 1947, according to which the Speaker of the House is third in line for the presidency in case of disaster.

Though we now say that the Speaker *leads* the House of Representatives, in 1789 they would have used another term: the Speaker *presides* over the House. In presiding, the Speaker would remain largely above the political fray. It was (and still is) the Speaker's job to oversee deliberations in the House, ensuring that the rules guiding the legislative process were followed fairly. By contrast, the real political leader of the House in the first Congress was not its Speaker, Thomas Muhlenberg, but James Madison, then a representative from Virginia, who used his influence to set the legislative agenda.

While early Speakers were expected to be almost apolitical in presiding over the House, that changed before long. The crucial development here was the rise of political parties, as Representatives split into competing camps. As this happened, the vote for a Speaker came to reflect party allegiances, with Federalists supporting their preferred candidate and Democratic Republicans supporting theirs. To this day, the Speaker of the House of Representatives, though elected by a vote of all House members, is always the leader of whichever party holds the majority of seats there.[72] Thus, as the office has evolved, the Speaker has come to have a dual role: as leader of his or her party and as the presiding figure over the whole House.

Any Speaker who honors both sides of this dual role will struggle with the tension between them. As party leader, the Speaker will favor his or her party's policies. But the office also carries responsibilities to the institution of the House of Representatives as a whole. For the House to function as intended—that is, to deliberate over bills carefully and to pass legislation that the nation needs— requires intricate rules to guide the process. It's the Speaker's job to see that the process works as intended.

For the House to function properly also requires some minimum of mutual respect among members. There are guidelines in place to maintain that basic level, either through formal rules or through an unwritten code of conduct, and the Speaker has a responsibility to see that House members toe the line.

*   *   *

Though the Constitution establishes the office of the Speaker, it is silent about its specific powers. The actual power of the Speakership has waxed and waned, then waxed again over time, dependent on each Speaker's personality and the rules governing the House. During much of the 20th century, for example, the Speaker was relatively weak, with much of the legislative of power within the House held at the committee level and by the committees' potent chairmen.

More recently, however, Speakers have gained in power. An interesting illustration comes from the career of Newt Gingrich. Gingrich, a Republican, was elected to the House of Representatives in 1978, during a long period of Democratic domination there. Fiery by temperament, he made a name for himself with aggressive attacks on Democrats in general and on their House leaders in particular.

By the 1990s, Gingrich had gathered a following among restive Republicans in Congress, who shared his yearning to break the Democratic hold on the House. With his swelling influence, Gingrich issued a notable initiative, the famous "Contract with America." This was a set of ten legislative actions that Republicans promised to take if elected. House candidates across the country could run on this contract in the 1994 elections, and many chose to do so. The result was a striking electoral victory, with Republicans winning a majority in the House for the first time in four decades.

This victory was something of a landmark, as it was the first time since Reconstruction, more than a hundred years earlier, that the House of Representatives provided the kind of unified, coherent policy leadership that Gingrich and the Contract with America offered. In its wake, and to great surprise, Gingrich found himself elected Speaker of the House and at the head of a political juggernaut. For better or worse, he was also a Speaker clearly defined by strong partisan commitments.

*   *   *

Speakers since Gingrich have inherited an office shaped by his legacy of centralized power within the House and strong partisanship. Some might have preferred otherwise, but with an evenly divided electorate and strong partisan currents running throughout our political system, Speakers have been pulled toward party-based leadership. As Dennis Hastert, who held the office from 1999 to 2007, put it, "The job of the Speaker is to rule fairly, but ultimately to carry out the will of the majority." In our times, that majority is most often defined by party loyalty.

While it might be tempting to blame Gingrich and other Speakers of the House for the strong partisanship currently found in the House of Representatives, the blame cannot be placed solely on them. Speakers are, after all, elected by members of their own party and must answer to them. If rank-and-file members want a Speaker given to compromise and bipartisanship, they can elect one. But current political forces are driving the House in a different direction, and in recent years, many House members have shown a desire for *less* compromising leadership rather than more. Indeed, recent Speakers, Republican and Democratic, have had to face down insurrections mounted by the most partisan wings of their own parties just to hold onto their office.[73]

Such strong partisanship is a fact of political life for the foreseeable future. Still, citizens who want more even-tempered, less bitterly divisive politicking in Congress have nowhere better to look for leadership than to the Speaker. The Speaker of the House is more than a party chieftain and has a clearer responsibility to act in the name of the whole institution, indeed in the name of the American people, than anyone else in Congress.

STATUTE

The Constitution overrides a statute, but a statute, if consistent with the Constitution, overrides the law of judges.

—Benjamin Cardozo, Supreme Court Justice (1932–1938)

A *statute* is, first of all, a law, but a law that comes from a particular source. Statutes are laws passed by legislative bodies, such as the United States Congress (or the Parliament of the United Kingdom, or the legislatures of our fifty states). When civics texts discuss bills that become laws, they have statutes in mind.

Since legislatures represent the people, the laws they pass express the people's will as well as can be. This imbues statutes with a special force, which is why, as Supreme Court Justice Benjamin Cardozo pointed out, they override what he called the law of judges.

What Cardozo meant was this. The law of judges, or the common law, is the law that has evolved through decisions made by judges, case by case. Its source is the judges themselves, who apply the law as they inherit it, but also adapt it as they apply it to specific cases. The result is a large body of law that has evolved within the courts and is dependent on the authority of judges.

Statutes differ. As acts of legislatures, they represent the will of the people more directly than laws that grow out of judges' decisions, and statutes trump those laws.

To see the difference, consider one case from the world of publishing—and murder. In the late 1970s, David "Son of Sam" Berkowitz was arrested for a series of grisly killings in New York City, for which he was tried and found guilty. After he was imprisoned for those crimes, however, rumors began to circulate that he was preparing to sell his story for publication.

According to the judge-made legal tradition, there was nothing to prevent Berkowitz from doing so, nor from earning money from the deal. But the notion that Berkowitz would profit from his crimes outraged the public. In response, New York's legislature passed a statute that called for proceeds from such deals to be set aside for victims of the original crimes. Thus, a statute was passed which overrode laws that had evolved in the courts.

Statutes, unlike judge-made laws, capture a definitive judgment at a particular time. They are an expression of the people's will, and must be seen in this serious light. In keeping with this seriousness, the Constitution makes it difficult to pass statutes, placing various hurdles in the way, including a bicameral legislature and the presidential veto. Our state constitutions do likewise.[74]

Despite the rigors of the legislative process, wrong-headed laws are occasionally passed. Legislatures will at times pass statutes that violate the standards of the Constitution. In such cases, as Cardozo noted, statutes are overridden by the Constitution. If the Supreme Court determines that a statute violates the Constitution, the statute will be nullified. This has happened well over a hundred times in this country to laws passed by Congress, and well over a thousand times to state and local laws.

*   *   *

Having distinguished statutes from constitutional and judge-made law, it is worth contrasting statutes with two other tools of government, both of which can be mistaken for statutory law. Statutes differ from governmental regulations, and they differ from executive orders.

Regulations are the rules that are generated by governmental agencies, such as the Environmental Protection Agency or the Securities and Exchange Commission. These agencies—and there are many of them at both the state and national levels—produce a vast number of regulations that reach into every corner of American life. If you find yourself on the wrong side of them, you will surely feel as if you have broken the law when they are enforced. But regulations are not laws in the sense that statutes are.

Likewise with executive orders. These are official statements through which a president can direct the way the agencies of the Executive branch enact policies. Like regulations, executive orders have real legal force, but they are not laws themselves.

The difference between statutes, on the one hand, and regulations and executive orders, on the other, is in the relative ease with which the latter can be changed. Regulations are produced by specific processes within given agencies, which can alter or remove them as well. These processes are separate from ones of the legislature and not subject to the hurdles of the law-making process found there.

Executive orders come from presidents, and they too can be changed without the involvement of the legislature. For example, when Barack Obama held the presidency, he used executive orders to set key immigration policies. Yet, without the force of statutes, his executive orders were open to reversal after he left office. When Donald Trump was elected, he was able to rescind elements of Obama's immigration policy with executive orders of his own.[75]

As the Constitution says, "All legislative Powers herein granted shall be vested in a Congress of the United States." Regulations and executive orders have important uses, but they are not statutes—not products of legislation—and therefore, they lack the force and stability of statutes.

Subpoena

A *subpoena* is a legal device, a written demand, that compels an individual to provide information to some legitimate authority, such as a court. Subpoenas take two basic forms: one is a demand for evidence, such as documents or computer hard drives; the other is a summons for a person to appear before an investigative body to answer questions. The word's roots mean "under" (*sub*) and "penalty" (*poena*). Anyone who receives a subpoena is under the threat of a legal penalty if they fail to meet the subpoena's demands. With the threat of penalties, subpoenas provide leverage to pry information from unwilling hands.

Subpoenas are most often issued in ordinary court cases. But they also play an important role in the political sphere. Government must police itself to some degree, which means it must investigate potential wrongdoing within its own offices. For example, Congress has oversight responsibilities in relation to the executive branch. If there is reason to suspect corruption there, a Congressional committee will launch an investigation and gather the pertinent facts. If necessary, the committee will use subpoenas to coerce testimony or evidence from the parties under investigation. In some cases, special prosecutors may also be named to investigate alleged governmental wrongdoing, and they too can issue subpoenas.

Given the legal force of the subpoena, there are rules to insure its proper use. If Congress launches an investigation, individual representatives or senators cannot issue subpoenas on their own initiative. They must be approved by committee vote. Nor can a special prosecutor issue a subpoena at will; he or she must submit a request to a three-judge panel with final say as to whether a subpoena will be issued or not.

*   *   *

The case of Richard Nixon and the Watergate scandal provides a good example of the use of the subpoena in a government investigation, and of the subpoena's power. The downfall of Nixon's presidency stemmed from a seemingly minor event, a break-in at a Democratic National Committee office at the Watergate building in Washington, D.C., which occurred during the 1972 presidential campaign. The break-in itself got little attention at first, but led to some pointed questions: Who were the burglars, what were they up to, and who sent them?

Congress called for an investigation of the matter, and as the investigation proceeded, an odd fact came to light. For years, Nixon had secretly taped conversations in his office. Once investigators found out about these tapes, they naturally wanted them and formally requested that the president turn them over. But few presidents have been less likely to submit to such a request than the combative Nixon, who refused.

Which brought the Watergate investigation to a crucial impasse. With Nixon unwilling to turn over the tapes, investigators took the next step, issuing a subpoena. By using its subpoena power, the investigators ramped up the pressure on the president enormously, and the demand set Nixon on a course to his political demise. Thus, the subpoena played a key role in the only presidential resignation in American history.

*   *   *

With a government as large and powerful as that of the United States, there are countless closed doors and a near certainty that behind some of them, people misuse their power in one way or another. The subpoena can open the doors and bring to light corrupt dealings.

However, we should consider the power of the subpoena in the context of our sharply divided and acrimonious political environment. Charges of corruption or gross incompetence in government seem to be daily media fare. Subpoenas, or the threat of subpoenas, provide investigators with one of the most effective weapons in their arsenal. Given the current political climate, we should not be surprised that the political world is being shaken to its core, nor that the subpoena is being used in the heat of battle. When the office of Special Counsel Robert Mueller investigated allegedly illegal relations between Donald Trump and the Russians, they delivered over 2800 subpoenas to relevant parties.

However, here is a related consideration, one with a Darwinian twist. In our dangerous political environment, we should also not be surprised if defenses against the subpoena evolve in response to its use. Already in recent years, the reports have surfaced of missing hard drives, alias e-mail accounts, deleted e-mail troves, and "homebrew" servers. As public officials face the threat of investigation, for good reasons or bad, look for them to take increasingly sophisticated measures to maintain the privacy of their political dealings.

SUPREME COURT

> Broadly speaking, the chief reliance of law in a democracy is the habit of popular respect for law. Especially true is it that law as promulgated by the Supreme Court depends upon confidence of the people in the Supreme Court as an institution.
>
> —Felix Frankfurter, Supreme Court Justice (1939–1962)

While the Supreme Court depends on popular respect for its effectiveness and upon the "confidence of the people," the relationship between it and the people is surely complicated. Of all our major government institutions, the Supreme Court is the least democratic and by design the most insulated from the currents of popular feeling. While members of Congress and the president are elected by the people and get their legitimacy from those elections, the courts are different. Their work depends instead on understanding and applying the law, a job best done without too much direct pressure from the public.

This is truest of the Supreme Court, which, as its name suggests, is the highest court in the land, sitting atop the federal judicial system. It is the nation's highest authority on the law, and thus has a final say on the nation's legal matters. The Court has a special responsibility to resolve those legal conflicts we call constitutional: whether the laws passed by state and national legislatures violate constitutional limits, for example, or whether they are executed according to protections guaranteed by the Constitution.

If this sounds abstract, the Supreme Court's actions are anything but. Because the Constitution limits government and the Supreme Court has a final say on how the Constitution is interpreted, it has great authority concerning what government can do for, or to, us. What, for example, are the limits of gun control, given the

Second Amendment protection of the right to bear arms? Or, how much rule-making power can regulatory agencies legitimately wield, given that they are unelected? How are civil rights to be understood, and how far does one person's civil right to, say, equal job opportunity limit the rights of business owners to hire and fire whomever they wish? These are concrete issues that affect us every day and have immense consequences.

With stakes so high, the Supreme Court has an especially sensitive role in American government. It stands in judgment over the government itself to ensure that it acts according to its deepest law, the Constitution. Therefore, its decisions are expected to guarantee the integrity of the system as a whole.

*   *   *

Given the heavy responsibility the Court bears, its justices must have those quali-ties that distinguish good judges in general. Ideally, they will have an authoritative, historically informed view of the law. They must be seen as impartial and cannot be personally involved in the matters they are judging. Nor should they feel the heat of direct political pressure. Their decisions must be based on principle, not on emotion, or expediency, or personal political views. For the legal system to maintain its authority, the people must have confidence that justice is adminis-tered fairly, so the Supreme Court has a special responsibility to make its decisions without favoritism of any sort, including party loyalties. "Clear heads, therefore, and honest hearts are essential to good judges," as James Wilson, one of the nation's Founders, put it.

The Court is made up of nine justices, including one Chief Justice, who has the responsibility to see that the Court operates smoothly as an institution. In accordance with the Constitution, Supreme Court justices are nominated by presidents and confirmed by a vote in the Senate. Before the Senate votes to confirm, senators have an opportunity to question the nominee and debate his or her qualifications. Once confirmed and sworn in, justices serve "during Good behavior," as the Constitution puts it. That is to say, justices serve as long as they themselves choose, barring any impeachable offense. This term of service is one of the ways justices are insulated from outside pressure.

The nomination process is crucial to the workings of the Supreme Court. Being nine in number, the power the justices wield is neither that of a single member nor of a very small group. What's more, with justices often serving long terms, it is unlikely that a majority of the justices at any one time will be appointees of a single president. In 2020, for example, justices of the Supreme Court included one nominated by George H. W. Bush, two by Bill Clinton, two by George W. Bush, two by Barack Obama, and two by Donald Trump. Since presidents nominate justices whose views they like, the appointment process, combined with long terms on the bench, tends to promote diversity of opinion within the Court.

*   *   *

Ideally, the opinions of Supreme Court members should have no bearing on their decisions, and the justices should have neither bias nor, indeed, any political will of their own. The Court exists to interpret the law, and the law rests on unchanging principles.

However, the Supreme Court has in fact played a major role in some of the most crucial political controversies of the past 70 years. Consider, for example, the school desegregation cases, especially *Brown* v. *Board of Education*, in which the Court took the lead in striking down discriminatory laws. Significantly, it was not Congress, the more popularly representative institution, that struck down school desegregation. It was the more politically insulated Supreme Court.

The *Brown* v. *Board of Education* decision was a landmark, not only on the civil rights front, but also for the direction the Supreme Court would take in the decades that followed. For many people, *Brown* revealed how much good the Court could do with the proverbial stroke of a pen. Its desegregation decisions, *Brown* and others, "shone like beacons," wrote Mary Ann Glendon, "lighting the way toward an America whose ideals of equal justice and opportunity for all would at last be realized" through the actions of the Court.

With its reputation strengthened by *Brown*, the Supreme Court entered a period of reformist activism unprecedented in our judicial history.[76] Under the leadership of Chief Justice Earl Warren, the Supreme Court seized opportunities to defend the rights of aggrieved individuals and minorities of all kinds. For example, acting on behalf of religious minorities, it struck down organized prayer in public schools; it extended the rights of accused criminals to due process when arrested (resulting in the famous Miranda rights); and it expanded the rights of individuals to free speech (which came to include, for example, a jacket bearing the words "Fuck the Draft," worn to a public high school).

Yet the Supreme Court's campaign for individual rights during the Warren years was not without dangers. As it pursued its often-unpopular string of civil liberties decisions, the Supreme Court provoked an impression that it was taking sides in political fights and using its prestige against the will of the majority. To its critics, the Court was "legislating from the bench": that is, imposing its preferences on matters which should have been left to elected legislatures.

Having become deeply involved in politically charged matters, the Supreme Court has also become a target in the nation's political conflicts. The nomination process for its justices, for example, has grown rancorous, as the nation observed in the famously bitter confirmation hearings for Robert Bork, Clarence Thomas, and Brett Kavanaugh.

The danger to the Supreme Court from its politicization runs deeper than the occasional unpleasantness. In recent years, citizens have come to see the justices as either "liberal" or "conservative" and expect those judges to decide cases in ways that advance a liberal or a conservative political agenda.

The fact remains that the Court's capacity to speak authoritatively on our highest legal matters depends on public faith in its judgments, which can only decline when it is seen as overtly politicized. If the Supreme Court is seen to be taking political stands in its decisions, it spends down its store of civic capital, upon which its own effectiveness depends. With the Supreme Court as a backstop of the whole government's legitimacy, real dangers would appear certain to emerge down this path.

TAXATION

Taxation is the source of life for the bureaucracy. ... Strong
government and heavy taxes are identical.

—Karl Marx

Since government cannot exist without its "source of life," we can safely
say that taxation, in some form, probably goes back as far as organized
government itself. Taxes are the monies (or goods) taken by the state out of
the general economy and used to support its activities. If we want government
to do much of anything, we must pay taxes to enable it. Taxation is "the vital
principle" of government, Alexander Hamilton wrote in *Federalist* 30, which
"sustains its life and motion."

In the United States, we have a good deal of government and therefore a
good deal of taxation. The governing operates at different levels: national,
state, and local, and each has its own streams of support from taxation.[77] The
sources are manifold. Income is taxed by the federal government and also by
many states. Property is taxed, especially by local government. There are sales
taxes, inheritance taxes, taxes on imports, and so-called "sin" taxes on goods or
activities that government wishes to discourage, such as cigarettes, alcohol, and
gambling.[78] If you want less of something, the thought goes, tax it.

Among the three levels of government, the national is the biggest tax
collector. In 2016, the total tax receipts for all of American government came
to $5.3 trillion, with 65 percent going to the federal government, 20 percent
to the states, and 15 percent to cities, counties and towns. With the total Gross
Domestic Product (GDP) of $18. 6 trillion that year, total taxes paid amounted
to around 28 percent of the nation's economic output. Though the rate of overall

taxation in the United States varies somewhat year by year, 28 percent is near the recent average.

Some comparisons will put these figures in perspective. The tax burden in the United States runs low compared to similarly developed countries. At the high end, France and Denmark collected taxes amounting to just over 45 percent of each country's GDP in 2017. In Germany the overall tax rate was 37.5 percent. In Japan, it was 30.6 percent. Among Anglosphere nations, the United Kingdom, Canada, and New Zealand total tax rate fell between 32 and 33 percent; and Australia came in at just under 28 percent, nearly the same as the United States.

Historical data for the United States, which would allow us to compare today's tax rates to those of earlier periods in our history, are harder to come by. However, in 1930, federal, state, and local taxes came to 11.1 percent of GDP, a good deal less than half of the contemporary rate. It seems highly likely that earlier rates were lower still. Federal revenues between 1820 and 1860, for example, generally ran from 1% to 2.5 percent of GDP. We asked much less of government in the past, so government was naturally less expensive.

*   *   *

Americans have had a rocky relationship with taxes since we cried "No taxation without representation!" and launched the Revolution. In truth, we've never been terribly fond of taxation, with representation or without.

The reasons are understandable. Paying taxes leaves us poorer as individuals, though perhaps better off as a society. Also, when we spend money—on a new car or a night out for the family—the reward is immediate. When we pay taxes, though, the gratification is generally indirect: an infrastructure project somewhere, more arms (hopefully unused) for the military, more regulatory staff in some obscure bureau, and so on.

So taxes provoke a good deal of indignation—not to mention stress—among taxpayers. Calvin Coolidge, famously frugal as president, spoke to this feeling in his 1925 inaugural address. "The collection of any taxes which are not absolutely required, which do not beyond a reasonable doubt contribute to the public welfare, is only a species of legalized larceny. Under this republic the rewards of industry belong to those who earn them."

A distaste for taxes is understandable, but when terms such as "larceny" are used to describe taxation, it casts the matter in an unduly sinister light. Government without revenue is a non-starter, like a car with no engine.

And while Americans do not much like taxes, they do demand, at the same time, lots of what government provides. These two conflicting impulses are carried by our representatives to their respective law-making bodies, local, state, and federal.

There, legislators hash out the issue as best they can and ultimately reconcile the conflict between dislike of taxes and appetite for government.

The results speak for themselves in the form of our legislation. Projections before the Coronavirus struck had the total tax burden in the United States reaching the not inconsiderable sum of $6 trillion by 2020, larger than the entire 2019 GDP of any other nation except China.

TORT

tort [noun]: A wrongful act other than a breach of contract for which relief may be obtained in the form of damages or an injunction

—*The Merriam-Webster Dictionary*

Tort is a legal term more than a strictly political one. As *Merriam-Webster* implies, it is a wrong done (to someone), for which the wronged party can seek compensation under the law. The word's etymology illustrates: in Latin, *tortus* means "twisted" or "crooked." Our words *contorted* and *tortured* come from the same root. The core idea with tort law is that someone has been harmed, and the law can force whoever is responsible to pay for the injury or loss.

Tort law applies to a wide variety of cases: the driver injured in an accident caused by a defect in the car; the patient who dies due to a medical misdiagnosis; the customer who slips on ice when entering a store. In such cases, the same basic notion applies. One party is injured and another party is liable. Through tort law, victims can file a suit seeking relief for the damages.

Although tort suits punish those responsible for harm done to others, tort law differs from criminal law. In criminal law, the government prosecutes wrongdoers, and does so on behalf of the public good. In tort law, private parties file suit for reasons of self-interest.

We can see how tort and criminal law differ by looking at the notorious O. J. Simpson murder case from the 1990s. When his wife and a male friend were found murdered, the retired football star was arrested for the crime. Simpson was charged with murder by the State of California and tried in a criminal court. When the trial ran its course, Simpson was found not guilty, the jury being unconvinced by the prosecutors' case.

But although Simpson was found not guilty in that trial, his legal troubles were far from over. After the criminal trial, the families of the two victims filed suit against him, seeking compensation for the harm they suffered from the murders. In the ensuing *civil*—not *criminal*—trial, the jury found Simpson responsible for that damage and ruled that he owed the families $33.5 million for their losses. This civil verdict was entirely separate from the criminal proceedings. Despite being found responsible for harms done in the civil trial, Simpson was still not guilty of the murders as a matter of criminal law. The $33.5 million award was pure "torts."

*   *   *

While tort law is in essence an affair between private parties, it still plays an important role in the broad project of governing. One of the primary responsibilities of government, for example, is to see that conflicts that arise among people are settled lawfully, and to ensure that some level of justice is observed in their settlement. Tort law helps achieve this, providing impartial judgments that sort out rights and responsibilities across a wide range of disputes that might not be addressed by criminal law.

Beyond this, tort law has other, broader social effects. By penalizing malicious, negligent, or otherwise liable behaviors, tort law provides an incentive for private parties to act responsibly. Toy manufacturers, for example, are more likely to test their products thoroughly if they know that any damage their products might cause could provoke ruinous lawsuits. In addition, tort law also provides a measure of justice for the public. When O. J. Simpson was found criminally innocent of the murder of his wife and friend, millions were outraged by the verdict, above all the families of the victims. The ruling in the civil trial assuaged that sense of injustice, at least to some degree.

*   *   *

Because tort law has effects that ripple out across the broader society, it sometimes becomes an issue in the political arena. Legislators grapple at times with the question of whether to reform the tort system. This is because tort cases, though fought between private parties, impose costs that are borne by all. If a manufacturer is found responsible in a tort lawsuit, a heavy penalty can be enough to destroy the company. To protect against such ruin, companies take out insurance to pay the costs should they find themselves on the receiving end of such a judgment. But insurance itself is expensive, and the cost of it is passed on to consumers through higher prices for goods and services. At least part of the dramatic rise in medical costs in recent decades comes from increases in doctors' malpractice insurance rates.

In response, lawmakers are tempted to reform tort law through legislation. Proposed reforms include caps that limit monetary settlements. Another suggested reform is to make it more difficult to launch tort suits in the first place, or to penalize lawyers who bring weak or frivolous suits to court.

To defenders of the current system, however, tort reform threatens to short-circuit a process that successfully imposes responsibilities on businesses that might otherwise ignore those responsibilities. Since tort suits fulfill this basic function, defenders argue, it serves no special purpose to reform the system—except to insulate businesses from their obligations.

As a matter a matter of political discourse, the term *tort* won't arise on a daily basis. But tort reform is a substantial issue, and is sure to return to the public eye from time to time, for the foreseeable future.

TREASON

Treason is generally deemed the highest crime, which can be committed in civil society, since its aim is an overthrow of the government. … Its tendency is to create universal danger and alarm; and on this account it is peculiarly odious, and often visited with the deepest public resentment.

—Joseph Story, Supreme Court Justice (1812–1845)

In its most dispassionate definition, *treason* is the effort to overturn a sovereign government. In less clinical terms, treason has always been seen as a special horror, a violation of deep commitments not only to one's government, but to one's whole society. According to William Blackstone, 18th-century commentator on English law, treason is a betrayal of natural, civil, and even spiritual law. Consider how frequently nations have been compared to homes, as in the terms *homeland* or *fatherland*. So treason, the betrayal of one's country, has historically aroused the same revulsion as parricide, the murder of one's father.

Accordingly, governments have punished treason in the harshest ways. It is a capital crime in the United States to this day. But mere execution seems a mild sentence compared to the horrific penalties meted out under traditional English law. Blackstone spelled out the "solemn and terrible" specifics:

1. That the offender be drawn to the gallows, and not be carried or walk…
2. That he be hanged by the neck, and then cut down alive.
3. That his entrails be taken out, and burned, while he is yet alive.
4. That his head be cut off.
5. That his body be divided into four parts.
6. That his head and quarters be at the king's disposal.

English law was the source of American law, and the Founders took treason seriously as well. Treason is the only crime mentioned in the Constitution, for example. But in contrast to the English example, the United States Constitution is restrained in dealing with treason. Appearing in Article 3, Section 3, the pertinent clause reads as follows: "Treason against the United States, shall consist only in levying War against them, or in adhering to their Enemies, giving them Aid and Comfort. No person shall be convicted of Treason unless on the Testimony of two Witnesses to the same overt Act, or on Confession in open Court."

Their restraint is significant. The Founders were acutely aware of the way treason laws could be used against innocent citizens by a tyrannical government. On this score, there was, again, a great deal to learn from English history. King Henry VIII, for example, was especially open-minded with regard to treason: it didn't take much to set him off. Clear cases, such as armed insurrection, fell under his definition of treason, but all of the following did as well: "burning houses to extort money; stealing cattle by Welchmen; counterfeiting foreign coin; ... refusing to abjure the pope; deflowering, or marrying without the royal licence, any of the king's children, sisters, aunts, nephews, or nieces, etc." All were treasonous, as were other offenses besides.

Due to their fear of abuse, the Founders were cautious in their approach to treason laws. Above all, they wanted the crime limited to specific conditions and not left open to imaginative interpretation. Thus, as noted above, treason would "consist only" in cases where the accused levied war against the United States, or clearly sided with an active enemy. Moreover, no one would be convicted of treason without the testimony of two witnesses, ruling out cases where the accusation of one was enough. And finally, in the case of confessed traitors, the confession must come in public court, to protect against confessions coerced behind closed doors.

*   *   *

The constitutional restraint shown toward treason has had its effect. Over the course of 230 years, we have had barely thirty prosecutions for the crime, with convictions numbering in the teens. Among those convicted, several were pardoned or paroled, and only a very few have actually been executed. The most recent treason trials in the United States took place over sixty years ago, stemming from the Second World War. Those included prosecutions against "Axis Sally," an American woman tried for promoting the Axis cause on radio, and Herbert John Burgman, a pilot who defected to the German Air Force during the war.

A great deal of turbulent history has passed since those last prosecutions. Among those who have *not* been tried for treason are various atomic spies and Soviet agents, the most violent anti-government protesters of the Vietnam War era, and more recently, American citizens such as John Walker Lindh who have taken up arms in pro-Islamist, anti-American causes. Even the Civil War, from which we might have expected a bumper crop of treason charges, yielded only a handful of actual prosecutions.

Judging by history, the language and spirit of the Constitution with regard to treason seem to have served us well. Our government has not, after all, fallen to any treasonous conspiracies, nor have we fully descended into cyclones of treason hunting, which have plagued other nations in difficult times. It is hard to imagine that a more expansive reading of what treason is, or a more aggressive pursuit of potential traitors, would have served the nation better than the constitutional approach we have taken.

This constitutional approach to treason may be useful in the future, as well. As fissures deepen in our society, political hotheads will be tempted to use any available weapon to destroy their opponents, including charges of treason. We are hardly above this temptation today. In the heat of Donald Trump's presidency, for example, the T-word made its ominous appearance. A former head of the CIA, John Brennan, called Trump's behavior in one instance "nothing short of treasonous," and others echoed the charge. Trump turned the tables, suggesting that the investigation of his presumed dealings with Russia amounted to a treasonous attempt to overturn his presidency.

Such charges—that a sitting president might be a traitor, for example—are concerning: first, because of any danger that a president might actually be treasonous; and second, because of the dangers presented by the cavalier use of a term dreadful in its literal sense. If, in the future, our political wars grow crueler, we would do well to recall the cool thought behind the Constitution and its treatment of treason.

TREATY

[T]here is no state so strong that it does not sometimes need
the help of others from outside it, either to support its trade
or to repel the force of foreign peoples marshaled against
it. Which is why even the most powerful nations and kings
desire to make treaties.

—Hugo Grotius

Treaties are the building blocks of the international order. They are agreements between sovereign nations that bind them to act in specified ways. So, for example, a commercial treaty between two nations might set low tariffs on goods traded between them, thus encouraging increased commerce. Or, several nations might sign a treaty that pledges mutual military support if any member nation suffers a foreign attack. This is one feature of NATO, the North Atlantic Treaty Organization.

Treaties are, as Alexander Hamilton put it in *Federalist* 75, contracts between nations.[79] Like contracts, they have the force of law. And like contracts, treaties by their nature serve the interests of each party that signs them. No nation will sign a treaty in which it gets nothing it values.

While treaties can be usefully compared to contracts, there is a crucial difference. With contracts, there is some controlling authority—a government—that can penalize breaches. Betray the commitments in your contract, and you will pay a legal price.

It is otherwise with treaties. They are made between sovereign powers, and there is no higher power to which the signatories answer (international organizations, such as the United Nations, being generally too weak to enforce much international law). If one side fails to live up to its terms, there has historically been little in the way of legal penalties to pay.

Consider the fate of the famous nonaggression pact between Nazi Germany and the old Soviet Union, a treaty signed in 1939. In it, the two nations agreed not to take military action against each other for ten years. But the treaty lasted only as long as Adolph Hitler cared to honor the German end of the bargain. Just two years later, in 1941, he decided time was up and sent an invading force of 3 million soldiers into the Soviet Union. This violation shocked the Soviets and much of the world. Yet there was no overarching authority to punish the Germans, no place for Soviet leader Joseph Stalin to plead his case against them. (Of course, Stalin had far graver concerns at the time than international arbitration.)

Having said as much, treaties tend toward self-fulfillment. As noted above, nations sign treaties that they expect will serve their interests. Thus, meeting their terms makes sense. Also, when nations sign treaties, they put their reputations on the line. National honor is at stake here, but remaining faithful to treaties is a practical matter as well. Nations that earn a reputation for dishonesty or unreliability will find it difficult to sign treaties in the future that could otherwise serve them well.

*   *   *

Treaties hold a particular place in American government, as spelled out in the Constitution: "[The President] shall have power, by and with the Advice and Consent of the Senate, to make Treaties, provided two thirds of the Senators present concur." Thus, the president is responsible for negotiating treaties with other states, which are then presented to the Senate for its consideration.[80] If two thirds of the senators vote in favor, the treaty is ratified and becomes law.

As is the case with all legislation, this constitutional process is not meant to produce treaties easily. Passing a treaty requires not just simple majority support in the Senate, but a significant majority—two thirds. Moreover, the Senate is an institution in which individual senators, or small coalitions, have the power to derail otherwise popular legislation, including treaties.

The Senate hurdle is meant to insure that treaties represent a broad spectrum of American support, that they reflect the will of the nation as a whole and not some narrower interest. It is a check on the capacity of the executive to make weighty international agreements on its own. Presidents naturally find this restraint frustrating, as it limits their ability to navigate the difficult terrain of foreign relations. But the Constitution was not designed to make life easy for presidents, nor for anyone else in government.

A recent case can clarify the place of treaties in the American system. One cherished goal of Barack Obama's presidency was to have the United States join in international efforts to control climate change. April 22, 2016, was therefore a milestone, the day when he signed the United Nations Paris Climate Agreement. By signing, Obama pledged the United States to "commit formally" to the terms of the agreement, and announced his confidence that this would "ultimately prove a turning point for our planet."

The president's signing of the Paris Agreement was thus "formal" and a "commitment." It was also, perhaps, very good policy. But the president's signature did not make it a treaty, and therefore the agreement was not American law in the sense that treaties are. By the same token, his signature carried less weight than a treaty would have done.

It was also less durable. When Obama's successor, Donald Trump, chose to pull the United States out of the agreement, there was little his opponents could do to prevent it. As it was not a treaty, Trump did not need Senate approval to bail on it.

Supporters of the Paris Agreement learned a painful lesson in this. For international agreements to have the stature and durability of treaties under United States law, they must run the gauntlet of Senate approval. Agreements that do not will lack the deep roots that ratified treaties earn through those trials.

UTOPIANISM

When I am asked where I would like to live, my standard answer is: deep in the virgin mountain forest on a lake shore at the corner of Madison Avenue in Manhattan and Champs Elysees, in a small, tidy town. Thus I am a utopian, and not because my dream happens not to exist but because it is self-contradictory.

—Lescek Kolakowski

Utopia means, literally, "no-place."[81] The word was coined in 1516 by Sir Thomas More in titling a book he wrote. *Utopia* describes a fictional island, far out in the Atlantic, where a perfectly organized society thrives. In More's telling, it is made up of several modest cities, each surrounded by fruitful farmlands. There is no private property in this Utopia, and the homes and dress of the people are identical. With no private property, More's Utopia has no theft and no need for locks on doors.

Utopia is fiction, but not mere entertainment. Its readers explore a state whose superior organization solves all the familiar social problems. In doing so, readers could hardly resist contrasting their own society with Utopia. In this way, the utopian no-place that More imagined served as a critique of his own society.

That first utopia was a harbinger, and many thinkers would follow Thomas More's example in imagining perfect societies. Though unreal, utopias have had a very real, indeed enormous, effect on history. The 19th century, for example, was something of a golden era of utopian thought. Compared with More and his book, however, these later utopians added a crucial twist. Not content with the imaginary, they formulated plans to build real "utopian" communities. The followers of one utopian, Robert Owen, founded a small colony in Indiana called New Harmony, for example. Followers of Charles Fourier gathered to form the Brook Farm near Boston. There were more of these small, rather eccentric, alternative communities.

Nineteenth century utopianism was not all quirks, however, as it bore some grave tidings for the future as well. Another figure conjuring up new worlds was Karl Marx, whose belief in a final, near-paradise of communist harmony mirrored those of other utopians.

Marx, unlike Owen and Fourier, had an enormous impact on history, especially in the rise of Marxist-inspired communist governments. These nations promised a future in which people would live in harmony, without the competition, exploitation, and suffering so common throughout human history. To get there, these communist states would require the wholesale reordering of institutions and the re-education of the people for their new life. But the result, believers promised, was sure to justify the struggle.

The essential elements of political utopianism can be seen here: that we can transcend social contention through deep reform; that human society is plastic and can be molded to fit some rational plan; and that we, or at least some of us, are smart enough to handle that planning. With the proper spirit and will, we can remake the world and turn the "no-place" of our hearts' desire into a reality.

*   *   *

High tide for political utopianism has ebbed, and nations are much less interested in trying vast social experiments of the 20th-century communism sort. However, our utopian dreams are not all dashed; they are just more a matter of retail than wholesale application as a rule.

We can see utopianism, for example, where modern technology meets the desire for personal transformation. Recent technological developments hold the promise of transcending human physical limitations in unprecedented ways, including, apparently, the possibility of uploading an individual's consciousness, from brain to computer, in a bid for "digital immortality." Or, to take another example, the use of surgeries and hormone treatments to accomplish a change in gender. With modern technology and the will to use it, we can carry out genuinely remarkable physical transformations, ones that reflect utopian inclinations.

While these examples are personal, even intimate in their point of reference, their effects are also, inevitably, social and political. No person, for example, can carry out a change of gender without affecting others. Family members and friends will always be deeply affected, as well as colleagues and medical providers. In addition, institutions must adjust to the presence of transgender individuals. The military is currently doing so, as are schools, prisons, and hospitals. Thus, while transgenderism takes a utopian attitude toward the adaptability of the human body, it involves the broader society in the effort as well. It assumes that society can re-make itself to accommodate transsexuality with something like a harmonious result.

Past experience, however, suggests that skepticism is in order regarding the ease of this transition. As one close student of utopianism wrote, "Utopia can be defined as life without alienation," but added a further blunt observation: "Alienation is reality." Utopianism rejects the conditions imposed by reality.

Historically, we have approached matters the other way around. Living in society means adjusting ourselves to all kinds of challenging, often recalcitrant realities. We fit ourselves into the world, accepting certain limits imposed by nature and the demands of life in a diverse society. This attitude has traditionally provided a starting point for social and political life. Confronting these challenges and navigating through them is the stuff of politics—and exactly what the stuff of utopia is not.

VETO

173 despots would surely be as oppressive as one.

—Thomas Jefferson, President (1801–1809)

Coming from Roman history, the Latin word *veto* means, literally, "I forbid," or "I prohibit." It's a notion full of potential applications in governance. The Romans found a particularly beneficial way to use it. During the era of the Roman Republic, there were two top leadership positions: the consuls. They had equal status but differing areas of responsibility. Crucially, however, each had veto power over the other's decisions. One could say to the other, when he tried to implement a given policy: *Veto,* I forbid it. With the veto, the Romans limited government power and presumably the amount of damage it could do to Roman society.

The same basic tool has been adopted in American government. Most often when we speak of it, we are referring to the presidential veto, which is the power of the president to block legislation that comes from Congress. It should be noted, however, that all our governors also have the veto power in state government. It is a staple of American constitutionalism.

At the national level, the veto power is granted by Article 1, Section 7 of the Constitution. It is not called the veto there, but the idea is clear. Every bill that passes Congress must be presented to the president. If the president approves the bill, he or she signs it into law. If not, the president refuses to sign, thus vetoing the legislation. This veto is not absolute, but "qualified," as the Framers of the Constitution put it. An absolute veto would kill the bill outright. With our more limited veto power, Congress can vote again on the bill. If two thirds of both houses of Congress vote in favor, the president's veto is overturned and the bill becomes law.[82]

The Constitution compels the president to do one thing more when vetoing a bill. The president must return the bill, with explanations for the veto, "to that House in which it shall have originated, who shall enter the Objections at large on their Journal." If Congress wishes to redraft the bill and they address the president's concerns, they will have every reason to expect that the rewritten bill will pass. And whether they redraft it or not, the president's comments on the bill are made part of the public record, adding to government transparency and presidential responsibility.

*   *   *

During the Constitutional Convention of 1787, the Framers discussed the veto thoroughly, but there was little opposition to the basic idea and never much doubt that when their work was done, the president would have the veto.

It's worth asking why there was such basic agreement about the veto—and for that matter, why the veto has remained unchanged over the 230 years since the Constitution was ratified. After all, the laws in question—the ones that the president would block—will have passed scrutiny by our democratically elected Congress. Why would the Framers of the Constitution give the president power to thwart the will of Congress, and thereby the will of the people?

It is, of course, because the Founders did not fully trust the democratic impulse. The veto reflects their concerns about how the will of the people, translated directly into legislation, could do real damage. They feared, among other things, a "tyranny of the majority," which, through self-serving laws, could infringe on the rights of the minority.

The trick of our government, one might say, is in taming the impulses of the people and channeling popular will toward stable, productive laws. It does so in part by submitting legislation to review from competing viewpoints—the two houses of Congress, for starters—as the law is being written.

The veto power imposes an added layer of scrutiny to the legislative process by requiring the president's review before any bill's final passage. Moreover, with the possibility of a presidential veto always in mind, Congress will generally take extra care in drafting legislation to take a president's views into account. Thus, well before a veto can even be enacted, it serves as a brake on the majority's legislative will.

These matters were more than theoretical to the Founders. When Thomas Jefferson warned about the dangers posed by 173 despots, he did not have in mind some gang of usurpers, waiting in the wings to overthrow the government. He was reflecting on his own experiences in Virginia, where he had served as governor and where the weak executive office was overmatched by a powerful legislature. Those legislators, all duly elected by the people, were Jefferson's dangerous "despots."

VICE PRESIDENT

I am Vice President. In this I am nothing, but I may be
everything.

—John Adams, Vice President (1789–1797)

Americans have a long tradition of mocking their government and
politicians. But the office of the vice presidency has been uniquely abused
and derided over its history. When Daniel Webster, the great senator, was
offered the position in 1839, he declined. "I do not propose to be buried until I
am dead," he said. Even vice presidents themselves saw fit to join in. Texas's John
Nance "Cactus Jack" Garner, who served in the office under Franklin D. Roosevelt,
said that the vice presidency "wasn't worth a bucket of warm spit." Despite the
disdain, however, many of our most formidable political leaders have served in the
position, including John Adams, Thomas Jefferson, Theodore Roosevelt, Lyndon
Johnson, and Richard Nixon.

The *vice* in the term *vice president* has a specific meaning. It refers to a person
who takes the place of another, or who represents another. In British political
history, the viceroy was a person who stood in place of, and represented, the royal
leader, king or queen.

So, in our system, the vice president is one who serves in the place of the
president. This often happens in ceremonial matters, with vice presidents famously
traveling the world, representing the nation at important funerals. But the "standing
in place of" has a deeper meaning. Article II of the Constitution puts it this way:
"In case of removal of the President from office, or of his death, or resignation,
or inability to discharge the powers and duties of the said office, the same shall
devolve on the Vice President." Above all, this is the job of the vice president: to

take the place of the president when he or she cannot serve, and insure continuity in that crucial office.

In addition, Article I of the Constitution grants that "The Vice President of the United States shall be President of the Senate, but shall have no vote, unless they be equally divided." As to formal duties, this is it for the office.

*   *   *

Providing continuity when the nation loses a president is a heavy burden. Apart from being prepared for that emergency, however, vice presidents have historically had relatively little to do. When James Madison was elected, his vice president, George Clinton, didn't show up in Washington, D.C. until weeks after the inauguration. Later, Clinton died with eleven months remaining in his term, and the office of vice president went unfilled the whole time. In those days, there "existed no provision for a replacement, either by election or appointment," as one historian wrote, "and few seemed to care or even to notice."

In recent decades, though, the vice presidency has undergone a transformation. This has been the result of presidents' willingness to grant their vice presidents a greater role in governing. Walter Mondale's term in the office under Jimmy Carter marked a turning point in these terms. Mondale, a prominent senator before becoming vice president, was a great help to Carter, a former governor, in learning the unfamiliar ways of Washington. Mondale was also the first vice president to receive the Presidential Daily Brief, a highly classified bulletin on foreign-policy intelligence; and he was given a standing invitation to any meeting on the president's schedule. These precedents in vice presidential responsibility have generally carried over to succeeding administrations.

The growing importance of the vice presidency is partly a reflection of the ever-expanding burden of the president's job. As Joe Biden put it during his term as vice president under Barack Obama, "The way the world has changed, the breadth and scope of the responsibility an American president has, virtually requires a vice president to handle serious assignments, just because the president's plate is so very full."

Yet any responsibilities that come to the vice president are the prerogative of the chief executive. If presidents choose not to delegate in the vice president's direction, there is little to be done. Unless the Constitution is amended, the office will remain technically weak.

WELFARE STATE

> There has been something crude and heartless and unfeeling
> in our haste to succeed and be great. Our thought has been
> 'Let every man look out for himself, let every generation
> look out for itself.' ... We have come now to a sober second
> thought.
>
> —Woodrow Wilson, President (1913–1921)

The term *welfare* has a central place in American political discourse, but a confused one, with no absolute definition and a variety of uses. For example, "welfare" often refers to direct government assistance to the poor. However, we also say that Americans have a *welfare state*, which means that we have a government whose programs provide a measure of economic security to all its people. The American welfare state, for example, includes Social Security, Medicare, and other programs benefitting the middle class, as well as various programs to serve the poor.

The United States was not the first nation to build a welfare state. Several European nations moved earlier to provide this public support, and Germany did an especially early and impressive job of it. Their system was largely set in place by their "Iron Chancellor," Otto von Bismarck (1815–1898), who described it as "state socialism" and said that the German people deserved aid in times of distress, "not as alms, but as a right." Thereafter, American reformers could look to Germany as a model, if they wanted to see what a coherent national system of welfare might look like.

The German model, however, proved difficult for the United States to emulate because our nation lacks something that Bismarck had in spades: massive, centralized political power. By contrast, American government diffuses power through its different levels of government and different branches at each level. Ours is a government well designed to confound the sort of comprehensive effort that Bismarck achieved in founding the German welfare state.

This diffusion of political power has shaped the American welfare state. Welfare has grown over time, with an improvised quality, as new layers have been added to old. In the early years of the republic, concern for the poor was a local responsibility. Cities, towns, and counties provided assistance to the most needy, often by placing them in "poor houses" or by providing "outdoor relief," consisting of necessities given directly to them.[83]

By the later decades of the 19th century, state legislatures jumped in, passing laws that compensated workers killed or injured on the job. For the elderly, a few states passed pension programs. For children, many states enacted child labor laws, compulsory education, and programs to resettle those living in the most troubled families.

And so it went. The early steps toward a welfare state were halting, addressing problems one by one and state by state, rather than comprehensively taken at the national level. Government tended to take action on the most egregious problems, serving maimed workers, widows, and the most deprived children. But under prevailing assumptions, economic insecurity was a manageable personal risk, not a systemic failing of the American economy.

*   *   *

It was not until the 1930s that the national government assumed a strong role in providing welfare and made the welfare state far more uniform across the country.[84] The crucial turning point was Franklin Roosevelt's election to the presidency and the New Deal he proposed to combat the Great Depression. Under the New Deal, the federal government enacted legislation, including the Social Security Act and Aid to Families with Dependent Children (AFDC), that provided the basis for the American welfare state for decades. AFDC was the central program for delivering direct financial aid, in the form of welfare checks, to struggling families.

Still more layers were added when, in 1965, President Lyndon Johnson declared a "War on Poverty." This built on previous welfare state programs, which remained in place and often received a much greater stream of funds. For example, AFDC tripled its spending between 1964 and 1970. The War on Poverty also added new programs, such as Food Stamps, Medicare and Medicaid, subsidized housing, school lunches, and more.

But the War on Poverty marked high tide for the American commitment to building a comprehensive welfare state. Its vast expense, combined with often discouraging results (we never achieved a clear victory in this fight), drained public support from the effort. Major events in the retreat from the War on Poverty included the election of Ronald Reagan to the presidency in 1980 (after he campaigned on reducing government) and the end of AFDC in 1996.

Yet, although public enthusiasm for it dropped, Americans have never showed much will to actually undo the welfare state. They hold tight to Social Security and Medicare, for example. And even the often-maligned AFDC was not so much abandoned as replaced.[85]

What remains today is something of a muddle. Historian Michael Katz describes it as "a complex, incomplete, uniquely American semiwelfare state." It reflects, all at once, American willingness to support the needy, a degree of disdain for those who depend on government support, traditional distrust of government, and a strong element of self-interest, especially in the middle class's passionate embrace of Social Security.

To the degree that the American welfare state is a system, it is one with something for everyone to hate. Depending on who is talking, it is too ambitious or too timid, too generous or too stingy. All agree it is too complicated and too inefficient. But if our legislation reflects the people's will, it is still the system we want.

WHIP

When people used to ask me about my duties, I sometimes joked that one aspect of my job (maintaining party discipline, the political scientists called it) reminded me of what one of my Bug Tussle teachers had said about correcting the behavior of an unruly farm boy:

You should appeal first to his honor,
Then to his pride,
Then to his conscience,
Then to his hide.

—Carl Albert, House Majority Whip (1955–1961)

The term *whip* comes to American politics directly from Britain, where its origins lie in the world of fox hunting. Out on a hunt, a "whipper-in" had the job of riding alongside the dogs and discouraging strays from leaving the pack. The metaphor in legislative politics is clear. A whip in politics is a party leader who works to keep party members together, working in unison like dogs on a hunt.

Carl Albert, one-time Democratic party whip in the House of Representatives, was actually well furnished for the role. When elected to the position, one of his Oklahoma constituents sent Albert a long, braided leather bullwhip to mark the occasion. Of course, it hung on the Congressman's office wall, much loved but never used. "No party whip would be caught dead using a bullwhip," he wrote. "Maybe that should read: 'One who tried to use a bullwhip could end up dead.'" Members of Congress, elected to their positions and responsible to their constituents above all, don't take kindly to threats from whips or any other party leaders—as Carl Albert knew.

More than simple disciplinarians, whips are first and foremost vote counters. They must know where party members stand on a given bill: whether they support it, oppose it, or stand undecided. Knowing the minds of the party's representatives, the whip can then help the leadership prepare for votes. Does the leadership have enough support to pass the bill? If not, how many votes do they need, and who might be convinced to switch over? It is the whip's job to know, and he or she knows by keeping in constant touch with rank-and-file party members.

The position of the whip is not mentioned in the Constitution, so it is not a constitutional office. The whip is a creation of the parties, and whips serve the interests of their party. Both Democrats and Republicans have whips in each house of Congress and have done so since the early 20th century. This was a time when the legislative burden on Congress was growing rapidly and the parties looked for ways to maximize their efficiency in passing legislation. Doing so meant that party leaders needed to keep close tabs on their members and tighten discipline over them.

The "whipping-in" image suggests that whip operations are top-down, with party leaders imposing their will on underlings. And in fact, whips will use their share of sticks and carrots to get their way. They can, for example, threaten to withhold funding from party mavericks in the next election cycle.

But the whip's job is more complicated than the mere imposition of the leadership's will. Naturally, leaders need to convey their wishes to rank-and-file members, but it is equally important for the leadership to learn what is on the minds of those members. Individual representatives will know the political realities of their home districts better than anyone else. Through the whip, they can transmit that information to the leadership, helping it better understand the nation's political landscape. Thomas P. "Tip" O'Neill, a Democratic whip from 1971 to 1973, and later Speaker of the House, compared the whip's role to that of a "service provider," adding, "the service we provided … was information."

The interplay between party leadership and the rank-and-file can be subtle. Suppose the party in power wants to pass a bill that is sure to be unpopular with an otherwise faithful party member. If the vote is going to be close, the leaders might pressure that representative to toe the line. But if the vote won't be close, and voting with the party will injure a representative back home, leaders can let them vote as he or she pleases. Why exert pressure when a victory is in hand? Such cases, however, depend on sound information. Everyone concerned must know the score, and it is the whip's job to make sure they do.

If, on the other hand, an upcoming vote on important legislation is likely to be close, the whip will likely take a less flexible approach. When the Democrats held a narrow majority in Congress during President Barack Obama's first term, the Congressional leadership made it a priority to pass the president's health-care plan, the Affordable Care Act. In a narrowly divided House of Representatives, the ACA had no support from Republicans, and the Democratic leadership needed every possible vote from their party to pass the bill.

However, a small handful of Democratic representatives from relatively conservative districts held back, concerned about the ACA's popularity back home. To bring these "Blue Dog Democrats" into line, the leadership put their whipping operation into overdrive. Not only the whip, but the majority leader, the Speaker of the House, the president, and his chief of staff, all had words with the reluctant members, putting enormous pressure on them to support the bill. In the end, a deal was struck that brought the "Blue Dogs" back into the pack, and the ACA passed on an extremely narrow, party-line vote.

This was judged as a great victory for the president and the Democratic leadership in Congress, but a historical footnote is in order. In the next election, the Blue Dogs, weakened by the ACA vote, either decided not to stand for reelection or took a beating. With these (and other losses), control of Congress shifted away from the Democrats and to the Republicans. This was an outcome the whip should have known was possible (and likely did), and it was the whip's job to make the risk clear to other party leaders. As Tip O'Neil understood, information is the whip's business.

NOTES

1   However, Alexis de Toqueville had a strong presentiment about the possible development of an administrative state. See Philip Hamburger's discussion of de Toqueville in his *Is Administrative Law Unlawful?* (University of Chicago Press, 2014), pp. 413–416.

2   Some agencies, though, are more independent of presidential control than others.

3   Adrian Vermeule makes this point in his *Law's Abnegation* (Harvard University Press, 2016). See p. 46, for example.

4   It's worth noting that "industry trade association" does not translate as "heartless corporate villain," and that industries might well have considerable useful experience and expertise in their given fields.

5   Discretionary spending does not include spending on entitlements, over which Congress has little discretion, since spending levels are built into the laws themselves.

6   However, it does mention specific rights. See Article I, Section 9, which protects the Writ of Habeas Corpus and prevents ex post facto laws and bills of attainder.

7   Of course, the limits of the enumerated powers proved highly elastic over time.

8   Ratification was the state-by-state process of accepting the Constitution.

9   Eisenhower also had a civilian career, serving as president of Columbia University between 1948 and 1953.

10 It was Walter Bedell Smith.

11 It should be noted here that this "social contract" theory of rights is especially derived from the work of English philosophers Thomas Hobbes and John Locke.

12 This is not to say that the U.S. government does not keep, and has not kept, an eye on potential enemies of the country, nor that it has not tried some of the tactics noted above (infiltration, disruption, etc.). It has done so in numerous cases, including a campaign that it mounted against Martin Luther King, Jr.

13 New Deal legislation, broadly considered to include state laws, included minimum wage laws, for example, and other labor-related legislation, impinging on traditional contract law.

14 Karl Marx famously opened his 1848 tract, *The Communist Manifesto*, with the words: "A spectre haunts Europe—the spectre of communism."

15 As an example of the politicization of nearly everything, we have the recent claim that "knitting has always been political," made on a fiberarts website (Ravelry.com): https://

www.theguardian.com/lifeandstyle/2019/jun/25/knitting-is-political-how-trump-forced-the-craft-community-to-confront-racism.

16 It should be noted that Kolakowski was not a "conservative" in any exclusive sense. He was as much a liberal and a socialist. See his marvelous essay, "How to Be a Conservative-Liberal-Socialist: A Credo," from *Modernity on Endless Trial* (University of Chicago Press, 1990), pp. 225–227.

17 Most prominently, the internment of American citizens of Japanese background was a clear affront to the Constitution; but there were others as well.

18 It is tempting to assume that the great power of the corporation led inevitably to the exploitation of workers, but Richard Epstein argues that workers' wages were actually rising substantially without legislative interference. See his *How Progressives Rewrote the Constitution* (Cato Institute, 2006), pp. 5–6.

19 See, for example, *The Death of Contract* by Grant Gilmore.

20 Note that the term *convention* has other political uses, such as its meaning as an agreement in international relations: the Geneva Convention, for example.

21 Although the state does provide the legal apparatus under which civil cases can be tried.

22 Of course, these parliaments will hold varying degrees of real power, and some, such as those in the old Soviet bloc, could not remotely be considered democratic.

23 It should be noted that this last mechanism, the Supreme Court's power to judge the constitutionality of laws, is not explicit in the Constitution, but was successfully asserted by Justice John Marshall in *Marbury v. Madison.*

24 Anti-democratic perhaps, but healthy and natural as well.

25 Elite in the sense of highly trained, informed, and experienced, not in the sense of membership in any particular class.

26 We should note that not all of our political leadership is elected. Federal judges, for example, are not, nor are cabinet heads and the powerful bureaucracies they lead.

27 The gathering is metaphorical. They do not get together in once place to do their work.

28 If no candidate wins a majority, the election goes into the House of Representatives to be decided by vote there. This means that if there is a substantial third-party bid that keeps any candidate from reaching the majority *of electoral votes*, it goes to the House.

29 Although, as political scientist Eric Schmidt points out, the popular vote has no constitutional meaning, and focusing on this "phantom," as many commentators have since 2016, is corrosive as well.

30 In the 1950s, when the Electoral College was under one of its periodic attacks, then-Senator John F. Kennedy raised this issue. His concern was not simply with the presidency, but with "the whole solar system of governmental power. If it is proposed to change the balance of power of one of the elements in the solar system, it is necessary to consider the others." See Judith Best's *The Case Against Direct Elections* (Cornell University Press, 1975), pp. 18–19.

31 We should always be careful in making such a judgment, however. Was the scholarly James Garfield a mediocrity? Or the laconic, strong-willed Calvin Coolidge?

32 This is a tendency. In 2016, the electoral system elected Donald Trump over Hillary Clinton, which hardly supports the thesis that the system punishes the mercurial and

demagogic.

33 Wikileaks is a nonprofit organization dedicated to publishing anonymous news leaks; it amounts to a high-tech, international, whistle-blowing operation; thus Assange's appeal for political sanctuary.

34 However, there are smaller states in the Caribbean that have diplomatic relations with the U.S., but where the embassy is located in a nearby country. See https://travel. state.gov/content/travel/en/us-visas/visa-information-resources/countries-limited-visa-services.html

35 Although we do hold territories and protectorates abroad.

36 We should also include the judicial function, as the Constitution does.

37 Under the Articles, as many historians point out, national government barely existed at all, with power held by the states.

38 Some states, it should be noted, choose to delegate the responsibility for redistricting to independent commissions, rather than have their legislatures deal with this politically difficult matter.

39 That is, a legislature with two separate bodies, such as the House of Representatives and the Senate in Congress.

40 It makes sense from their own points of view that such major powers would be reluctant to cede powers to the U.N. or to other international agencies.

41 This construction comes from David McLellan's *Ideology* (University of Minnesota Press, 1986), p. 6.

42 Congress has other means than impeachment to keep itself—the legislative branch—in order.

43 The Monroe Doctrine, by which the United States claimed Latin America as a special sphere of interest, is a great exception, and we have indeed been involved in that region's affairs more deeply than Washington might have approved.

44 The Constitution, however, gives the federal Supreme Court the power of judicial review over state law as well as federal law.

45 In keeping with the primacy of the legislative, the judiciary was created through an act of Congress.

46 This does not mean that the Supreme Court's decisions are final. It, too, is human and thus fallible. The *Dred Scott* decision is an example, and it was opposed for years by many people, including Abraham Lincoln.

47 Even in 2008, the two major Democratic candidates for president, Barack Obama and his primary opponent Hillary Clinton, refused to support same-sex marriage during their campaigns, despite their party's general support for gay and lesbian rights.

48 This was not a black-and-white matter. Many states passed laws supporting civil unions or mutual benefits for same-sex partners; and Vermont's legislature passed a law supporting same-sex marriage, though it was vetoed by the governor.

49 Zenger's lawyer put it this way: "They have the right beyond all dispute to judge both the law and the fact ..." and "Where they do not doubt the law, they ought to do so."

50 Labor can still be quite powerful, though, in local or state politics.

51 While it's natural to always want better educational performance, we might consider whether our public education gets enough credit. A lot of thought and effort have

gone into producing our system.

52 So, for example, environmentalists have sought to use national policy to address problems of pollution.

53 This was actually a complex matter, since American involvement in Vietnam came through the efforts of liberals; for example, those in John F. Kennedy's administration.

54 See, for example, http://news.bbc.co.uk/2/hi/uk_news/politics/82529.stm

55 On "bearded god-killers," I am familiar with the term from the work of the scholar of religion, Martin Marty; see, for example, https://religionnews.com/2017/10/04/freud-and-other-god-killers-are-here-to-stay/

56 Note that Reynolds was writing specifically about ideas promulgated by the Soviet Union as part of its ideological warfare against the West. See https://pjmedia.com/instapundit/336559/

57 Opposition also came from members of Congress and other sources.

58 This is not to say that the United States has none of the "blood and soil" sort of nationalism, which does have roots here and may well be on the rise, as we have seen with increased "white nationalism" in recent years.

59 For similar reasons, parties are also wary of outside support for their candidates. They prefer centralized coordination and fear the effects of loose cannons.

60 Al Gore, most prominently, in a 1994 speech.

61 See *The Oxford Companion to American Law*, p. 607, which calls the police in the United States the most decentralized in the world.

62 This definition of legitimate government comes from Max Weber, *Politics as a Vocation,* but the basic idea has deeper roots.

63 It should be mentioned here that, along with primaries, some states hold caucuses where party members can vote on their preferred candidates.

64 Of course, Native Americans held a very different view on the matter of American land as cheap property for colonists.

65 The initials refer to the Security and Exchange Commission, the Food and Drug Administration, and the Federal Trade Commission.

66 Though far from all Athenian residents held citizenship.

67 Madison's concern about this point was strong enough that in the Constitutional Convention he proposed granting the federal government veto power over laws passed by state governments.

68 The historian was G. M. Trevelyan. See Crane Brinton's *The Anatomy of Revolution* (Vintage Books, 1965), p. 168.

69 This, I believe, is the implication of Walter Berns's comments on the matter in *Taking the Constitution Seriously:* " ... with every right created they [the Supreme Court] have narrowed the range of our public or political area."

70 The Senator in question was Ted Kennedy of Massachusetts.

71 This does not mean that every "socialist" state socializes all decision-making. Scandinavian nations, for example, do not. But to the degree that they leave decisions in private hands, they are not entirely socialist.

72 In theory the Speaker could be elected on a nonpartisan basis, but nothing like that

has happened for generations.

73 For Republican John Boehner, the challenge came from the "Liberty Lobby"; for Democrat Nancy Pelosi, it came from Alexandria Ocasio-Cortez and like-minded progressives.

74 Though Nebraska has a unicameral legislature, the only one in the nation.

75 It should be noted that the legality of some of President Trump's executive orders concerning immigration have been contested in the courts.

76 As Christopher Wolfe put it in *The Rise of Modern Judicial Review*, "The Warren Court ... expanded the category of 'fundamental rights' dramatically and undertook to establish broad social policy in a number of controversial areas. It became the most activist Court in American history and left a profound imprint on American life and law."

77 Although money is in some cases shared between the levels, as when the federal gives block grants to the states for given purposes, or when the states share revenues among localities.

78 Governments also tax "sins" because they are confident that these will be a solid source of revenue.

79 See *Federalist* 75.

80 In negotiating treaties, presidents will naturally depend to some degree on the Department of State and its leadership.

81 "No place" is the most common translation, but it has also been translated as "Good place," since the Greek root could be either *ou* or *eu*.

82 This, however, is rare and dependent on both houses of Congress agreeing by wide margins to overturn the veto.

83 Outdoor relief was that given to people who did not live in "poor houses" but maintained their own homes in some form.

84 One exception was pensions for veterans, a big project in the decades after the Civil War.

85 By the more limited, less generous Temporary Assistance to Needy Families.

ACKNOWLEDGMENTS

Taking on a project of this scope meant relying on any number of people for help. Simply getting hold of the necessary books and articles for research was a job in itself, and for this I relied on two libraries in particular. First was the Maynard (MA) Public Library, where research librarian Jeremy Robichaud provided me with a steady supply for years. Later, having moved to northern New Mexico, I depended on the Española Public Library for the same service, and there Lucy Peña and the rest of the staff did a splendid job meeting those needs.

In addition, I conducted a handful of interviews to gather information on specific topics. I want to thank Bill Kauffman and Paul Garver for taking the time to talk with me. In this regard, I also want to thank the late Dennis Rapp. I spent an enjoyable afternoon with Denny, an old family friend, who reminisced about his work on the Public Land Law Review Commission with my father, and also about time spent in Washington working for the Carter Administration and in Albany for the New York State Government.

I knew early on that I would need scholarly support in this project and was fortunate to find John Kitch, currently teaching at the University of Missouri. John offered hundreds of comments on the manuscript as it progressed, all much appreciated. The entries also received a review from Eric Schmidt, of Kentucky Wesleyan University, and his suggestions were also excellent and useful. In addition, I want to thank the writer Eugene Pool, a good friend, whose comments likewise proved very helpful. Finally, late in the editorial process, historian Michael Sherman reviewed the manuscript and submitted an exceptionally thoughtful report to me, with many excellent suggestions for improving the text.

Of course, responsibility for the final product and any of its failings is mine alone.

Starting late in 2018, this project received an unexpected boost when I joined a writer's workshop here in northern New Mexico led by the award-winning novelist and historian Lesley Poling-Kempes. The discipline of reading my entries aloud to the group was enormously helpful, as were the discussions that followed the readings. Among the members of the group, I want especially to thank Beth Ferguson, whose comments were particularly insightful.

Finally, I want to thank my partner Helen Byers, not only for her support and encouragement, but for her practical suggestions and editorial input. Without her help, this book could not have been done.

ABOUT THE AUTHOR

Ed Hagenstein is a writer and editor with long experience in educational publishing. In addition, he was co-editor of *American Georgics: Writings on Farming, Culture, and the Land* (Yale University Press, 2011). After many years in the Boston area, he now lives in northern New Mexico with his partner, Helen Byers.

9 781578 690350